7

Education, Unemployment and Labour Markets

Education, Unemployment and Labour Markets

Edited by
P. Brown and D.N. Ashton

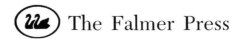 The Falmer Press

(A member of the Taylor & Francis Group)
London, New York and Philadelphia

(e) **UK**   The Falmer Press, Falmer House, Barcombe, Lewes, East Sussex, BN8 5DL

USA   The Falmer Press, Taylor & Francis Inc., 242 Cherry Street, Philadelphia, PA 19106-1906

First published 1987

Library of Congress Cataloging in Publication Data

Education, unemployment and labour markets
  Bibliography: p.
  Includes index.
    1. Youth—Employment—Great Britain. 2. Occupational Training. I. Brown, P. II. Ashton, D. N.
HD6270.F53   1987   331.3′42592
ISBN 1 85000 177 4
ISBN 1 85000 178 2 (pbk.)

Jacket design by Caroline Archer

Typeset in 10½/12 Caledonia by Imago Publishing Ltd, Thame, Oxon

Printed in Great Britain by Taylor & Francis (Printers) Ltd, Basingstoke

Contents

Contents

Acknowledgements

A number of the chapters which appear in this volume were presented as papers at the British Sociological Association's Annual Conference at Loughbourgh University in March 1986. Other chapters by Blackman; Church and Ainley; and Turbin and Stern, were commissioned by the editors, and the chapter by Raffe was prepared for the International Labour Organization (Geneva). We are extremely grateful to all contributors for their cooperation and willingness to meet tight deadlines.

We would also like to thank Malcolm Clarkson of the Falmer Press, and Elizabeth Brown and Maureen Ashton for their enduring patience and encouragement.

Introduction

Those 16-year-olds leaving school in 1987 entered primary school in the same year that James Callaghan, then Labour Prime Minister, lauched the 'Great Debate' on education at Ruskin College. The Great Debate raised a series of key questions about the role, organization and content of schools, including the question of whether the educational system was adequately preparing pupils for economic life. The Great Debate was launched amidst a rising tide of criticism from the media, and the Conservative Party, who believed that comprehensive reorganization had resulted in a decline in educational and moral standards, and a concern shared with employers, that the educational system was failing to meet the 'needs' of industry.

At that time parents, teachers, politicians and academics could not have anticipated the extent of changes which are now taking place in secondary education, and the changes which are now affecting the transition of these young people into adulthood and economic life. A large proportion of these young people will not find permanent, full-time jobs and will be forced to make the transition from school on Youth Training Schemes (YTS) or go on the dole. Others who had intended to leave school will remain in full-time study in order to delay their entry into the labour market in the hope of improving their chances of full-time employment. In the longer term, many of these young adults will have made the transition into economic life with their occupational ambitions unrealized, and extended periods of unemployment will, for some, become a normal part of their transition into adult life.

A significant proportion of their parents have experienced unemployment for the first time, and many of the jobs which they took for granted, and which were seen as desirable for their children, have now disappeared. Few teachers could have envisaged the scale of expenditure cuts in education and the extent of changes now taking place as a result of educational institutions being identified as a major contributory factor to Britain's economic decline and the high rates of youth unemployment

associated with it. Politicians of all political persuasions grossly underestimated the extent and significance of the collapse of demand for
labour and the structural changes which the economy is undergoing. The
ideological stance of the main political parties has provided no shortage of
answers and panaceas for the ensuing problems. Foremost amongst these
has been the attempt by the Thatcher government to introduce radical
reform in the education system and the labour market. Yet the policies
which are being pursued pay scant regard for the empirical evidence
which has been accumulated on these issues.

Sociologists would have anticipated that during the years of the
Great Debate, the transition from school to work would not have proved
particularly traumatic for the vast majority of school leavers. In the light
of subsequent events, they have had to redefine their research questions
and open up new areas of enquiry which have entailed crossing
disciplinary boundaries. The most obvious example of this is the study of
the labour market, which previously remained a sociological 'black box'.
There are a number of chapters in this volume which reveal the fruits of
recent attempts to overcome this deficiency and the volume as a whole
provides evidence of the nature and consequences of changes in education
and the labour market. It also raises certain critical questions about the
objectives and unintended consequences of government intervention in
the school and labour market since the Great Debate.

The first two chapters look at attempts to tighten the bond between
school and the labour market through the introduction of what has been
termed the 'new vocationalism'. Such initiatives as the Technical and
Vocational Education Initiative (TVEI) and YTS have blurred the institutional boundaries between school and employment. Brown examines the
previous relationship between school and employment as understood by
ordinary working class youth. This study shows that the instrumental
attitudes of these pupils led them to reject much of the academic
curriculum for their future lives. This has two consequences for our
understanding of the new vocationalism. The view that school-leavers are
unprepared for the world of work is not supported by the evidence.
Brown's conclusions was 'not that these school leavers must be educated
once more to know their place; it is that they do know their place, but
that they see the school as a useful aid in attaining it, but have become
increasingly frustrated and angry when they discover that there are
insufficient places to accommodate them'. However, if youth
unemployment is not an educational problem it is clearly a problem for
education, particularly because the instrumentalism of the ordinary kids
presents a major threat to their continued willingness to make an effort.
This creates personal troubles for the ordinary kids, and professional
troubles for teachers who find it increasingly difficult to justify both to
themselves and their pupils their everyday practices in the classroom. In
this context the new vocationalism offers teachers a way of maintaining

the compliance of the ordinary kids (at least in the short-term), but at the cost of increasing class and gender inequalities in the school at a time when a fundamentally different educational policy is required. The conclusion that the new vocationalism may lead to increasing class and gender inequalities was also reached by Blackman who attempts to trace the continuity and discontinuity between the TVEI and Newsom Report. Blackman identifies the radical case for the new vocationalism which rests on an integration curriculum, new forms of assessment and evaluation such as profiling, and a new pedagogy of experiential learning and problem solving. Moreover, Blackman argues that the radical case for the new vocationalism amounts to the 'velvet glove' over an 'iron hand'. Another argument supporting the radical case for the new vocationalism is that it provides an opportunity to breakdown gender divisions in education and training, but because of unemployment this is not happening, and indeed, the TVEI is encouraging both gender divisions in the choice of subjects studied in school, and the earlier establishment of gender specific occupational identities.

The importance of social and occupational identity as a factor in understanding labour market experiences is also examined by Furlong, and Church and Ainley. Furlong raises the hypothesis that with the recurrence of youth unemployment we would expect the experience of the transition from school to be extremely traumatic. He argues that in the initial stages of their labour market careers this is not the case. The reason for this is not because school leavers are adapting their aspirations to labour market conditions, but rather that they have developed different types of image maintenance strategies which allow them to continue to maintain their pre-existing occupational identities in circumstances in which they will not necessarily be realised. These strategies enable young people to resist pressure on them to reduce their aspirations on first entering the labour market, but may have created greater personal troubles for those who, due to the realities of the labour market, are unable to realize their ambitions.

Church and Ainley also argue that the occupational ambitions of their sample of school leavers in London's dockland have not been reduced as a result of high rates of youth unemployment. Indeed, some of the males in their study had shifted from wanting 'a trade' to wanting non-manual jobs which have been created by the arrival of office firms in the locality. They also found tentative evidence of males displacing females in certain types of non-manual employment.

In the docklands labour market Church and Ainley found little evidence of an under-class of permanently unemployed youth. What they did find was a significant minority of school leavers with 'chequered' labour market careers, which involved spells of unemployment and periods on government schemes. They conclude that despite the absence of a growing under-class, as found in other parts of Britain, this does not make unemployment any less of a problem during the transition to adulthood.

The problem of making the transition from school to adulthood is specifically examined by Hutson and Jenkins, and Wallace. Hutson and Jenkins argue that the young unemployed are not left in limbo and that there is no evidence of a culture of unemployment emerging in their sample of young adults in South Wales. Despite all the odds that are stacked against them and the impossibility of achieving full adult status and social membership whilst they are unemployed, life of a sort goes on. Life is made bearable due to a willingness on the part of parents, particularly the mother, to manage the problem of their child's unemployment. They argue that the picture of a warm close relationship between mothers and children identified by Leonard in South Wales in the 1960s had not changed very much in leaner times. However, there was a tension between the mother's desire to cushion their children from the hardships of unemployment and 'keeping them hungry' (making them willing to continue to search for work).

Although 'life goes on' for unemployed youth, Wallace notes major divisions between young working class adults. She looks at the impact of high rates of unemployment, particularly in terms of the domestic life cycle. She examines the traditional pattern of the ways of making this transition, which were previously seen to depend upon differences in the type of employment young workers entered. This sort of model, she argues, is no longer applicable. There are new forms of social division among the working class which are no longer based on occupational differences but upon differences between the mainly employed and mainly unemployed. Central to these differences are new forms of domestic arrangement.

One of the main government initiatives to combat youth unemployment and re-shape Britain's training provision has been the introduction of the Youth Training Scheme as a 'bridge between school and work'. In examining the link which the Youth Training Scheme forms between school and work, Lee *et al.* identify it as a surrogate labour market which is placed alongside the real labour market of depressed youth employment. This study was conducted in an area of relatively low unemployment, where the chances of success for the scheme were relatively favourable. Despite these circumstances it was found that YTS could not compensate for the deficiences and inequalities of the real labour market. Like the real labour market the YTS schemes were highly stratified providing a series of very different opportunities for school leavers. Young people were aware of these differences which resulted in intense competition for entry to those schemes which led to good jobs and a reluctance to enter those schemes with poor employment prospects. The experience of YTS and whether it led to employment was not understood by the school leavers to be a result of inequalities of opportunity within YTS but, as several other chapters in this volume indicate, a result of the personal and moral qualities of the individual's concerned.

Ashton, Maguire and Spilsbury explore some of the reasons why the sociology of the youth labour market has remained a 'black box'. They argue that developments in segmentation theory provide the most fruitful means of conceptualizing the relationship between youth and adult markets. They identify the main dimensions of labour market segmentation and highlight the significance of age segmentation in creating the particular features of the youth labour market. These consist of eight major segments each of which has its own distinctive entry criteria. Using evidence from surveys of employers and young adults they argue that once young people enter their first job the forces of labour market segmentation then have a powerful influence on their pattern of job movement, training opportunities and career chances. In analyzing the changes currently taking place, in and between these segments, they suggest that YTS, rather than transforming the structure of the youth labour market has, at least in its early phases, been constrained in its operation by the forces of labour market segmentation.

Most of the research that has recently been undertaken into the youth labour market has been in an urban context, with the implicit assumption that rural circumstances are the same. Turbin and Stern, on the basis of a study of four rural labour markets, challenge this assumption. They point to the significance of seasonal work, the small size of local firms, and the pattern of ownership and independence in shaping the opportunities for youth in rural labour markets. In general, rural areas were found to have poor opportunities for work which were seen to be a cumulative outcome of the recruitment policies of employers, poor training provision and the absence of firms with internal labour markets recruiting a significant proportion of their 'career' jobs from the locality.

Another dominant thrust of the Thatcher government has been the attempt to push down the level of youth wages in an attempt to generate a greater demand for young workers. Roberts, Dench and Richardson tested this idea by asking urban employers how they fixed wage rates and how these affected their recruitment. They found, as did Turbin and Stern in rural areas, that employers do not respond uniformly to common external labour market conditions and that pay is only one of several influences on employers' recruitment practices, and is decisive in too few cases to sustain hopes of cheaper youth labour draining the current pools of unemployment. They also argue that low pay does not encourage employers to create bridges to adult rates of pay and occupations, low paid youth employment is currently leading young adults into dead ends, exposing them to an unemployment/poverty trap from which claimant roles may offer the most realistic prospect of adult life styles.

In the final chapter Raffe reviews the main sources of evidence on the level, rate, duration and distribution of youth unemployment between 1979–84. He concludes that 'over this period youth unemployment has changed from a relatively short-term, frictional problem to one of much longer duration, where such labour market movements as still occur tend to be in and out of schemes rather than in and out of jobs. The unequal distribution of youth unemployment persists and may have been intensified'. He suggests that the problem of youth unemployment is increasingly one of young people's failure to secure jobs rather than a failure to keep them. Raffe also challenges the view that unemployment needs to be understood in terms of segmented labour market theory which makes a clear distinction between youth and adult labour markets. Instead he argues that the factors which caused adult unemployment are those which also caused youth unemployment to rise disproportionately. Thus 'specific remedies for youth unemployment — whether focused on training, wages, or any other target — can have only a modest effect on the problem, except insofar as they simply remove young people from the workforce, if adult unemployment is not also reduced'.

1   Schooling for Inequality? Ordinary Kids in School and the Labour Market

Phillip Brown

Introduction

The institutionally arranged passage into adulthood has been seriously disrupted for large numbers of school leavers due to the collapse of the transition from 'school to work'. Many pupils are delaying entry into the labour market by opting to stay-on in full-time education; many are being forced on to government schemes for unemployed youth in order to bridge the gap between school and work; and many are experiencing long periods of unemployment.

The collapse of occupational opportunities for school leavers has generated what C. Wright Mills (1971) has called 'private problems of milieu' and 'public issues of social structure'. In this chapter I will consider the private troubles confronting 'ordinary' (Kahl, 1961) working class boys and girls as they prepare to leave school and enter the labour market.[1] It will be argued that the changing relationship between the reward structures of the school and the labour market signals a major threat to the ordinary kids' understanding of their *being* in school and of what they hope to *become* when they leave.

The public issues which will be addressed concern the production and reproduction of educational and social inequalities. More specifically, it examines the way in which the state has defined the problem of youth unemployment and what it is doing about it. This is a public issue because as Mills tells us in a well-known passage from *The Sociological Imagination* (1971):

> When, in a city of 100,000, only one man is unemployed, that is his personal trouble, and for its relief we properly look to the character of the man, his skills, and his immediate opportunities. But when in a nation of 50 million employees, 15 million men are unemployed, that is an issue, and we may not hope to find its solution within the range of opportunities open to any one

individual. The very structure of the problem and the range of possible solutions require us to consider the economic and political institutions of the society, and not merely the personal situation and character of a scatter of individuals (p. 15).

The question of youth unemployment therefore, is a public issue because the state has sought vocational solutions to the problem, which I will argue, represents an attempt to maintain existing patterns of educational and social inequalities, and to avert an impending legitimation crisis both in and outside the school.

Class, Culture and Schooling

Considerable interest has been shown in the transition from 'school to work' in the post-war period, and more recently, the consequences of youth unemployment, partly because the passage into adulthood has been seen to depend on acquisition of employment. In the 1970s some writers were concerned with finding ways of 'smoothing the transition (Bazelgette, 1978; Clarke, 1980), whilst others were more concerned with revealing the processes which ensure the reproduction of educational and economic inequalities (Willis, 1977; Corrigan, 1979). Despite such differences in emphasis, British research has consistently found that the school has been very successful in regulating the ambitions of school leavers so that they fit the available opportunities in the labour market (Carter, 1966; Roberts, 1974; Ashton, 1986).

In the 1980s similar studies have examined the personal and social consequences of youth unemployment (Kelvin and Jarrett, 1985; Ashton, 1986). The main concern of this discussion, however, is to evaluate the likely consequences of youth unemployment for working class responses to the school, and particularly those of the ordinary kids. One confronts a major problem when attempting such an endeavour in that contemporary theories of schooling the working class have failed to provide an adequate account of the range of working class orientations to school and the labour market. The ordinary kids have remained invisible from such accounts (with some important exceptions: Kahl, 1961; Ashton and Field, 1976; Jenkins, 1983), because of a tendency for sociologists to *describe* variations in working class responses in terms of pupil acceptance or rejection; conformity or nonconformity (Hargreaves, 1967; Willis, 1977; Corrigan, 1979), and because of a failure to include female pupils in such analyses.

Moreover, those differences in working class responses which have been acknowledged are usually explained in terms of what will be called a process of *educational* or *cultural* differentiation. Consideration of ordinary kids reveals that both these approaches are singularly inadequate, because if an adequate explanation of working class responses to the school and occupational structure is to be developed, it is the interplay between the processes of *educational* and *cultural* differentiation which needs to be understood.

My reason for identifying the problem with existing sociological accounts is not to lead into a description of what an alternative explanation would look like. This task is undertaken elsewhere (Brown, 1987a). What I do want to show is that because sociologists have studied working class responses to the school in terms of pupil acceptance and rejection, and as a result of explaining differences in pupil orientations to school and the occupational structure in terms of a process of *educational* and *cultural* differentiation, they have failed to provide an adequate account of working class responses to the school which would provide a basis for evaluating the likely impact of changing labour market conditions for schooling working class pupils in the 1980s.

Explanations in terms of the process of *educational* differentiation have emphasized the school's role as a sifting and sorting mechanism which ensures that pupils from middle and working class backgrounds arrive at educational and occupational destinations appropriate to their class membership. The apparent acquiescence of working class pupils as they move into the market for working class jobs is seen as a by-product of their educational location, given the apparent success of the school in its role of 'cooling out' unrealistic expectations. Therefore, both marxists (Bourdieu and Passeron, 1977; Bowles and Gintis, 1976) and non-marxists (Hopper, 1971; Roberts, 1974) who seek to explain working class experiences in school in terms of the process of *educational* differentiation identify the school as performing a central role in determining differences in educational attainment and give it an important role in the pre-occupational socialization of working class school leavers.

Alternatively, there are a number of writers who have challenged this orthodoxy, and have attempted to explain working class educational and labour market experiences in terms of class *cultural* differences in attitudes and aspirations. Explanations couched in terms of a process of *cultural* differentiation correctly emphasize cultural differences in the *demand* for education and in the definition of desirable occupational goals. For example, in Willis's book *Learning to Labour* he argues that the difficult thing to explain about how working class kids get working class jobs is not how the school allocates working class kids to the lower bands, but why working class kids voluntarily 'fail' themselves. Rather than attempt to explain educational failure in terms of the available *means* to succeed within the school. Willis views middle and working class pupils as already culturally distinct. What happens in the school is simply an expression of cultural differences originating outside it. Working class kids do not evaluate their relationship with the school in terms of what the school might offer given their location in the academic order, but in terms of the consequence of academic success for *being* a working class adult as understood in their 'parent' culture. It is the class cultural definition of a future in manual labour offering little intrinsic reward, he argues, which leads to the basic exchanges on offer within the school — 'Knowledge for qualifications, qualified activity for high pay and pay for goods and services' (p. 64) — being rejected. Despite recognizing class culture as important for understanding pupil responses to school and the transition into the labour market, a major difficulty with *cultural* explanations such as Willis's is how to explain why large numbers of working class pupils do *not* develop an anti-school subculture. This difficulty results from a characterization of middle and working class pupils as culturally distinct, and the assumption that the development of pro- and anti-school sub-cultures is a manifestation of these cultural differences. This leads Willis to understand the counter-school sub-culture as the *normal* working class response to the school. And it is because the counter-school culture is assumed to be the *normal* working class response to the school that he is led to lump together other working class responses as *conformist* responses, and to an explanation of the working class conformists (ear'oles) in terms of the school's success in ideologically incorporating these working class kids into bourgeois modes of thought. However, the range of working class responses to the school cannot be explained simply in terms of working class culture because pupil responses to the school will, at least in part, reflect a *selection* from that culture, unless we regress to a form of explanation which relies on differences in working class family 'types' (Carter, 1966; Ashton and Field, 1976) or, like Willis, condemn the majority of working class kids to the status of ideological dupes as the price for celebrating 'the lads' as cultural heroes.

Ordinary Kids

The study of comprehensive schooling which I conducted in Middleport, South Wales, revealed that a simple bi-polar distinction between those who accept or reject the school is a misleading oversimplification of classroom life (Brown, 1987a). Within the informal pupil culture found in the two working class comprehensive schools, pupils recognized three different ways of *being* a working class pupil in school. These were commonly recognized in terms of the rems, swots and ordinary kids. While it is legitimate to identify the rems as those pupils who reject the school, and the swots as those who accept the school the ordinary kids (who comprise the largest category of pupils from both schools), neither simply accept or reject the school, but nevertheless comply with it. The ordinary kids' compliance with school is not based upon the premise that if they worked hard in lessons they could 'get out' of the working class, seduced by the knowledge that a few do succeed, but on their own class cultural desire to become a working class adult in a respectable fashion. The ordinary kids believed that modest levels of endeavour and attainment (usually leading to CSEs) would help them 'get on' which, in the working class neighbourhoods of Middleport, typically meant boys entering craft apprenticeships and girls low-level clerical and personal service occupations. The educational incorporation of ordinary working class girls and boys was based on an *'alienated instrumental'* orientation which led the ordinary kids to reject much of the academic curriculum which was believed to be irrelevant to their present and future lives.

> Martin: We got maths lessons, they're putting in, like, all different things like algebra, cross-sections and trigonometry and all that. But like me, I want to be a welder, won't need none of it. Might have somethin' like adding up, to measure a piece of metal to which you're goin' to weld to it. But you don't need nothin' like statistics like, things like that ... like science, you don't want to know all the different things.
>
> Mark: History, with history now, say somebody wants to be a motor mechanic say, I can't see where history comes into it, you know, I can't really see what history has got to do with school, you know ... with learnin' 'cos history is ... it ... just deals with the past.

Despite their resistance to the school's definition of 'useful knowledge' and 'success', the ordinary kids were willing to make an effort in school because limited commitment and modest levels of attainment were seen to offer the opportunity to 'get on' in working class terms. If this interpretation of the ordinary kids' compliance to school is correct, then it needs to be understood to be as much a working class response as that which leads to a rejection of the school. It also raises serious objections to the way Willis and others restrict the possibility of a 'truly' working class response to the 'cultural few' whom he identified as adopting a counter-school sub-culture, thus denying the existence of any other form of class culture/schoool structure mechanisms which acts to reproduce or threaten class and/or school stability.

The most important point to note about the ordinary kids' compliance with school is that it has depended upon certain historical conditions in which the reward structure of the school and labour market have corresponded sufficiently to allow pupils to predict the likely outcomes of efforts in school. The problem this generates for schooling ordinary kids in the 1980s is that unless they perceive a clear relationship between the products of 'making an effort' in school and rewards in the labour market these pupils will see little point in bothering to comply, because their interest in much of what is taught is limited to those 'practical' subjects which are believed to have some relevance and interest to them. Any situation where the ordinary kids can no longer predict rewards in the labour market for efforts in school, therefore, not only threatens the social order of the school but also presents personal troubles for the ordinary kids.

The Personal Troubles of Milieu

C. Wright Mills (1971) suggests that *troubles* concern the personal problems confronting the individual and those areas of social life of which he or she is directly and personally aware. 'A trouble is a private matter: values cherished by an individual are felt by him [or her] to be threatened' (p. 15). the personal troubles which threaten the ordinary kids stem from the fact that their future frame of reference reflects past processes and practices rather than present circumstances. Inherited beliefs, attitudes and values, including an understanding of the school and their future place in society are becoming a less adequate basis for maintaining personal dignity in the school and personal survival in the labour market.

At School

Between the time the ordinary kids were deciding what examination subjects to study for CSE in the fourth year and the time they reached school-leaving age, their chances of finding 'any' job declined to a quarter and their chances of finding an apprenticeship declined to an eighth of the proportion of those who had left school three years earlier. The responses of the ordinary kids to this changing situation have not been uniform. Some of them now believe that there are few opportunities and little point bothering to make an effort in school.

> Amy: All the teachers are the same, they say 'oh you should get this, you could pass in this', but they're no good to you, when you're leavin'. I don't see the point in havin' em ... people these days have got qualifications but they still haven't got jobs.

However, over two-thirds of the 225 ordinary kids still believed that they could get a job if they made an effort to find one. The need to maintain a sense of purpose and predictability in their life provided a powerful raison d'être for continuing to believe that they could find suitable employment. It also provided a compelling reason for continuing to 'make an effort' in school. Therefore despite questioning its 'value' there are a number of reasons why the ordinary kids' compliance with the school has not been completely withdrawn.

Firstly, the rapid decline in occupational opportunities occurred when the ordinary kids were in secondary education. It was only as they approached school leaving age that they began to realize how difficult it might be to get a job, by which time it seemed pointless to 'give up' completely, because qualifications gave them something to show for their years at school. 'Havin' you somethin' to show for your years at school' was believed to convey the 'right' attitude to employers, and therefore improve the chances of getting any job. Among younger working class pupils who are entering secondary education with a knowledge that there is little hope of them getting a job when they leave school, 'making an effort' will refer to a much longer time-span. Were they to ask themselves whether it is worth 'making an effort' for five years when there is little chance of a job at the end of it, the answer from a large proportion of working class pupils would probably be 'No'. In these circumstances there is likely to be a fundamental change in the attitudes of even junior school pupils in the direction of an alienated orientation.

Secondly, although qualifications were seen to be of little help in getting the jobs they wanted, making an effort in school was now justified as a way of improving their chances of getting 'any' job,

> Liz: When you leave school with no qualifications and the unemployment is as it is now, you won't be able to get a job, they're looking for school leavers with, you know, qualifications.
>
> Mark: Well the job situation … well it's worse now and there's not much chance of you gettin' jobs because of the situation, but if you've got qualifications behind you, the employers will take somebody who's got qualifications before someone who hasn't got qualifications.

Thirdly, the way the ordinary kids understood the relationship between employment and 'being' in school provided them with a sense of personal dignity because academic success had never been necessary to 'get on' in working class terms. The ordinary kids could achieve their occupational ambitions without being like pupils whom they identified as the 'swots' and who were seen as spending all their time doing school work and 'never going out in the nights', or like the 'rems' who had not bothered to 'make an effort' in school and who condemned themselves to a life in unskilled jobs or government schemes.

> [Talking about the rems]
>
> Amanda: They spent all these years at school haven't they, you know. They could have tried, if they had CSEs at least it's somethin '… at least they're tryin' ent they?
>
> Mark: I don't really have no disrespect for 'em, but if you want to be a layabout, job creation and all that, what's the future in that, diggin' a garden … what security for your family is

> that, you know. What prospects have you got for the
> future, right 'I'll be famous [imitating some of the rems],
> you see 'em out of school … 'Oh I've got a job, I've got
> forty quid a week in Burgerland', what's the point in that?

To 'give up' and leave school without qualifications would be an extraordinary act, which would make them little better than rems, forfeiting any legitimate claim to what occupational opportunities now remain for school leavers.

In the Labour Market[2]

Despite the ordinary kids' efforts in school, table one shows that under 20 per cent found employment within three months of attaining school leaving age. Twice this proportion of ordinary kids stayed in full-time education, while others entered government schemes or became unemployed. Over a year later the proportion of ordinary kids in employment had more than doubled, but remained at under 40 per cent. The proportion of unemployed ordinary kids has also more than doubled to almost a fifth, but the percentage of ordinary kids on goverment schemes had declined by two-thirds to under 10 per cent. Almost a third of the ordinary kids opted for a second year of additional study. The large proportion of ordinary kids opting to stay in full-time study signals the failure of these pupils in their attempt to find suitable employment at the time they had intended to leave school. The primary motivator for the ordinary kids' staying in education was their perceived chances of finding employment and a desire to avoid having to go on a government scheme or on the dole.

The majority of ordinary kids (57 per cent) did enter the labour market and almost two-thirds (62 per cent) of these went on at least one government scheme (a third had been on more than one scheme). This was despite finding that 40 per cent of those who entered a scheme did *not* state a willingness to do so while at school. A large proportion of ordinary kids have therefore been forced to bridge the gap between school and trying to find employment with the entry onto a scheme.

> *Jane:* I was determined not to go on a scheme because, you know, the
> money for a start, £25 a week it's nothin' is it? The way that
> people were takin' advantage of them, I was determined not to
> go on one. But in the end it got so bad, you know, it was terrible,
> you know, you never realise it's going to be that bad … when I
> came out of school, and no job, I thought it couldn't be that bad
> and I could get a job easy … my mother she was havin' me up
> before nine every morning and goin' down to the job centre, but

Table 1: *Destinations three months and eighteen months after attaining school leaving age (percentage)*

	Ordinary Kids		Total	
	Three	*Eighteen*	*Three*	*Eighteen**
Full-time employment	18	38	13	32
Unemployment	9	19	6	16
Government schemes	29	9	27	9
College/school	43	32	53	41
Other	1	3	1	2
Totals (number)	163	162	317	316

* Number of months after attaining school leaving age

> it was just useless, so I didn't have no alternative, it was either a government scheme or just you know, laze about on the dole and do nothin' about it.

The majority of ordinary kids, although hoping that a scheme would improve their chances of getting the sort of job they want, believe (particulary after the first scheme) that they were a means of making the most of no job. They were also a way of keeping in circulation and a demonstration that they were doing something rather than being on the dole. Yet some of the ordinary kids who left full-time study preferred to seek employment while they were on the dole and many of those who went on a scheme found themselves joining the dole queues.

Over a quarter of the ordinary kids with labour market experience had been unemployed for more than three months, and almost half of these for more than six months (not including time spent on government schemes). Responses to unemployment obviously depend upon its duration. If it is short-term it is unlikely to threaten social identity. However, despite the relatively short time the ordinary kids have been in the labour market it is the group of long-term unemployed whose social identity may be particularly out of tune with their understanding of what they *could* have become, or could now be becoming. The experience of long-term unemployment not only threatens the ordinary kids' chances of 'getting on', but indefinitely postpones their acquisition of the status of working class adult, previously arranged through the transition to employment and, eventually, marriage (Leonard, 1980; Jenkins, 1983). The social significance of engaging in paid employment in order to secure adult status is perhaps lessened for female school leavers (Gaskell and Lazerson, 1980). Yet, in the early years of post-school life, finding 'suitable' employment is important to both sexes (Griffin, 1985).

One of the concerns of this chapter has been to describe how the ordinary kids confront the personal troubles which have resulted from the collapse of the transition from 'school to work'. It has been shown that many of these young people have postponed their transition into the labour market or are now unemployed. It can also be shown (although not here) that most of those ordinary kids who have found employment are not in the jobs they want. A detailed analysis of the ordinary kids' responses to their labour market experiences is beyond the scope of this chapter (see Brown, 1987a), but what I want to show is that despite sharing a common understanding of *being* in school, it is possible to identify important differences between ordinary kids on the basis of labour market experiences. The ordinary kids who are unemployed, although registering a decline in the perceived importance they ascribe to school performance in finding jobs, remain more likely than those in jobs to emphasize *technical* differences in 'human capital' (i.e. having enough qualifications) as a reason for their failure to find jobs, rather than a *moral* failing involving a willingness to 'make an effort'. Alternatively, those *in* jobs emphasise that the reason why some of their peers are unemployed is not a *technical* but a *moral* issue. They are unemployed because they have not been willing to 'make an effort'.

The belief among the ordinary kids who are *in employment* that finding employment depends primarily upon a willingness to 'make an effort' is consistent with the way in which the ordinary kids *in school* legitimated their right to whatever jobs were available, compared with the rems who had not bothered to 'make an effort'. The same cultural understandings in school, which united the ordinary kids by distinguishing them from the morally inferior rems now threaten to divide the ordinary kids in the labour market.

Differences between jobs in terms of level of skills, training, working conditions and money, previously represented a division between 'respectable' and 'rough' working class youth (Willmott, 1966; Jenkins, 1983). In a period of declining occupational opportunities, the manifestation of a willingness to 'make an effort' increasingly depends upon being in a job whether or not it is the one preferred. Sennett and Cobb (1977) have argued that there is no more urgent business in life than establishing a sense of personal dignity, and this certainly appears to underlie the attitudes of the ordinary kids who are in jobs. They may not be in the jobs they want, but at least they have made the effort to find a job rather than being on the dole. It is through employment that the ordinary kids can demonstrate their moral worth both to themselves and to others. The experience of unemployment therefore circularly reinforces the attitude that to be unemployed is not to show willing, because by definition you can only show willing once you are in a job.

As the duration of unemployment increases it is also increasingly difficult to do — and to be seen to be doing — something to demonstrate one's social worth: one is forced to leave the vagaries of the market to determine an increasingly uncertain and bleak future. A major problem in the experience of unemployment is the threat of falling to a position normally felt to be below one, and is not only a social descent but a moral descent.

Being unemployed *is* interpreted as a moral descent among the ordinary kids in jobs, but those on the dole are more likely to reject the view that their unemployment is the result of a failure to 'make an effort'. There was a substantial increase among the unemployed ordinary kids in the proportion who believed that there are no jobs regardless of how hard they try to find one, and it may well be that a small proportion of the ordinary kids who are currently unemployed may not be prepared to take jobs they do not want. However, although the ordinary kids recognize the lack of occupational opportunity for school leavers, their response to unemployment is fatalistic (if only they had better qualifications, worked harder at school, or if only mum or dad could put a 'word in' for them). The crucial link between personal predicament and labour market conditions is rarely made in a consistent manner. However there may be a growing sense of alienation among the ordinary kids in employment as well as those on the dole. The ordinary kids have not simply accommodated previous understandings of who they are and what the future has to offer according to changing circumstances, or according to labour market conditions. Despite the tendency to understand personal experiences in individualistic and fatalistic terms, 'their apparent acquiescence should not be confused with contentment' (Runciman, 1966, p. 26). Sennett and Cobb (1977) have also noted that the psychological motivation instilled by a class society is aimed at healing a doubt about the self rather than creating more power over things and other persons in the outer world. Despite the fact that what has happened to many of the ordinary kids since leaving school directly challenges their sense of social justice based on a willingness to 'make an effort', their transition from school seems set to lead to increasing divisions amongst working class youth, rather than to the creation of collective understanding of their collective problems.

Public Issues of Social Structure

In this section I will suggest that the personal troubles experienced by the ordinary kids are, in the main, a manifestation of public issues of social structure. A *public issue*, Mills tells us, is a public matter which often involves a crisis in institutional arrangements. The crisis in institutional arrangements which this chapter addresses concerns the political incorporation of large numbers of working class people into the school and the reproduction of social and educational inequality. It will also be argued that:

1   The collapse of the transition from 'school to work' is not an

educational problem but a problem for education (Watts, 1978; Roberts, 1984), and the main reason why working class youth are unable to find employment is a result of a collapse in the *demand* for young workers.

2   The attempt to find vocational solutions to economic and social problems by restructuring secondary education is not only a justification for increasing inequality of opportunity, it is a blue-print for the future educational system of the 1990s which is as redundant as many of the jobs the Thatcher government now feels it needs to prepare school leavers to enter.

3   There is an urgent need to establish a new politics of education if any semblance of social justice is to remain in British secondary schools. But changes in the educational system cannot compensate for society (Bernstein, 1969), broader changes will be necessary if a 'new deal' for Britain's youth is to be achieved.

Education and Economic Efficiency

In the era of the welfare state and continuing economic growth, the educational system was identified as holding the key to Britain's future prosperity. It was widely believed that the better educated the workforce, the greater the level of economic efficiency. Moreover, for the investment in education to yield its potential economic returns, it was argued (particularly by liberal reformers) that the educational system must be restructured in order to improve opportunities for pupils from a working class background to draw upon an hitherto untapped 'pool of ability'. However, economic recession and the growth in youth unemployment are seen to undermine the view that investment in education will ensure continuing economic prosperity. By the middle of the 1970s the dual objective of equality of opportunity and economic efficiency could no longer be sustained as an argument for more investment in education. The liberal movement of the 1960s and 1970s were mortally wounded by their own two-edged sword. Investment in education did not prevent recession or unemployment, but was increasingly assumed to be a contributory factor to Britain's economic problems. The attempt to use the educational system as an instrument for orchestrating social reform was believed by conservative writers such as Boyson (1975) to have gone too far, too fast. There was growing anxiety, fuelled by the media, that the comprehensive reorganization of secondary education had led both to a decline in educational standards, and presented a growing threat to the very fabric of British society. Therefore, whilst Britain's economic prosperity was seen to depend on the school's ability to tap the 'pool of ability' in the 1960s, by the late 1970s such efforts were identified as a source of economic liability.

Despite such claims, the existence of *some* relationship between 'educated' labour power and economic efficiency has not been questioned.

What has been questioned is any *simple* relationship between economic efficiency and investment in 'human' capital. It is because the school has given the wrong medicine, in the wrong dosage, to the wrong children, that a disproportionate number of school leavers are now unemployed. As a result of this diagnosis the Thatcher government (partly under the guise of falling rolls) has performed major surgery on the educational budget. There have also been efforts to remedy the apparent mismatch between the needs of industry and the products of the school, by restructuring the secondary school curriculum. The Manpower Services Commission (MSC) (rather than the Department of Education and Science (DES)) has been provided with funds to introduce new forms of technical and vocational education. TVEI began during September 1983 in fourteen areas in England and Wales. The current total is now over 100. The main purpose of TVEI is to make the school curriculum more relevant to the world of work, and it is intended to be available for all pupils who want to take part regardless of sex or educational attainment (MSC, 1985).

The Limits of the New Vocationalism

Initiatives such as the TVEI, it can be argued, manifest a contradiction between the state's attempt to maintain existing patterns of educational and social inequalities, and the potential for social and educational change which is resulting from the restructuring of the economy. My reasons for this assertion are given below.

Firstly, the argument that the current crisis in schools and the market for young workers results from the school engendering anti-industrial attitudes and unrealistic expectations of working life is not supported by the evidence (Bates *et al.*, 1984; Brown, 1987b). The study of school leavers in Middleport leads to the conclusion that the current crisis in schools results from the fact that there has been a decline in the type of employment opportunities through which the ordinary kids can 'get on' in working class terms, and become adult in a respectable fashion. Its conclusion was *not* that these school leavers must be educated once more to know their place; it is that they *do* know their place, that they see the school as a useful aid in attaining it, but have become increasingly frustrated and angry when they discover that there are insufficient places to accommodate them.[3]

Secondly, attempts to restructure the educational system in order to meet the 'needs' of industry must be treated with considerable scepticism. As long age as 1947 the Central Advisory Council for Education stated:

> Schools can prepare their pupils for industry only to a very limited degree, because it is in practice almost impossible to do more and would be highly undesirable on the grounds of educational

principle. The practical objection to basing education on the needs of the scholar's future employment is the variety and frequent change of occupations, and rapidity of technical change (p. 50).

Indeed when it comes to specifying what the 'needs' of industry are and how they can best be met, employers express considerable uncertainty (CPRS, 1980). What they do seem to agree about is the need for a flexible and adaptable workforce capable of responding to changes in the work process (Parsons, 1985; MSC, 1985). I will say more about this in a moment.

Thirdly, if there are anti-industrial attitudes harbouring among Britain's youth today, they are to be found not among ordinary kids but within the middle class (Wiener, 1981). Yet it will be middle class parents and pupils who will resist any interference with the school curriculum which affects the acquisition of paper qualifications giving access to higher education and the professions. Therefore a likely outcome of the state's attempt to be seen to be 'doing something' about youth unemployment (given a definition of the problem as one of supply rather than demand), will be the use of such initiatives as TVEI to appeal to working class pupils as part of the attempt by teachers to keep the post-war settlement (between large numbers of working class pupils and the school) alive.[4]

In the previous section I tried to show that the school compliance of the ordinary kids has depended upon certain historical conditions in which the reward structure of the school and labour market have corresponded sufficiently to allow pupils to predict the likely outcomes of efforts in school. The teachers I spoke to in Middleport acknowledged much of what is taught in comprehensive schools has always been irrelevant to the future lives of working class school leavers. Until recently they could justify what they were doing on the ground that modest levels of academic achievement appeared to provide access to the types of jobs these pupils wanted. This rationale for a far from satisfactory situation can no longer be sustained, and the realization of this fact is seriously affecting teacher morale and forcing teachers to find ways of justifying their day-to-day practices to both themselves and their pupils. Coupled with the prevailing climate of government cutbacks and falling school rolls, the financial incentives offered to local education authorities and schools makes TVEI an all-too-inviting innovation (Watts, 1983; Bates *et al.*, 1984). The TVEI offers teachers the opportunity of bolstering their own sense of purpose and pupil compliance by placing less emphasis on the value of qualifications which can be traded in the market for jobs, and more upon the *direct* relevance of school learning to employment. This emphasis upon the extrinsic value of school *learning*, rather than school certificates, is seen as providing the opportunity for making the move to increase the *practical* content of the curriculum more *intrinsically* meaningful and interesting. But if more involvement in practical endeavour is the carrot dangled in front of the ordinary kids, there is also a stick. The more sinister aspect of recent attempts to reform the educational systen involves a shift from relatively impersonal and objective (although academic) systems of educational assessment, to one where the school increasingly emphasizes the 'personality market': where pupils' subjective attributes are assessed on a highly subjective basis. It is the whole person which is now on show and at stake in the market for jobs. It is the personality package (Fromm, 1962) which must be sold in the market place. This trend, epitomized by the growing popularity of 'pupil profiles', emphasizes — as the kids do themselves — that it is not only 'what you know' which gets one a job.

This response by teachers is not surprising because we would expect teachers and careers officers to advance what they see to be in the best interests of *their* pupils or clients in the hope that it is they who will get a job (Kirton, 1983). Yet a consequence of teachers attempting to resolve their personal and professional troubles, and having to work within the constraints imposed by the 'chalk face', is that the question of school leaver 'employability' is not defined as it should be, as relative to the *demand* for labour, but as a personal trouble which can only be overcome at the expense of other teachers' equally deserving (or undeserving) pupils.[5]

The important point here, is that the absence of an alternative politics of education to Thatcherism — which emphasizes the freedom of the individual to be unemployed as a price of market competition, and the restoration of *social* rather than educational authority and discipline *through* the classroom (Hall, 1983, p. 3) — amounts to a roaring silence. One of the reasons why the teaching profession and others concerned with the present trends in British education have failed to mobilize popular support for an alternative politics of education results from an apparent inability to counter the argument that the school has failed to meet the 'needs' of industry and consequently needs to be trimmed and restructured. The issue of the relationship between the educational system and the economy must be confronted head on if an alternative educational strategy is to gain credibility and 'work'! There are at least three reasons for this.

Firstly, the reduction of social and educational inequality is a political, not an educational goal. It has to be set *for* education, not just *in* education (Hall, 1983, p. 6).

Secondly, popular support for educational reform and investment in education has always been couched in terms of its beneficial impact for Britain's economic development (Halsey, Floud and Anderson, 1961; Vaizey, 1962).

Thirdly, many of those whom the school serves will evaluate being in school with an eye to their future economic and social roles beyond the school gates (Ashton and Field, 1976; Griffin, 1985).

The real issue is *not* whether any connection should exist between education and industry but *how* the connection is made. There is a considerable difference between teaching *about* industry and teaching *for* industry (Jamieson and Lightfoot, 1981). Moreover, if we are going to meet the social and economic demands of an advanced capitalist democracy, we will require young women and men to be capable of responding to new opportunities, which will include periods of retraining, but also allow them to benefit constructively from a shorter working week and a shorter working life (Watts, 1983; Handy, 1984; Williams, 1985). If Britain is to meet these demands it is not more *vocational* education which is required during the compulsory school years, but a more *general* education of *all* pupils.[6] The way to ensure the provision of a workforce to meet the *social* and economic needs of the late twentieth century requires that we *break down class and gender inequalities, not impose them, which I believe will be the result of the TVEI in many schools.*

The reason why I believe this to be the case, partly stems from the unsurprising finding that pupils construct their social identities (to which occupational identity is central), in class and gender specific ways. For example, although the ordinary kids shared a frame of reference towards the future in terms of 'getting on' in working class terms, the types of employment and ways in which they can become adults in a respectable fashion varied between the sexes. If we are genuinely interested in producing the 'labour force of the future', the educational system must attempt to breakdown sexism in schools which operates against both boys and girls and fosters the development of gender specific occupational preferences and expectations by, for example, *reinforcing* the processes through which boys enter metalwork, woodwork, and design, craft and technology and, for girls, home economics, childcare and office practice (Whyte *et al.*, 1985).

A study of the ordinary kids in Middleport also shows that because categories of pupils are so closely related to class cultural understandings of being a working class adult, it is only when the school offers an 'out' both subjectively and objectively that the costs and benefits of being defined as a swot and 'getting out' of the working class are truly posed for the majority of these pupils.[7] Conservatives such as Hampson (1980) however have argued that:

> Young people's perception of jobs are often outdated and their aspirations circumscribed by social and cultural factors. The problem is to overcome the pupil's family, background and peer group influences (p. 93).

This lack of openness to new possibilities he considers to be a problem of 'ignorance' to be overcome by better careers advice and sources of occupational information. But when ordinary kids discuss school and adulthood they are not expressing attitudes based on an *ignorance* of alternatives;

they are expressing collective *knowledge* of ways of being a working class pupil and an adult in Middleport. Their orientations are grounded in the material practices of working class people, transmitted from generation to generation, and are the basis for establishing personal dignity,[8] social identity and social status in a class society. They will not easily give up understandings which serve to define who they are, and to maintain a sense of social dignity, unless there are genuine opportunities to make a *new* future. The importance of this point reminds us that the educational system cannot compensate for society (Bernstein, 1969), and so long as sexual discrimination is practised by employers against any application for employment which does not conform to appropriate gender specification, or as long as the attempt to encourage the ordinary kids to conceptualize their future in 'new' ways is not supported by equal access to a comprehensive education or genuine opportunities beyond the school gate, the school's impact on pupil attitudes and preferences will be small.

Conclusion

The scenerio of the educational system I have briefly sketched in the latter part of this chapter is far removed from the current trend in secondary education, and from the problems of 'growing up' if one is a working class teenager in the 1980s. In the present political climate the stage is set for increasing inequalities of educational opportunity (Dale, 1983). I have argued that efforts to find vocational solutions to social and economic problems are part of an attempt (for whatever reason, or indeed lack of reason), to maintain the existing patterns of social and educational inequalities. The burden of the growing contradiction within capitalist Britain — which in marxist terms can be expressed as a contradiction between the forces and relations of production — has fallen heavily on working class youth.

It remains unclear what will be the long-term consequences of contemporary economic and social change. What we can conclude is that it is not only the political consensus concerning the role of the educational system which has collapsed (and awaits appropriate political responses to Thatcherism): it is also a working class understanding of being in school and becoming adult. The personal problems this has caused have been defined as private problems which the individual must look to him or herself to resolve, rather than as a public issue of social structure which raises uncomfortable questions about the sort of society we have and the sort of society we want.

It has also been shown that ordinary boys and girls usually define these personal troubles in individualistic and fatalistic ways. However, the inability of the labour market to provide them with a means of maintaining a sense of personal dignity and achieving adult status challenges their sense of social justice. The allocation of middle class kids to middle class jobs has not led to working class revolts; the schools' attempt to determine who gets a job and who is unemployed on the basis of school performance may meet with far greater resistance. For the first time in British history the school will become an ideological battle ground where the legitimation of educational outcomes — as much as the school's day-to-day practices — must be won among working class youth, because it is no longer a matter of educational outcomes determining the type of jobs pupils will enter, but increasingly, of determining who gets any job. The new battle over 'education', like the ordinary kids' fight to become adult in a respectable fashion, is only just beginning.

Acknowledgements

I would like to thank Chris Harris for his comments on an earlier draft of this chapter.

Notes

1   The data which inform this study were collected between 1981 and 1984. All fifth-form pupils from two coeducational working class schools were given a self-completion questionnaire, along with selected classes of mainly 'academic' pupils from a third school catering for pupils from a middle class background. 451 fifth-form pupils (223 males and 228 females) completed the questionnaire. A sub-sample of 120 pupils were then interviewed. On the basis of these interviews and observations in Thomas High School (one of the working class schools) it was clear that pupils distinguished three ways of *being* in school, which were characterized as being like 'rems', 'swots' or 'ordinary kids'. These are not the author's terms but those of the pupils. The term rem is taken from the term 'remedial'. However, it is important to note that although the term remedial is used with reference to non-examination pupils by teachers, when the term rem is used by the ordinary kids it has moral connotations. It is not that the rems are believed to be 'thick', but that they are unwilling to 'make an effort'. It was the members of the conspicuous male anti-school sub-culture in Thomas High School who were most likely to be referred to as rems. The swots are alternatively those pupils located in the upper bands of the school and who were identified as spending all their time working and never having a laugh or getting into trouble with teachers. In Thomas High School to be studying for 'O' levels was almost by definition to be a swot. The ordinary kids stand between the rems and swots. They are defined with reference to what they are not, rems or swots, rather than what they are, 'ordinary' or 'average'.
    The questionnaire data were used in an attempt to quantify how many rems, swots and ordinary kids there were, because these different ways of being in school were closely related to different pupil orientations. On the basis of pupils' attitudes to school, future educational plans, occupational preferences, and school performance, it was possible to distinguish forty-nine rems; 177 swots; and 225 ordinary kids (see Brown, 1987a).
2   The main source of information was a postal questionnaire administered 18 months

after attaining school leaving age. Three hundred and eighteen of the 451 young people in the original sample responded.

3　However, these are still expressed in individualistic and fatalistic terms.

4　In some circumstances TVEI may overcome this problem by linking into the academic studies which will exclude many of the rems and ordinary kids from participating. The point is that it is not for *all* pupils.

5　And there is evidence that by continuing to tie teacher authority closely to the exchange value of school learning for jobs, it highlights rather than resolves contradictions in the school's attempt to win the compliance of ordinary working class kids.

6　This is particularly appropriate given the time for skills training after the age of 16 in colleges and on the extended two-year Youth Training Schemes.

7　Even then there is no guarantee that location in the upper-band will lead working class pupils to conceptualize their futures in this way.

8　Albeit frequently at the expense of other working class pupils who they define as morally inferior.

References

ASHTON, D. (1986) *Unemployment Under Capitalism*, Brighton, Wheatsheaf.

ASHTON, D. and FIELD, D. (1976) *Young Workers: From School to Work*, London, Hutchinson.

BATES, I. *et al.* (1984) *Schooling for the Dole?*, London, Macmillan.

BAZALGETTE, J. (1978) *School Life and Work Life*, London, Hutchinson.

BERNSTEIN, B. (1969) *Class Codes and Control Vol 2*, London, Routledge and Kegan Paul.

BOWLES, S. and GINTIS, H. (1976) *Schooling in Capitalist America: Educational Reform and the Contradictions of Economic Life*, London, Routledge and Kegan Paul.

BOURDIEU, P. and PASSERON, J.C. (1977) *Reproduction in Education, Society and Culture*, London, Sage.

BOYSON, R. (1975) *The Crisis in Education*, London, Woburn Press.

BROWN, P. (1987a) *Schooling Orindary Kids: Inequality, Unemployment and the New Vocationalism*, London, Tavistock.

BROWN, P. (1987b) 'The new vocationalism: A curriculum for inequality?' B. COLES, in *The Search for Jobs and the New Vocationalism* Milton Keynes, Open University.

CARTER, M. (1966) *Into Work*, Harmondsworth, Penguin.

CENTRAL POLICY REVIEW STAFF (1980) *Education, Training and Industrial Performance*, London, HMSO.

CLARKE, L. (1980) *The Transition from School to Work: A Critical Review of Research in the United Kingdom*, London, HMSO.

CORRIGAN, P. (1979) *Schooling the Smash Street Kids*, London, Macmillan.

DALE, R. (1983) 'Thatcherism and education', in AHIER, J. and FLUDE, M. (Eds) *Contemporary Education Policy*, London, Croom Helm, pp. 233–56.

FROMM, E. (1962) 'Personality and the market place', in NOSOW, S. and FORM, W.H. (Eds) *Man, Work and Society*, New York, Basic Books, pp. 446–52.

GASKELL, J. and LAZERSON, M. (1980) 'Between school and work: Perspectives of working class youth', *Interchange*, 11, pp. 80–96.

GRIFFIN, C. (1985) *Typical Girls?: Young Women from School to the Job Market*, London, Routledge and Kegan Paul.

HALL, S. (1983) 'Education in crisis', in WOLPE, A.M. and DONALD, J. *Is There Anyone Here from Education*, London, Pluto, pp. 2–10.

HALSEY, A.H. FLOUD, J. and ANDERSON C.A. (Eds) (1961) *Education, Economy and Society*, New York, Free Press.

HAMPSON, K. (1980) 'Schools and work', in PLUCKROSE, H. and WILBY, P. (Eds) *Education 2000*, London, Temple Smith, pp. 85–94.

HANDY, C. (1984) *The Future of Work*, Oxford, Robertson.

HARGREAVES, D. (1967) *Social Relations in a Secondary School*, London, Routledge and Kegan Paul.

HOPPER, E. (1971) 'Notes on stratification, education and mobility in industrial societies', in HOPPER, E. (Ed.) *Readings in the Theory of Educational Systems*, London, Hutchinson, pp. 13–37.

JAMIESON, I. and LIGHTFOOT, M. (1981) 'Learning about work', *Educational Analysis*, 2, pp. 37–51.

JENKINS, R. (1983) *Lads, Citizens and Ordinary Kids*, London, Routledge and Kegan Paul.

KAHL, J.A. (1961) 'Common man', in HALSEY, A.H. *et al*. (Eds) *Education, Economy and Society*, New York, Free Press, pp. 348–66.

KELVIN, P. and JARRETT, J.E. (1985) *Unemployment: Its Social Psychological Effects*, Cambridge, Cambridge University Press.

KIRTON, D. (1983) 'The impact of mass unemployment on careers guidance, in the Durham coalfield', in FIDDY, R. (Ed.) *In Place of Work*, Lewes, Falmer Press, pp. 99–112.

LEONARD, D. (1980) *Sex and Generation: A Study of Courtship and Weddings*, London, Tavistock.

MANPOWER SERVICES COMMISSION (1985) *TVEI Review 1985*, Sheffield, Manpower Services Commission.

MILLS, C.W. (1971) *The Sociological Imagination*, Harmondsworth, Penguin.

MINISTRY OF EDUCATION (1947) *School and Life*, London, HMSO.

PARSONS, D. (1985) *Changing Patterns of Employment in Great Britain — A Context for Education*, Sheffield, Manpower Services Commission.

ROBERTS, K. (1974) 'The entry into employment: an approach towards a general theory', in WILLIAMS, W.M. (Ed.) *Occupational Choice*, London, George Allen and Unwin, pp 138–57.

ROBERTS, K. (1984) *School Leavers and their Prospects: Youth and the Labour Market in the 1980s*, Milton Keynes, Open University.

RUNCIMAN, W.G. (1966) *Relative Deprivation and Social Justice*, London, Routledge and Kegan Paul.

SENNETT, R. and COBB, J. (1977) *The Hidden Injuries of Class*, Cambridge, Cambridge University Press.

VAIZEY, J. (1962) *Education for Tomorrow*, Harmondsworth, Penguin.

WATTS, A.G. (1978) 'The implications of school-leaver unemployment for careerss education in schools', *Journal of Curriculum Studies* 10, pp. 233–50.

WATTS, A.G. (1983) *Education, Unemployment and the Future of Work*, Milton Keynes, Open University.

WHYTE, J. *et al*. (Eds) (1985) *Girl Friendly Schooling*, London, Methuen.

WIENER, M.J. (1981) *English Culture and the Decline of the Industrial Spirit, 1850–1980*, Cambridge, Cambridge University Press.

WILLIAMS, S. (1985) *A Job to Live*, Harmondsworth, Penguin.

WILLIS, P. (1977) *Learning to Labour*, Farnborough, Saxon House.

WILLMOTT, P. (1966) *Adolescent Boys of East London*, London, Routledge and Kegan Paul.

2 The Labour Market In School: New Vocationalism and Issues of Socially Ascribed Discrimination

Shane J. Blackman

Introduction

There are three sections to this chapter but one essential issue of discussion, that is, equality of access for working class girls and boys in education and the labour market. Section 1 traces the working class struggle to gain 'secondary education for all' and how state intervention through vocational guidance attempts to restrict access within education and establish a specialized relation between social classes and occupational sectors; special attention is given to the continuities and discontinuities between the Newsom Report and the Technical and Vocational Education Initiative (TVEI).

Section 2 presents the views of some educational practitioners on the issues of schooling and training, in particular I investigate what is the radical case for TVEI. The data in this section is drawn from the Girls and Occupational Choice research project[1] (University of London, Institute of Education, Sociological Research Unit), local labour market study. This includes interviews with TVEI unit coordinators, TVEI evaluators, careers' advisers, careers' teachers, classroom teachers, trade unionists, specialists and policy makers at the Manpower Services Commission (London), Youth Training Managing Agents, employers, training board advisers, pupils in school, ex-YTS workers, and employed and unemployed youth.

Section 3 is an analysis of girls and boys sexual and occupational identities which are shaped by stereotypes which operate to inhibit pupil perceptions within school and between occupational sectors. The data in the final section is drawn from the Girls and Occupational Choice research project[2]: a study of girls' and boys' occupational choice based on a largely working class sample[3] of 1000 girls and boys from the ages of 11 to 16.

Section 1

Access Within Education

The introduction of the new vocational education into the secondary school curriculum raises important issues concerning access within education. The status and purpose of vocational education in school is a subject of considerable controversy. The origin of this debate derives from the establishment of free access for working class pupils to secondary schooling and the nature of comprehensive development in the 1960s and 1970s.

Tawney's (1922) proposal of *Secondary Education for All* became a central part of the pre-war Labour Party education policy. Banks (1955) points out that the policy has a long history:

> The idea dates back from at least the 1890s, when it emerged as part of the programme of the Trade Union movement. In a resolution 'emphatically' condemning 'the education policy of the present government' the Trade Union Congress in 1897 demanded 'equality of opportunity' (p. 116).

The proposal stems directly from the demands of formal working class organizations of labour. The pre-war period saw the publication of a number of education and sociological studies (Laski, 1928; Nightingale, 1930; Lowndes, 1935; Cattell, 1936; Hogben, 1938) which documented evidence of class inequalities, class discrimination and class privilege. Glass (1961) argues:

> In one important respect the situation today has no pre-war parallel. There is now a recognition that secondary education is a proper subject for discussion and for study. This is in striking contrast to the pre-war position, when attempts to investigate access to the various stages of education tended to be looked at by the Government as attacks on the class structure. And indeed they were, for, as I have indicated, secondary and higher education were in large measure tied to the middle classes (p. 403).

Both Banks and Glass demonstrate that the gaining of secondary education for the working class was fraught with struggle and direct opposition from government. Before the Education Act 1944, which abolished fees in all maintained secondary schools, the Spens and Norwood Committees envisaged a tripartite system of secondary education, where three schools would cater for three occupational levels and also three types of ability and aptitude.

On a practical level the working class population would receive free secondary schooling, but access within education was based upon 'arbitrary' selective principles which reinforced the differences both between and within social classes by directly organizing pupils' vocational aspirations through attendance at strictly different types of secondary school.

On an ideological level the government assertion was that the three schools enjoyed parity of esteem but in the eyes of working class parents equality of prestige was impossible between high status selective and low status non selective schools.[4]

In Britain during the 1950s educational research within the social demographic and political arithmetic traditions paid close attention to the 'new secondary schools'. The approach was to investigate forms of social discrimination and injustice through four macro sociological variables, social class, educational opportunity, educational attainment and social mobility. The quantitative analysis of empirical data showed that the grammar school prepared its pupils for the professions and other salaried occupations carrying middle class status, and the modern school prepared the majority of its pupils to take up skilled or unskilled manual occupations. The studies[5] of pupils in secondary schools concluded that each specific school had a more or less specialized relation to the occupational structure. Floud and Halsey (1961) state 'The selective system of secondary education continues to set artifical limits to both the range of employment opportunities and the occupational aspirations of juveniles' (p. 86).

Taylor (1963) also identifies the status problem between the two secondary schools and Musgrave (1965) argues 'The difference is based on the fact that the modern school recruits its pupils from the low status parents and channels them into jobs that are of low status' (p. 218). The type of school experience determines an individual's range of job aspirations but also structures his or her approach to employment and understanding of how the labour market operates.

The Newsom Report and the Technical and Vocational Education Initiative

The position of vocational education within the modern school both pre- and post-Newsom is important because it raises a number of current issues. A central recommendation of the Newsom Report (DES, 1963) was to increase vocational education: 'The curriculum in the fourth and fifth years at school should be such that pupils are able to see a relevance to adult life over at least a substantial part of their work' (p. 40). However, Dent (1961) points out that by the late 1950s 'The dominant trend in secondary modern schools was to provide "special" courses, most of them with a vocational or semi-vocational bias' (p. 119). The combination of vocational bias and the fact that examinations were not a requirement (Kneebone, 1957) led working class parents to regard the modern school as a 'dumping ground'. By the late 1950s and early 1960s the idea that the state had not tapped a pool of working class talent in the modern school became a subject of earnest enquiry. This issue resulted in what Dent (1961) identifies as:

> A burning desire to prove to the public that the Secondary Modern School was definitely not a *School for failures* — an increasing number of teachers turned to external examinations to justify their belief that the intellectual ability of their pupils was far higher than generally believed and to give children the opportunities their abilities merited (p. 122).

Formal educational qualifications provide the entrée to the different levels of the labour force, the selective structure of the secondary system, in particular the position of the modern school, functioned to deny access to marketable certificates and offered courses with a predetermined occupational destiny. This meant that the working class pupil in the modern school did not have a key to equal economic opportunity through the comprehensive principle of equality. Carter (1966) clearly sees the purpose and consequence of the Newsom Report to maintain selective schooling and rigorously channel the working class pupil to specific sites in the occupational structure. He states:

> There are clear signs, however, that vocationally biased courses may be extended to many more schools in Britain. Indeed, the idea seems to be gaining popularity amongst educationalists that vocational courses should be the basis for education of senior pupils in all secondary modern-type schools (p. 29).

The post-war history of vocational education has been the history of the school experience for the 'less able' working class pupil. The terms of reference for the Newsom Report were 'To consider the education between the ages of 13 and 16 of pupils of average and less than average ability' (p. xv). The Report was concerned with pupils only in secondary modern and comprehensive schools, and the 'less able' pupils in the grammar school. One of the justifications for the current emphasis on vocational training is to increase pupil employability in the light of high levels of youth unemployment. This problem did not exist in the late 1950s and early 1960s, but are there continuities as well as discontinuities in the approach of the Newsom Report and TVEI?

The material results of the Newsom Report were the Newsom departments, Newsom teachers, Newsom courses and Newsom pupils. Burgess (1983) who conducted an ethnographic study of Newsom resources within a school states:

> Being a Newsom pupil carried a social stigma which was, in part, transferred to their courses and their teachers ... As the Newsom

department and pupils were common currency in the staff-room gossip, I found they were used as the subjects of jokes which were told in the staff-room at the end of the day. Newsom pupils were put into foolish situations displayed in cages and put behind bars (p. 130).

Also see Burgess (1986) for a reassessment of where the Newsom pupils are now. There were important checks on the Newsom expansion of vocational education into the curriculum coming from Wilson's Labour government proposals to establish comprehensive secondary schooling, from the growing hostility towards streaming, the focus on strategies of educational transmission such as learning in mixed ability classes, and the raising of the school leaving age to 16.

The TVEI proposals have been seen as an attempt to reestablish some of the principle aims of Newsom, primarily to bring schools closer to the world of industry. Jamieson (1985) understands this proposal as possibly representing corporate hegemony. The rhetoric of TVEI as in the recent government White Paper *Working Together — Education and Training* (1986) is couched in the very words of Newsom: opportunities, choices, motivation, relevance, broader achievement, challenging and stimulating. The White Paper announces the necessity to:

Secure a change of attitude towards learning, and the achievement it makes possible, as well as an improvement in the standards of competence, so that more young people see the value of entering the labour market (p. 5).

What is the government's understanding of the purpose of secondary education? Newsom and TVEI are based on the same implicit assumptions: first, that young people do not possess the correct type of attitude, second, that they cannot reach the required standards of ability and competence and third, that they do not recognize the value of work. The government's assessment of the pupil issues within school relate to a particular conception of the labour market. The document argues 'It is manifestly not desirable for young people to leave school or college and take jobs in which there are no opportunities for further education and training' (p. 5).

This assessment of the job opportunities is rather different from the Newsom Report's (DES, 1963) understanding of the *realities* facing the school leaver:

It is important not to mislead them into thinking that they are acquiring qualifications for a skilled trade which they have no prospect of obtaining. And it would be dishonest not to acknowledge that large numbers of young school leavers at present enter employment which invokes no skill or special knowledge which cannot very quickly be learned on the job (pp. 34–5).

Unlike Newsom, the new vocationalism is based on an unrealistic assessment of labour market possibilities for young people and has evoked criticism from economists of education. For example, Mace (1986) disputes the government's theoretical and empirical basis for their intervention into secondary schooling through the use of labour market arguments. The TVEI programme inflates the notion of worker autonomy in the labour process at a time when the introduction of new technology is resulting in a loss of worker autonomy rather than a gain. Cohen (1984) has a more critical understanding of the TVEI idea of worker autonomy:

> It represents an attempt to construct a more mobile form of self-discipline, adapted to changing technologies of production and consumption, and to link this to a modern version of self-improvement aimed at the reserve army of youth labour (p. 105).

Two central issues which vocational education raises are, first does it narrow pupils' access within education and second, does it become the exclusive area for the less able pupil and the site to place the troublesome deviant pupil.

Chitty (1986) argues, 'By its implicit operation TVEI will result in the reemergence of the old hard-line tripartite system in school' (p. 82). TVEI brings us back full circle to the original issues surrounding the 'new secondary schools' and as Glass (1961) understood it the social problem of class privilege within education. The proposition of the tripartite system operating within the comprehensive school is not a new idea, nor is the construction of vocational courses with a specialized relation to occupational destinies for working class pupils. Gleeson (1985) maintains that 'Despite the publicity given to core areas and transferable skill training, early specialization narrows the options open to young people later on in life' (p. 70). A closer investigation into the Newsom proposals indicates that their initiatives were not only based on an awareness of labour market processes but, in contrast to the TVEI proposals were opposed to early specialization. Newsom (DES, 1963) states:

> We do not think it educationally in the pupils' interest to introduce the specialized work before the fourth of a five year secondary course nor do the greater number of employers appear to wish for the return of trade-training schemes (p. 35).

In discussion with careers teachers and advisers a problem spotlighted was the use of TVEI courses to accommodate pupils who were no longer interested in school. Chitty (1986) considers TVEI will 'Be a dumping ground for the pupils that the school wants to get rid of' (p. 81). This interpretation is expressed by Dale (1985b) who suggests:

Those turned off schools by an academic diet are frequently reported as blooming when carrying out relevant or practical work, and to become different people on work experience (p. 49).

The justification of giving working class pupils specific work experience under the formal guise of schooling, used as a means to demonstrate ability and skill, even of the most deviant or less able pupil is an ideological sleight of hand: it withdraws the working class pupil not only from access within education but denies access to an increased range of sites within the occupational structure (see Reynolds, 1986).

The Labour Market Curriculum

Marxist educational case studies burgeoned in the 1970s from both the macro and the micro positions to identify divisions within secondary school as totally necessary to the nature of capitalist society. The macro understanding related to the processes of ideological and cultural reproduction of the division of labour (Althusser, 1971; Bowles and Gintis, 1976) while the micro understanding related to class cultural forms such as anti-school pupil groups (Willis, 1977; Corrigan, 1979). Both types of interpretation of secondary schooling share a concern to show how the social order is reproduced and maintained. These studies implicitly deal with the definition of working class educational failure but explicitly deal with cultural reproduction and resistance. In the mid-1970s Marxist theorists saw schooling as *indirectly* reproducing the social and sexual division of labour; this is in marked contrast to the government introduction through TVEI of work experience into school which *directly* reproduces the labour force.

Corrigan (1979) interprets school in terms of a hidden political battleground where working class culture is attacked every day by an alien, that is, middle class cultural imposition. He directs the discussion away from practical pedagogic problems of learning, banding, mixed ability and vocational education, to the interpretation that pupils do not view schooling as a vehicle to achieving social mobility. School demonstrates subordination and a clash of different sets of values. Corrigan does not see any purpose in identifying how to teach pupils of different abilities within school because the centre of the discussion on education revolves around the celebration, if not glorification of how male working class culture can be saved in the face of symbolic violence by state intervention in the classroom. The ideological starting point of Corrigan's marxist interpretation of schooling does not permit discussion of educational transmission because schooling is defined as a middle class imposition which the working class pupil must resist.

In *Learning to Labour*, Willis (1977) is not concerned with assessment but experience. He attempts an 'Inward appreciation of the lads' culture and subjective orientation within it' (willis, 1975, p. 8). For Willis the interpretation of the male anti-school group culture linked to male shop-floor culture demonstrates informal practices of creativity. The cultural practice of 'the lads' is understood as a complex, interactional form of working class communication ritual. Unlike Corrigan he does ask why educational transmission is a problem for working class boys who manipulate subordinate groups such as females and ethnic groupings, to support 'the lads' masculine ethos of manual labour over the educational pursuit of mental labour.

The social demographic tradition drew attention to class privilege and class inequalities, and the right of the working class to receive and have access within education. The Marxist educationalists (organic intellectuals) assert that the school is a middle class institution transmitting middle class culture through a bourgeois educational paradigm. These two approaches towards education and the working class have different objects of enquiry, different starting points and different priorities which result in completely different interpretations of the processes of secondary schooling. The Marxist educational position excludes the possibility that the secondary school can provide access within education, because schooling is structured to reproduce divisions. Those pupils who are labelled as the 'Newsom pupils' who are troublesome, deviant and working class are understood not in terms of learning or pedagogic difficulties and ability but in terms of their creative deviant actions against the schools' middle class form of indoctrination. The theoretical framework only permits working class pupils to be understood as heroes on the battleground of cultural imposition. On the subject of TVEI Chitty (1986) points out perceptively:

> At first sight it is not easy to unite the left on this particular platform. Contributors to *Schooling for the Dole?* for example argue rightly that the current controversy centres on whether schools should produce ideal workers to help solve the economic crisis or critical and independent people who can develop their own capacities to the full (p. 91–2).

He states that they reject both models in favour of a more radical approach. However, Chitty (ibid) concludes:

> Despite the attempt at an honest appraisal of working class attitudes, all this comes across as being somewhat patronizing and condescending, as well as betraying a very limited view of the role of education in society (p. 92).

The Marxist interpretation of secondary schooling at the level of curriculum material provides a valuable means of assessing the structure and operation of the way in which access within education is shaped or restricted for the working class. Rees and Atkinson (1982), and more recently Moore (1984), demonstrate that social and life skills or personal effectiveness within TVEI use materials which are clearly based on a deficit model of working class culture, to provide a legitimate rationale for forms of compensatory education. It was Bernstein (1970) who identified the inadequate rationale and the unsatisfactory idea of compensatory education, because it directs attention away from the issues of school resources, the internal organization and the context for learning. He asserts 'If the culture of the teacher is to become part of the consciousness of the child, then the culture of the child must first be in the consciousness of the teacher' (p. 347). Bernstein's call is to examine the social assumption underlying the organization, distribution and evaluation of knowledge; such a demand is relevant to TVEI. There is one assumption which unites both Newsom and TVEI proposals, as Finn, Grant and Johnson (1977) argue:

> It is the future work situation which is the determining factor — it
> is the natural and unproblematic needs of the labour market which
> structure the suggested educational reforms (p. 182).

Bernstein claimed that education cannot compensate for society; we need to add further that education cannot compensate for discriminatory practices within the labour market. An unregulated labour market supports and reinforces the selective principles of schooling which creates a double bind for working class girls and boys who are structurally directed to specific occupational sectors. The labour market does not operate on a principle of free allocation which permits choice and equal access. Offe (1985) insists that the labour market cannot be considered as an ordinary commodity market because it is never insulated against the impact of organized structural discrimination. There is a similarity between the selective processes of schooling and the discriminatory functions of the labour market in that education and employment are reduced to nothing more than supposedly free choices or procedures around an arbitrary criterion of suitability but are based on principles which legitimate exclusion from access.

The next section will examine the way in which different practitioners within the field of education interpret TVEI, paying special attention to the perspective of TVEI unit coordinators.

Section 2

Training Over Education

In this section I shall begin by examining the relationship between education and training and later investigate what is the radical case for

TVEI in terms of first, integration and second, non-traditional options.

The DES document *Supporting TVEI* (1985) states that 'Vocational education is to be interpreted as education in which the students are concerned to acquire generic or specific skills with a view to employment' (p. 57). The NUT (1983) considers that the TVEI proposals present a valuable opportunity to investigate vocational guidance but fear that implications would be hidden inside this trojan horse. Of the recent Government White Paper *Working Together* The NAS/UWT (1986) asserts:

> The Government's aim is to use the MSC as the medium through which to link the curriculum in Years 4 and 5 of secondary education to the requirements of employers. This aim is totally incompatible with the repeated assertions of the Secretary of State and HMI that the curriculum in schools should be broad, balanced, relevant and differentiated (p. 11).

One of the major problems which both the major teacher's unions have had to come to terms with is the power of the Manpower Services Commission to set limits to the debate about the 'relevance' of the school curriculum. The MSC's TVEI proposals for vocational guidance are shaping educational reform. A trade unionist working in the field of education argues:

> Work experience in school; I think that is one of the most appalling things that's ever been introduced into state education. Taking kids out from school and saying, this is the function of your existence, of your EDUCATION.

A policy adviser at the Greater London Training Board considers:

> The training field was in a mess, it needed changing, the needs of either side, industry or young people were not being met. But we did not need a change with this political emphasis, that leads back to the free market forces.

The TVEI proposals are changing the relation both within and between the secondary school and the labour market. Another aspect of the changing relationship of young people to the labour market has been the growth of YTS.

A policy maker at the MSC in South London states:

> One of the problems with TVEI is that young people going through that programme at the moment are getting features of YTS while they are at school, so it's perfectly possible that if they come out of school and are unemployed and want to go on YTS, that YTS won't meet their needs, because the coverage, core skills, transferable skills, personal effectiveness, work experience was part of their TVEI programme.

This is a clear example of how vocational training rather than vocational education has moved into the school curriculum. Training over education necessitates early specialization where pupils are presented with images of worker autonomy which have little relevance to their eventual form of employment (Gleeson, 1985). The point is not whether YTS is TVEI in school, but how far do courses on vocational initiation, preparation and guidance predetermine a pupil's job selection, at an age too early to permit a broad assessment and evaluation of the pupil's ability and skill. The NAS/UWT (1986) criticize the government proposals in the White Paper *Working Together* because it 'Focuses on the need for initiatives in the field of education and training to underpin the present employer led training strategy' (p. 11). The introduction into the secondary school curriculum of a general course relevant to employers' needs not only puts the comprehensive principle into reverse, but conflicts with the liberal principle of individual equality. Gross generalizations such as the assertion that employers now determine the school curriculum or that employers are using education for their labour requirements, keep the debate on education and the labour market at the level of rhetoric. Employers are not a homogeneous group nor are their specific labour requirements similar. Throughout the country the types of work situation vary and are importantly related to the local characteristics of an area and its history of employment. A TVEI unit coordinator argued that new vocationalism:

> Cannot create employment opportunities in Sunderland, Teesside where they're talking about vocational education in terms of general educational objectives which may be coping with employment, doesn't necessarily mean paid employment, it may be coping with the problems of unemployment.

At the practical level of trying to find work an ex-YTS worker states:

> Vocational training — sometimes seems like a good idea, but other times you feel that they're pushing people into industry or whatever, and *limiting your choice*. If they're not academic, they must be vocational. If TVEI is industry, train the workers, what happens where there is no industry.

What is the purpose of vocational education? What is being argued above is that TVEI does not train for employment, but for unemployment. This is clearly not an educational issue but a fundamental labour market problem: why have employment opportunities for school leavers vanished?

Jones (1984) considers that training for transferable skills within YTS on the model of occupational training families, presents a major problem. There is no reliable evidence on the ways in which transferable skills can be taught, if indeed such skills exist. Underlying the introduction of the

TVEI courses in school are two elements: one, a pedagogic model of transferability based on 'exposure' to new experiences and environments and two, a deficit model of the pupil who is seen as an empty container which requires filling to the required level to demonstrate competence in applying a generic skill. This model of educational transmission can be understood as horizontal learning through a passive pedagogy, leading in the form of YTS to forms of employment training which can be understood as horizontal adaptability. Both horizontal forms within the school and the occupational site, function to reinforce an individual's entrapment within a particular occupational sector (Braverman, 1974).

The flexible learner/worker is capable of being employed or reemployed in a variety of jobs, but all at the same level. To blame employers for inadequacies in their training programmes is a formulation which directs attention away from the major shifts in work processes and labour market policies. Generic skills training is not an expression of employer demands but, as Gleeson (1985) argues, it is 'An idealized conception of how industrial relations ought to function under free market conditions' (p. 64).

In the next section I will consider two contrasting views on the effect of the introduction of new vocationalism in school.

The Radical Case for New Vocationalism

Integration or bifurcation This initiative will mean that the values of the world of work will permeate the school curriculum. It is a radical approach to curriculum development in education. A TVEI unit coordinator claims:

> The implications of TVEI for the curriculum and for educational processes are far more radical and more far reaching. It's taken a bit of time for the penny to drop. One of the overt aims of TVEI is that it is meant to be an integrated curriculum approach, and if you're head of Maths or English within a secondary school, traditionally single subject based, then it is quite threatening, the implication of that.

The radical case for TVEI rests on three educational proposals: first, an integrated curriculum against a collection of separate subjects, second, pupil assessment and evaluation such as profiling against formal external examination and third, the new pedagogy of experiential learning and problem solving against traditional or academic learning.

But whose curriculum is to be integrated? An academic selective curriculum for able pupils, side by side with an integrated curriculum for the less able pupils is not a radical initiative. In fact to suggest that integration can occur while maintaining a selective curriculum is to ignore the evidence of past educational studies[6] of pupil polarization and withdrawal. Reform in secondary school in a context of urgency could result in a 'new curriculum' where possibly neither staff nor pupils have a sense of order and purpose, and which could create resentment in depth; such was the experience of the Newsom initiative. A TVEI unit coordinator stated:

> The first round or two of TVEI was about low ability, and you do get the impression it is low ability projects in Wigan or Sandwell. The MSC is very aware of those kinds of criticism.

A TVEI evaluator suggested that the divisions between the able and less able pupils could not be applied to the new initiative.

Whether TVEI goes across the curriculum or is for lower ability pupils depends on four features: first, the TVEI submission, second, the local education authority, third, the school and fourth, the definition and purpose of vocational education. The construction of unstreamed TVEI course units within a streamed or banded curriculum does not face the direct problems of pupil ability levels or status relations between pupil groupings.

If the only lesson where pupils are equal is in the TVEI courses the creation of limited pupil integration creates the potential space for disturbance or conflict, and withdrawal or non-cooperation. One point of consensus amongst the TVEI evaluators interviewed was the possible implication of curriculum development leading to a bifurcated curriculum, traditional academic curriculum for able pupils with limited vocational guidance, and a separate 'new curriculum' vocationally led for the less able non-academic pupils.

The major issue becomes separate integration; both the able and the less able pupils receive a new integrated curriculum but within either an implicitly or explicitly streamed system; this ensures that different pupil ability levels receive separate and different courses. To achieve equality of access within education it is insufficient to change merely the label or content of the course. What should be changed are the divisive principles of selection which inhibit, divide, and guide pupils into courses which restrict access to knowledge and to future occupational choice. A senior careers teacher suggests:

> But as far as curriculum change goes I think that we've got to be careful that TVEI does not channel people into a particular *form of technical service*, for example because at that particular moment the government feels they need more of something else. I feel very strongly we would end up with a *Brave New World* situation if you're not careful, which is much more subtle than it was in the book.

This is what Willis (1986) calls the new social conditions of youth.

What is the new pedagogy of new vocationalism? The implication of

TVEI for pedagogy and curriculum change can be both positive and negative. Some TVEI unit coordinators appear to be ignorant of modern teaching approaches, claiming as new the methods employed by TVEI:

> We are going to take a much more classroom activities based approach, much more problem solving, rather than a traditional humanities — history and geography approach.

This perspective shows that some TVEI unit coordinators appear to be insulated from the realities of classroom teaching and development of new teaching methods.

However, TVEI is facilitating the introduction of assessment techniques unrelated to the written external examination, an advance welcomed by many teachers. A TVEI unit coordinator states:

> The impetus for TVEI means that schools are doing a lot more about profiling and implementing that kind of change within the curriculum much quicker than they would otherwise. That's trying to achieve far more responsibility and autonomy in young people for their own development and their own progress.

Profiling could be valuable as a learning process for pupils but it needs to be seen as a form of assessment which is available to all pupils and not restricted to an identifiable minority. Further, profiling offers a possibility to extend child-centred learning or discovery, but it raises three issues: first, the preparation of teachers to provide close guidance and counselling to all ranges of pupils; second, profiling could be used to increase surveillance on pupil activities and to police their attitudes, thus operating as a powerful means of social control; and third, profiling demands extensive and expensive teacher time in supervision of each pupil which school heads' argue is unavailable under present circumstances. On the problem of adequate resources in school a TVEI unit coordinator states 'We need to have smaller numbers, better equipment, better staffing if we are going to make learning more effective.' This statement will leave a bitter taste in the mouth of classroom teachers at a time when local authorities and schools are starved of resources, and when capitation for each TVEI pupil is more than four times that allocated to other pupils in school (NAS/UWT, 1986).

What is the relationship between TVEI and GCSE? The new secondary school examination at 16 combines both the GCE and CSE. It has three major similarities with TVEI: first, an integration curriculum; second, less emphasis on formal examination and more emphasis on 'new' forms of assessment such as continuous assessment and profiling; and third, an attempt to make the curriculum more relevant to the world of work.

The major educational reform of the GCSE is understood by most teachers as an advance within comprehensive education. However the

GCSE shares many of the problems associated with the new TVEI programme. The central issue of controversy concerning the GCSE is that it remains as divisive as the two old forms of examination: for pupils of high status the GCE and for pupils of low status the CSE. In the GCSE pupils not only take different examination papers within the same subject but certain pupils are excluded from particular subjects, and contents differ according to pupil ability.

The important status division in school from the pupil perspective still remains the difference between the pro-school pupils and the anti-school pupils. Educational case studies within secondary schooling in the 1950s (Oppenheim, 1955), the 1960s (Lacey, 1966; Hargreaves, 1967), the 1970s (Willis, 1977; Woods, 1979) and the 1980s (Ball, 1981; Turner, 1983), trace the major relations of pupil polarization which are substantially determined by the schools' structural hierarchical organization of pupils into able and less able pupils. Some of these studies suggest that the possibility exists within mixed ability teaching not only to challenge the emergence of coherent anti-school groups but to raise standards in all ranges of pupil activity, through the close contact and interaction of teacher and pupil. The area of mixed ability is where the GCSE could have made a major pedagogic advance within comprehensive education. The necessity to face the issues and problems of streaming, banding and mixed ability has been side-stepped by the GCSE. Clare (1986) states:

> GCSE does not herald the extension of mixed ability teaching across the curriculum up to the age of 16. Although many schools are extraordinarily reluctant to admit it, they will continue to divide children by ability (at about 13) so that they can be taught in different classes at different paces to reach their differing levels of ability, just as they are now (p. 4–5).

Non-traditional options and discrimination   Possibly, the most radical feature of TVEI is that it provides an excellent opportunity to increase the involvement of girls in traditionally male education and skill training. A careers officer states of TVEI 'A very useful project to help change attitudes amongst the community and parents, in giving girls the experience of doing non-traditional types of work.' This view is supported by a TVEI unit coordinator:

> Developing TVEI has pushed that process further along, and that has increased the range of options. Boys have opportunities for catering and business studies; girls for graphical communication and electronics, and you've got take up. One example of equal opportunities is perhaps more access to things which in the past had not been available.

What evidence do we have of girls (or boys) branching out into non-traditional areas? Millman (1985) argues, 'Many TVEI programmes in their first year had explicitly set "male" and "female" options against each other' (p. 62). TVEI courses can have a marginal effect on gender stereotyping attitudes and this effect can be particularly poignant during the time of pupil option choice (Weiner, 1985). A girl's exposure to non-traditional components common to TVEI courses will have a moderate effect on stereotypical subject choices. A TVEI evaluator suggests that through counselling with pupils there is a reinforcement of stereotype selection of option choices. Courses and job opportunities are sold to pupils on a discriminatory basis where official rationales socialize pupils into an acceptance of gender, class and ethnic types of selection. A University of Lancaster report (1986) on TVEI states:

> Indeed it could be argued that TVEI in some ways exacerbates sex differentiation in that large numbers of students are opting for sex-stereotyped subjects, and the gap between the numbers of each sex taking such subjects is consequently wider (p. 2).

In discussion with TVEI coordinators (all men) there was considerable commitment to equal opportunity but at the expense of a policy of positive discrimination. Marsh (1986) argues 'The MSC began the 1980s with the objective of equality, but very much a policy stance rather than a programme of action' (p. 156). Our evidence supports both Marsh's argument and Millman's (1986) point 'Faced with a need for rapid innovation in a multitude of areas, it is unlikely that the predominantly male teams will make equal opportunities a priority and identify positive action strategies for themselves' (p. 67).

In discussion with pupils, even in the first year of secondary school their fear of unemployment was a predominant issue raised when assessing their future school careers. The introduction of TVEI may heighten the pupils' scramble for occupational identity and currency, consequently, vocational courses in school rigidify pupil job choice to first hand knowledge of adult work roles in their local labour market which offer 'safe' employment. In this way new vocationalism emphasizes the segmented and segregated labour market, where the school curriculum encourages and legitimates pupils' acceptance of inferior work roles. Socially ascribed discriminatory assumptions within the world of work are brought into the classroom where the power of stereotypes and the pupils' own collusion 'to get a secure job' reinforce their location in the social and sexual division of labour. The schools' selective processes combine with the discriminatory labour market functions to act as dual relations which inhibit equality; working class pupils, girls and pupils from ethnic groupings are denied access within education by being presented with specialized relations to specific occupational sectors (Griffin, 1985).

Pupils speak highly of TVEI work experience or vocational courses;

they provide a new confidence and give school a positive purpose. The rationale for comprehensive education is turned on its head by an appeal to commonsense legitimation, which is empirically evident in the pupils' changed attitude. The purpose of education is no longer provision of equality of educational opportunity but provision of training for pupils which will allow them the opportunity to gain employment in relation to their social class, gender or ethnic origin. For the working class pupil the real world, namely the adult world of work is the world of status and access to commodities. The pupils identify with work experience because they are treated as equals, not children. Their initiation into work experience provides a framework for them to socialize and fix their class and gender identity even when this means acceptance of discriminatory work relations. Inside school the opportunity for taking non-traditional courses is related to four factors, first, the pupils' sexual stereotype of masculinity and femininity, second, the reaction of self and opposite sex pupils in the classroom, third, familial work role models, and fourth, the pupils interpretation of the difference between their own work aspirations and work expectations. The threat of unemployment both outside and inside the secondary school curriculum can result in pupils lowering their educational experience and job expectation, where they choose 'safe' stereotypical jobs which are assessed as providing them with maximum opportunity for the future.

TVEI is operating in terms of class and gender bias, despite a formal policy of equal opportunities, and the pupils are actively colluding with this process. In the next section I will examine in more detail the ways in which pupils' own class and gender stereotypes influence their aspirations and expectations for work.

Section 3

Female and Male Labour Market Expectations

Two central issues have been raised in the earlier sections of this chapter; first, the limited access of working class pupils in secondary school to equality of educational opportunity because of implicit or explicit selective processes and structures, and second, how recent (TVEI) and past (Newsom) curriculum developments have brought socially ascribed discrimination in the form of the values and barriers of the labour market into the secondary school. In order to examine the relationship between these two issues and the contribution of the pupils' own class and gender stereotypes to the labour market I will draw on empirical data relating to three areas: first, a statistical and interpretative assessment of pupils aspirations and expectations of the labour market; second, an analysis of the pupil's sexual stereotypes of self sex and opposite sex; and third, possible spaces to combat pupil sexual stereotypes.

What are working class girls' and boys' immediate impressions of jobs in the labour market? We asked pupils to write ten jobs which they thought of.

Table 1 shows the pupils' most frequently mentioned jobs, and indicates that they are looking at the adult work role models within the household/extended family and the local labour market. The pupils are taken from a largely working class sample and the list reveals typically male and female work. The two professional jobs mentioned of teacher and doctor are of high profile in the pupils' local environment.

The pupils were then asked to write three jobs which they would most like to have.

Table 2 shows the girls are clearly located in a female 'occupational ghetto'. The jobs chosen by the girls are like the jobs which they identified as being highly visible in their immediate perception of the labour market. The pull of traditional female adult work roles is the major influence which guides the girls' stereotypical selection of employment opportunities. The boys, like the girls, are strongly situated within a particular traditional occupational sector. However, unlike the girls, the boys not only have access to a wider selection of jobs but have monopolized a new occupational site in new technology. Overall, both girls and boys are located within a narrow occupational sector, which is not only diminishing but the position of women within this site of labour is one of low status in comparison to men.

What are the realities of the labour market for working class girls and boys as perceived by these pupils? Here I wish to look at the past desires, current aspirations and future expectations, of third and fifth form pupils in relation to their stereotypical choice of traditional or non-traditional work roles.

Table 3 shows that the boys' past desires for jobs in the 'escapist categories' of glamour and sport are reduced when checked by their future expectation. The boys' past desires of traditional male non-manual work show a high level of stability which carries through to their current aspirations but rapidly declines in the face of future expectations. The boys' past desires for traditional male manual work remain relatively steady in comparison with their current aspirations and future expectations, with the exception of an increase for third year boys in future expectations.

To summarize, few boys expect traditional male non-manual work. The threat of unemployment is very apparent, and in fact may contribute to reinforce the boys' selection of work in traditionally male 'safe' areas of employment. The male pupils' employment expectations are typically masculine stereotypical and located within a narrow and declining sector of the labour market. The boys scramble for the 'safe' male working class jobs in traditional manual areas; the result of this is to exclude women and

Table 1: Pupil perception of the labour market

Occupation	Percentage mentioning
Teacher	66
Secretary	49
Doctor	36
Nurse	36
Hairdresser	27
Shop assistant	24
Lorry driver	19
Plumber	19
Bus driver	19
Milkman	19

Table 2: Jobs most frequently mentioned

Girls		Boys	
Job	Percentage	Job	Percentage
Secretary	17	Computers	15
Nursery/Nurse	17	Footballer	13
Hairdresser	16	Mechanic	12
Work in a Bank	13	Lorry driver	10
Air hostess	10	Police	9
Nanny/ childminder	9	Forces	9
		Electrician	7
Beautician	7	Journalist	7
		Taxi driver	7

Table 3: Past desires, current aspirations and expectations for work

Boys		Main categories of response (percentage)			
		Glamour/ sport	Traditional male non-manual	Traditional male manual	Dole/DK
Past desires	Third year	16	59	25	
	Fifth year	8	38	42	
Current aspiration	Third year	13	42	38	
	Fifth year	9	34	41	
Future expectation	Third year	6	22	35	11
	Fifth year	7	3	45	28

ethnic groupings, who face problems of socially ascribed discriminations with respect to stereotypical assessment of appropriate female and male employment roles.

Table 4 shows that the girls' past desire for work in the high status female service area becomes dramatically diminished, when related to their future expectations. The statistic on the girls' past desires for employment in the female service middle range, remain largely the same in comparison with their expectations. The evidence concerning the girls' past desires for work with children, animals or in male/female areas, also shows a decline as leaving school becomes a reality. The most significant statistic is that of the girls' low past desires for work in the female low level service sector in comparison with the greatly increased number of girls whose future expectations is for work in this low status female occupational area. The girls' current aspirations for employment in the traditional male non-manual areas amounts to a positive statistic but is considerably overshadowed by the overwhelming expectation of inferior low status female work.

To summarize, most of the girls in the sample realize that they will be working within a range of female stereotypical low status employment. The structure of the girls' future work roles shows an alarmingly narrow picture. The range of jobs in the labour market which are identified by the girls as 'appropriate' are not only few and in decline but they are located in sectors where little training or future training is either available or required. The occupational sectors which are seen as appropriate for girls and women are determined by the patriarchal practices of discriminatory labour market processes which create and maintain both visible and invisible barriers to the entry of women. Working class girls are directed to and located within an occupational sector, which unlike that for many working class boys, represents no future. A girl's realization of this context may lead her to attempt individual solutions which are not located within the formal labour market, such as dependency within a domestic relation, for example family of origin or marriage, or a work relationship based upon bodily and personal forms of exploitation, such as prostitution or pornography.

Pupil Sexual Stereotypes Which Affect Occupational Entry

The data in this section are drawn from an analysis of some pupil responses to an anti-sexist curriculum unit[7] developed by the GAOC team in collaboration with respective teacher teams in different comprehensive schools in inner London.

We found that the GAOC programme brought out the pupils' explicit and implicit sexual and occupational stereotypes. Outside school, the learning of social and sexual stereotypes is constant and rarely challenged

Table 4: Past desires, current aspirations and expectations for work

Girls		Main categories of response (percentage)						
		Fem' service high	Fem' service middle	Fem' service low	Kids and animals	M/F	Traditional male non-manual	Dole D/K
Past desires	Third year	29	25	1	4	6	16	
	Fifth year	10	21	5	16	14	12	
Current aspiration	Third year	3	17	3	17	13	28	
	Fifth year	7	26	3	20	4	24	
Future expectation	Third year	1	21	34	7	5	5	15
	Fifth year	0	23	50	3	2	3	13

or questioned. Inside school, there are a range of stereotypes operating at different levels. These can be identified as the stereotypes of the school ethos and organization, teachers' stereotypes, those embedded in the curriculum, and the pupils' self and opposite sex stereotypes; the stereotypes of the wider class culture in which the school is located are also pervasive.

It was found that the girls held contradictory sexual stereotypes of boys in the present and boys in the future as men. In general, the girls had a relatively realistic and low opinion of men. In their view men got the best pay, better and more interesting jobs, had more freedom to spend money and access to pleasure. The girls saw men as unreliable and incapable, 'You can't trust them'. They categorized the boys as men as children: boys are unable to look after themselves, they require female service to make them men, because they behave like children. The girls assessed men as irresponsible, for example they would not leave men in charge of children because they would 'go off with mates' or 'down the pub'. But in addition the girls did not want men to stay inside the home. There were contradictory elements which adhered to the crucial areas of work and sexuality. For example: first, boys who wanted to take non-traditional male occupations, close to the female sphere, were understood as being 'silly' or 'sissy', it was not tough for men to do such work, and second, the girls were adamant that boys should not be given dolls to play with as it would change the boys' adult heterosexual career. But third, at the same time girls insisted that boys should be expected to look after children and babies and share the domestic labour in the household both as boys and men. The girls want males both to look after children and not to look after the children.

Boys enjoy the portrayal of sexual stereotypes because they reinforce male power and status. The boys in this study displayed symbolic and actual aggression, sometimes with violence to demonstrate that they have control over girls. The boys not only expect the girls to be submissive but demand that girls accept the boys' definition of social categories which refer to the girls' femininity (Lees, 1986). The boys have no necessity to challenge stereotypes because they are resources which already provide them with power. In an all-male discussion group a boy pupil who made any suggestion of non-traditional masculine employment was greeted with excessive sexist bravado which insulted his manhood. In large all-male groups the boys were not prepared to speak on or reveal non-traditional male behaviour. But in smaller all-male groups the boys found it possible to speak about taking part in domestic labour. One boy's statement high-lights the power of the male peer group: when he did the hoovering in the house he had delicately to manoeuvre the machine in such a way that when he passed the window, no person from outside the house could observe him engaged in domestic work.

This evidence can be presented in a tentative hypothesis of how sexual and occupational stereotypes operate for self and opposite sex.

For Girls

The girls' stereotype of the male is as macho. The girls' stereotype contains facets of sexuality and occupational identity: there is a strict division between appropriate masculine and feminine work roles. The girls' stereotype of a boy's masculinity is strongly held for boys seen as men. Where the boy's behaviour blurs the sexual/occupational division, that is, there is an uncertainty in the 'macho' image held by the girl; because the boy shows a non-traditional interest in, and contact with, a female sphere, tension is created. The girl heightens her male stereotype and her female stereotype to maintain the distance between herself and boys in the present, and the projection of herself in the future in an adult sexual relationship and in an adult work role.

For Boys

The boys' stereotype of the female is as 'passive/submissive'. The boys' stereotype contains facets of sexuality and occupational identity; there is a strict division between appropriate feminine and masculine work roles. The boys' stereotype of a girls's feminity is strongly held for girls seen as women. Where the girls's behaviour blurs the sexual/occupational division, that is, there is an uncertainty in the 'passive/submissive' female image held by the boys; because the girl has non-traditional interest in and contact with the male sphere, tension is created. The boy heightens his female stereotype and his male stereotype to maintain a distance between himself and girls in the present, and the projection of himself in the future in an adult sexual relationship and in an adult work role.

At school the pupils are developing their individual sexual identity but are only just beginning their sexual careers. The pupils' understanding of appropriate female and male sexuality is linked to adult life style through occupational identity. Both girls and boys hold rigid sexual/occupational stereotypes for the same and opposite sex which act to inhibit the possibility to select non-traditional routes within education and between occupational sectors. The pupil's selection of an option which might have reference to a non-traditional adult work role is seen in the present context as suggesting that this person has an ambiguous sexual identity and occupational future.

Spaces to Combat Stereotypes

There are contradictions in the girls' and boys' sexual and occupational stereotypes for self and opposite sex. The oppositions exist in their own different relations, learning experience, and future projections of men's and women's work roles. Spaces are social sites created by the opposition of contradictions which allow the possibility to legitimate and validate other or alternative ideas.

The girls and boys play with and make fun of the contradictory elements within and between self and opposite social and sexual stereotypes. During one lesson of the GAOC programme the girls and boys were paired off, the girl having to persuade the boy that she was capable of bricklaying. The only argument that the boys put forward was that of the male stereotype of strength. The girls challenged and disputed this, leaving the boys with nothing else to say, except to deny the girls their stereotype of feminine beauty, namely, girls do not like to get their hands dirty because it is unfeminine. The girls, however, could play around with this idea of the female stereotype of cleanliness; they sensed the opposition between beauty and makeup and dirty hands, messy hair and working clothes: a sort of 'makedown' rather than makeup. The girls made fun of their self stereotype and opposite sex stereotype, they also valued the traditional male work which meant getting your hands dirty, not being told off and getting well paid for the work.

Some of the boys in one school were taken on a trip to a children's nursery. The boys enjoyed the visit, helping, looking after babies and young children, playing with them showing tenderness and expressing feeling, supposedly of a non-traditional male nature. On the return to school the boys stated that they would not mind working in the future with children. A boy asked 'Why can't we have some of the girls along on the next trip'. There was an immediate argument in which it was suggested that the girls would push the boys out, telling them 'You can't do that with babies', and would humiliate them for playing with children, since it was an unmanly thing to do.

Some of the examples have shown that boys and girls can combat the contradictions of the sexual and occupational stereotypes. The space is available in the girls' and boys' thinking, and experience. Stereotypes are socially learned contradictions, oppositions which create the space to enter in order to legitimate and validate other or alternative ideas of female and male social, sexual and work role identities. In this space there is the potential for making change part of the girls' and boys' everyday experience. One possibility of the anti-sexist curriculum is that it provides a means and a clearly defined method for using spaces and opening other areas by questioning the conventions of female and male sexual stereotypes in school and in the labour market.

Summary

The chapter attempts an initial exploration of the relations within and between the labour market, secondary schooling, new vocationalism and pupil sexual and occupational stereotypes.[8]

I have tried to demonstrate that 'secondary education for all' came about in the context of consistent class opposition and class privilege. The form and content of the new secondary schools envisaged by government education committees did not bear a close relationship to principles of equality. The schools would accommodate pupils according to their social class and prepare them for specific occupational sectors. In the 1960s and 1970s the challenge from the comprehensive school, with the demands for equality of educational opportunity and new teaching methods such as mixed ability highlighted the selective and divisive nature of secondary schooling.

The recent history of TVEI in school does not solely relate to the Manpower Services Commission, the Conservative government or even the Great Debate, but rather there is a continuity with the original aims of the Spens, Norwood and Newsom educational reports, concerning what should be relevant education for the working class. The radical case for the new vocationalism must surely amount to the 'velvet glove' over an 'iron hand'. There are positive and progressive features, such as the new forms of assessment, development of new teaching styles, an integration curriculum approach and new pedagogic relations between teacher and pupil. New possibilities with new potentials, but are there drawbacks? There has been a major shift in the ground of the educational debate. Within new vocationalism lies a fundamental danger to the principles of equality, where education merely becomes training to enable pupils to gain skills which direct them to employment relevant to their social class, gender or ethnic origin. State education becomes imbued with a common-sense rationale which directs attention away from the biased order and meaning within principles of selection which direct an individual's future opportunities to a limited occupational sector.

In order to maximize their employment opportunities young people actively choose to enter a smaller range of occupational categories. There is a reduction in non-traditional choices by boys and girls in the school or the labour market because of the threat of unemployment and declining employment within certain occupational sectors, which forces pupils into an assessment where stereotypes play an important role guiding pupils into typical female and male work. The GAOC anti-sexist curiculum unit provided a means and a vehicle to open spaces for potential change in how pupils use and identify with sexual and occupational stereotypes. The world of work is not neutral, the labour market is strictly segmented and segregated by class, gender and race. We found that our programme brought out pupils' explicit and implicit stereotypical understandings. The introduction of work experience and vocational courses without a thorough check on the transmission of the values and relations from the world of work may possibly exacerbate class and gender differentiation.

Acknowledgements

I would like to thank Professor B Bernstein, Lynne Chisholm, Dr Janet Holland, Norah Marks, Sara Wall and in particular Phillip Brown, who all played different but valuable roles in the production of this chapter.

Notes

1   The research team was Lynne Chisholm, Tuula Gordon, Janet Holland, Shane Blackman and Jean McNeil. The GAOC research project has been funded by the Economic and Social Research Council, with additional funding from the ILEA, EOC and the University of London's Institute of Education Research Fund.

2   The Girls and Occupational Choice project has two interrelated strands: first, research into the processes through which girls of 11 to 16 come to decisions about their future work. Boys are included in the study but the focus is on the girls. Questionnaires and recurrent interviews are the major techniques employed in this aspect of the study; second, an action research component which involved working in close collaboration with teachers on the development of intervention strategies designed to break down sex stereotyped occupational choice for both sexes, directed towards first and third year pupils in three London schools. This aspect of the study necessitated long periods of immersion in schools in interaction with teachers and pupils, developing, transmitting and evaluating tailor made curriculum intervention programmes, and using a wide range of research techniques. These included pre-and post-intervention questionnaires for participants and control pupils, post-intervention interviews for participants, observation, participant observation, feedback from teachers involved in the programme and others in the school via formal and informal discussion and interview. The entire process has been documented in detail by the members of the research team. For further details see GAOC Working Paper Series, University of London, Institute of Education, Sociological Research Unit.

3   The data in the tables in section three were first presented by Holland, J. (1986) 'Girls and occupational choice: In search of meanings', paper given at a conference at St Hilda's College, Oxford, September. The data are derived from a *sub-sample* of 271 third and fifth year pupils, 88 male and 183 female.

4   Currently, within certain secondary schools in the London area outside the ILEA, the school governors and the parent/teacher association have been placing political letters in the school register via pupils to mobilize parental support to retain selective and discriminatory schooling.

5   Himmelweit, Halsey and Oppenheim (1952); Floud, Halsey and Martin (1956).

6   Lacey (1966); Hargreaves (1967); Willis (1977); Corrigan (1979); Woods (1979); Ball (1981); Turner (1983); Griffin (1985); Hammersley (1985).

7   The GAOC anti-sexist curriculum intervention unit will be published by Basil Blackwell, Oxford, in 1987 (forthcoming).

8   See my two GOAC working papers: first, 'Doleful schooling' (1986b) which investigates new vocationalism, secondary schooling, pupil sexual and occupational

stereotypes and labour market issues, and second, 'Schooling Labour', (1987 forthcoming) an analysis of the Youth Training Scheme, Manpower Services Commission and the labour market.

References

ALTHUSSER, L. (1971) 'Ideology and ideological state apparatuses' *Lenin and Philosophy*, London, New Left Books, pp. 122–73

ASHTON, D. (1986) *Unemployment Under Capitalism*, Brighton, Wheatsheaf Books Ltd.

BALL, S.J. (1981) *Beachside Comprehensive*, Cambridge, Cambridge University Press.

BANKS, O. (1955) *Parity and Prestige in English Secondary Schools*, London, Routledge and Kegan Paul.

BATES, I., CLARKE, J., COHEN, P., FINN, D., MOORE, R., WILLIS, P. (1984) *Schooling for the Dole?*, London, Macmillan.

BENN, C. and FAIRLEY, J. (Eds) (1986) *Challenging the MSC*, London, Pluto Press.

BERNSTEIN, B. (1970) 'Education cannot compensate for society', *New Society*, 26 February, pp. 344–7.

BERNSTEIN, B. (1977) *Class, Codes and Control, Vol 3*, revised edition, London, Routledge and Kegan Paul.

BLACKMAN, S.J. (1986a) 'Stereotypes, sexuality and spaces: the challenge for anti-sexist schooling', paper presented at the University of London Institute of Education, University Teachers Centre, May.

BLACKMAN, S.J. (1986b) 'Doleful schooling: Youth labour market issues', *GAOC Working Papers*, no. 8, University of London, Institute of Education, Sociological Research Unit.

BOURDIEU, P. and PASSERON, J.C. (1977) *Reproduction in Education, Society and Culture*, London, Sage.

BOWLES, S. and GINTIS, H. (1976) *Schooling in Capitalist America*, London, Routledge and Kegan Paul.

BRAVERMAN, H. (1974) *Labour and Monopoly Capital*, New York, Monthly Review Press.

BURGESS, R.G. (1983) *Experiencing Comprehensive Education: A Study of Bishop McGregor School*, London, Methuen.

BURGESS, R.G. (1986) 'Whatever happened to the Newsom course', paper presented at a conference St. Hilda's College, Oxford, 15–17 September.

CARTER, M. (1966) *Into Work*, London, Penguin.

CATTELL, R.B. (1936) 'Is national intelligence declining?' *Eugenice Review*.

CENTRE FOR CONTEMPORARY CULTURAL STUDIES (1977) 'On ideology', *Working Papers in Cultural Studies*, 10, University of Birmingham.

CHISHOLM, L. (1984) 'Comments and reflections on action research in education', *GAOC Working Papers*, no. 2, University of London, Institute of Education, Sociological Research Unit.

CHITTY, C. (1986) 'TVEI: The MSC's trojan horse' in BENN, C. and FAIRLEY, J. (Eds) *Challenging the MSC*, London, Pluto Press, pp. 76–98.

CLARE, J. (1986) 'Exam nerves: The new GCSE', *The Listener*, 116, 2978, 18 September, pp. 4–5.

COHEN, P. (1984) 'Against the new vocationalism', in BATES, I. *et al. Schooling for the Dole*, London, Macmillan, pp. 104–69.

CORRIGAN, P. (1979) *Schooling the Smash Street Kids*, London, Macmillan.

DALE, R. *et al.* (Eds) (1976) *Schooling and Capitalism*, London Milton Keynes, Routledge and Kegan Paul/Open University Press.

DALE, R. (Ed.) (1985a) *Education, Training and Employment*, Oxford, Pergamon Press.

DALE, R. (1985b) 'The background and inception of the technical and vocational education initiative', in DALE, R. *Education, Training and Employment*, Oxford, Pergamon Press, pp. 41–56.

DALE, R. (1986) 'Examining the gift-horse's teeth: A tentative analysis of TVEI', in WALKER, S. and BARTON, L. (Eds) *Youth, Unemployment and Schooling*, Milton Keynes, Open University Press, pp. 29–45.

DENT, H.C. (1961) *The Education System of England and Wales*, London, University of London Press.

DES (1963) *Half Our Future* (The Newsom Report), London, HMSO.

DES (1985) *Better Schools* (Cmnd 9469) London, HMSO.

DES (1985) *Supporting TVEI*, London, Further Education Unit, School Curriculum Development Committee.

DOE, and DES (1986) *Working Together — Education and Training*, (Cmnd 9823) London, HMSO.

FINN, D. (1982) 'New deals and broken promises: Young workers: the school leaving age and youth unemployment', unpublished PhD thesis, University of Birmingham, CCCS, Faculty of Arts.

FINN, D. (1984) 'Leaving school and growing up: Work experience in the juvenile labour market' in BATES, I. *et al. Schooling for the Dole*, London, Macmillan, pp. 17–64.

FINN D., GRANT, N. and JOHNSON, R. (1977) 'Social democracy, education and the crisis, in CCCS', On Ideology, *Working Papers in Cultural Studies*, 10, University of Birmingham, pp. 147–98.

FLOUD, J. and HALSEY, A.H. (1961) 'English secondary schools and the supply of labour', in HALSEY, A.H. FLOUD, J. and ANDERSON, C.A. (Eds) *Education, Economy and Society*, New York, The Free Press/Collier-Macmillan, pp. 80–92.

FLOUD, J., HALSEY, A.H., MARTIN, F.M. (1956) *Social Class and Education Opportunity* London, Heinemann.

GLASS, D. (Ed.) (1954) *Social Mobility in Britain*, London, Routledge and Kegan Paul

GLASS, D. (1961) 'Education and social change in modern England', in HALSEY, A.H., FLOUD, J. and ANDERSON, C.A. (Eds) *Education, Economy and Society*, New York, The Free Press/Collier-Macmillan, pp. 391–413.

GLEESON, D. (1985) 'Privatisation of industry and the nationalisation of youth', in DALE, R. (Ed.) *Education, Training and Employment*, Oxford, Pergamon Press, pp. 57–72.

GOLLAN, J. (1937) *Youth in British Industry*, London, Victor Gollancz Ltd

GRIFFIN, C. (1985) *Typical Girls?*, London, Routledge and Kegan Paul.

HALSEY, A.H., FLOUD, J. and ANDERSON, C.A. (Eds) (1961) *Education, Economy and Society*, New York, The Free Press/Collier-Macmillan.

HAMMERSLEY, M. (1985) 'From ethnography to theory; a programme and a paradigm in the sociology of education', *Sociology*, 19, 2, pp. 244–59.

HARDING, J. (1986) 'Different labels same options', paper presented at a conference at St. Hilda's College, Oxford, 15–17 September.

HARGREAVES, D.H. (1967) *Social Relations in a Secondary School*, London, Routledge and Kegan Paul.

HIMMELWEIT, H.T., HALSEY, A.H. and OPPENHEIM, A.M. (1952) 'The views of adolescents on some aspects of the social class structure', *British Journal of Sociology*, III, pp. 148–72.

HOGBEN, L. (Ed.) (1938) *Political Arithmetic*, London, Allen and Unwin.

HOLLAND, J. (1981) *Work and Women*, London, Bedford Way Paper No. 6, University of London, Institute of Education.

HOLLAND, J. (1986) 'Girls and occupational choice: In search of meanings', paper presented at a conference at St. Hilda's College, Oxford, 15–17 September.

HOLLAND, J., BLACKMAN, S.J. GORDON, T. and TEACHER TEAM, (1984) 'A woman's place: strategies for change in the educational context', *GAOC Working Papers*, no. 4, University of London, Institute of Education, Sociological Research Unit.

JAMIESON, I. (1985) 'Corporate hegemony or pedagogic liberation: the schools-industry movement in England and Wales' in DALE, R. (Eds) *Education, Training and Employment*, Oxford, Pergamon Press, pp. 23–39.

JONES, P. (1984) 'What opportunities for youth?, *Youthaid Occasional Papers*, no. 4, London.

KNEEBONE, R.M.T. (1957) *I Work in a Secondary Modern School*, London, Routledge and Kegan Paul.

LACEY, C. (1966) 'Some sociological concomitants of academic streaming in a grammar school', *British Journal of Sociology*, XVII, 3, pp. 245–62.

LASKI, H. (1928) 'The British Cabinet', *Fabian Tract*, no. 223.

LEES, S. (1986) *Losing Out*, London, Hutchinson.

LONDON EDUCATIONAL REVIEW (1975) 'From theory to practice, from school to work', 4, no. 2/3, University of London, Institute of Education.

LOWNDES, G.A.N. (1935) *The Silent Social Revolution*, London, Oxford University Press.

MACE, J. (1986) 'Education, the labour market and government policy', paper presented at a BEMAS National Seminar, University of Birmingham, Easter.

McROBBIE, A. and NAVA, M. (Eds) (1984) *Gender and Generation*, London, Macmillan.

MARSH, S. (1986) 'Women and the MSC' in BENN, C. and FAIRLEY, J. (Eds) *Challenging the MSC*, London, Pluto Press, pp. 153–75.

MILLMAN, V. (1985) 'The new vocationalism in secondary schools: Its influence on girls', in WHYTE, J. DEEM, R., KANT, L. and CRUICKSHANK, M. (Eds) *Girl-Friendly Schooling*, London, Methuen, pp. 45–70.

MOORE, R. (1984) 'Schooling and the world of work', in BATES, I. *et al.* *Schooling for the Dole?*, London, Macmillan, pp. 65–103

MUSGRAVE, P.W. (1965) *The Sociology of Education*, London, Methuen.

NAS/UWT (1986) 'Education and training for young people', in *Schoolmaster and Career Teacher, Journal of NAS/UWT*, Spring. pp. 9, 11–12, 14, 34–5.

NIGHTINGALE, R.T. (1930) 'The personnel of the British Foreign Office and Diplomatic Service 1851–1929', *Fabian Tract*, no. 232.

NUT (1983) 'TVEI-extension of pilot scheme', *NUT Circular*, 392/83, London.

OFFE, C. (1985) *Disorganised Capitalism*, Cambridge, Polity Press.

OPPENHEIM, A.H. (1955) 'Social status and clique formation among grammar school boys' *British Journal of Sociology*, IX, pp. 288–45.

PERKINS, T.E. (1979) 'Rethinking stereotypes', in BARRETT, M., CORRIGAN, P., KUHN, A. and WOLF, J. (Eds) *Ideology and Cultural Production*, London, Croom Helm Ltd, pp. 135–59.

REES, T. and ATKINSON, P. (Eds) (1982) *Youth Unemployment and State Intevention*, London, Routledge and Kegan Paul.

REYNOLDS, D. (1986) 'Education and training at the periphery', paper presented at a conference at St. Hilda's College, Oxford, 15–17 September.

ROBERTS, K. (1984) *School Leavers and Their Prospects*, Milton Keynes, Open University Press.

TAWNEY, R.H. (1922) *Secondary Education for All*, London, Labour Party/Allen and Unwin.

TAYLOR, W. (1963) *The Secondary Modern School*, London, Faber.

TURNER, G. (1983) *The Social World of the Comprehensive School*, London, Croom Helm Ltd.

UNIVERSITY OF LANCASTER TVEI EVALUATION PROGRAMME (1986) 'Characteristics of

TVEI and non-TVEI students with particular reference to gender', Institute for Research and Development in Post-Compulsory Education, Lancaster.

WATTS, A.G. (1983) *Education, Unemployment and the Future of Work*, Milton Keynes, Open University Press.

WEINER, G. (1985) 'What the customers have to say: Interviews with pupils who have made non-traditional option choices', Open University, unpublished paper.

WILLIAMS, W.M. (Ed.) (1974) *Occupational Choice*, London, Allen and Unwin.

WILLIS P. (1975) 'The main reality: Transition school/work', *Stencilled Occasional Paper*, no. 38, University of Birmingham, CCCS.

WILLIS, P. (1977) *Learning to Labour*, Farnborough, Saxon House.

WILLIS, P. (1986) 'Unemployment: The final inequality' *British Journal of Sociology of Education*, 7, 2, pp. 155–69.

WOODS, P. (1979) *The Divided School*, London, Routledge and Kegan Paul.

YOUTH REVIEW TEAM (1985) *The Social Condition of Young People in Wolverhampton*, Civic Centre, Wolverhampton.

3   Coming to Terms with the Declining Demand for Youth Labour

Andy Furlong

The transition from adolescence to adulthood is a topic which has captured the interest of sociologists for many years. In particular they have tried to account for the ease with which the transition tended to be made, and how young people came to accept jobs which offered few prospects for the future. This tended to be explained as being due to a continuity of experience between early expectation and future reality. That is, young peoples' early experiences within the family, school and peer group adequately prepared them for their future position within the occupational hierarchy. However, the bulk of the work on the transition from school to work was undertaken in a period when occupational opportunities for youth were quantitatively and qualitatively different from what they have become in the 1980s.

On the basis of this model, we would expect a rapid rise in youth unemployment to result in a disjuncture between the expectations of young people and their labour market experiences. This disjuncture would be expected to result in a traumatic transitional period for those who failed to fulfil their prior expectations. Yet I will be suggesting that, in the short-term, this is not the case for many young people.

In this chapter I will examine the extent to which previous theories are still able to explain youth transitions in a declining market for their labour. Despite some shortcomings I will suggest that existing 'socialization' theories of the transition remain essential to a complete understanding of the process. Such theories enable us to explain the seemingly erratic labour market behaviour of young people, and their resistance to the limited opportunities available.

This chapter is based on a study undertaken into the effects of youth unemployment on the transition from school in Leicester. This involved a longitudinal study of a group of 100 adolescents who entered their final year of compulsory education in the academic year 1983/84. The sample is composed of fifty males and fifty females who were selected at random from two Leicester schools. One of these schools, 'Newtown', has a predominantly middle class intake, whilst the other, 'Crescent', has a predominantly working class intake. The pupils in the sample were first interviewed at school in January and February 1984, and then again a year later in their own homes. This chapter is based on the results of the first two interviews, and reports the young peoples' initial reactions to their experience of the transition.

Socialization Theory

The early sociological studies on the transition from school to work tended to follow the psychological work in seeing the transition to work as being a stressful period in a young person's life. As young people made the move from school to work, it was argued, they encountered 'considerable frustration' as their previous aspirations were 'beaten down' to fit the realities of the occupational world (Miller and Form, 1951).

Yet by the 1970s sociological analysis (perhaps reflecting the buoyant economy) had come to a broad consensus that in most cases the transition to work could not be characterized as a period of 'stress and strain'. The experiences of young people occurring in the home and the school, it was argued (Ashton and Field, 1976), provided them with adequate preparation for the realities they will encounter as they enter the world of work. Thus the smoothness of the transition was explained in terms of 'congruence of experience'

As the young person makes the transition from school they are forced to take stock of the degree to which prior impressions of the world of work match with the reality they now face. Whether the transition is made with ease or frustration depends to a large extent upon the discrepancy that exists between a young person's prior impressions and this reality.

Ashton and Field (ibid), for example, argued that most young people experience a continuity of experience in the home, at school and at work. As a result, the transition from school is not a period of stress. In most cases young peoples' previous experiences adequately prepare them for the work situation they will enter. Thus the initial 'frame of reference' which has been acquired in the home and school directs them towards different bands of occupations. As a result of their experiences within the home and school young people from lower working class families tend to come to seek their pleasures in the immediate present. On the other hand, those from middle class families tend to learn to postpone gratification in order to enhance their career prospects.

In a large part, these 'socialization' theories rested on the notion of the self concept, and in particular, the centrality of the occupational self concept within the overall self concept. A young person's interpretation and understanding of their position (of how they fit into society in general and the occupational structure in particular) is known as their occupational self concept. People gain impressions about themselves through making comparisons with significant others. And it is by means of these relationships that the self image is developed. Cooley (1922) described this as the 'looking glass self' in that people see themselves reflected through their relationships with significant others, and these reflections enable them to test the validity of their beliefs. For reasons we shall see, it is important to remember that self concepts are not purely subjective constructs, but develop out of a person's experiences within objective structures.

It is due to their experiences within social structures, such as the family and school, that young people gain impressions of the opportunities available to themselves in the local labour market (Ashton and Field, 1976), and form ideas about the desirability of certain types of work (Willis, 1977). As such, these impressions, being rooted in experience, reflect the realities and constraints of the local labour market. They result in smooth transitions for most young people, as entry into the labour market tends to confirm their prior expectations.

Opportunity Structure Theory

The socialization model was developed at a time when levels of youth unemployment were much lower than they are now. Consequently, young peoples' expectations could be translated into jobs much more easily. As a result of deteriorating employment prospects for youth, the validity of a model which rests on the assumption that young people enter jobs which confirm prior expectations must be called into question.

Roberts (1984) has suggested that throughout the industrial age, the transition to work has been a problem for most young people. In fact, he suggests that the smooth transitions of the post-war decades were exceptions to the rule. Because of this, Roberts rejects the validity of occupational self concepts for aiding our understanding of occupational entry. In its place he substitutes the term 'opportunity structure' which he sees as providing a more adequate theory of occupational entry. 'Neither school leavers nor adults', he suggests, 'typically choose their jobs ... they simply take what is available' (Roberts, 1977, p. 3).

However, the traditional 'socialization' approach, and the 'opportunity structure' model advanced by Roberts, are not as radically opposed as it would seem at first. According to Roberts (1968 and 1977), occupational plans are based upon our impressions of occupations open to us. Yet the gathering of impressions of our future work roles is exactly what others (Ginzberg *et al.*, 1951) have referred to as the occupational self concept; a term which Roberts rejects.

The 'opportunity structure' model, in effect, depicts humans as the more or less passive products of socializing forces. Yet humans are capable of acting upon their impressions of a situation. Self concepts are not purely subjective, but show us how a young person comes to terms with the objective elements of the social structure. In other words, it is through the development of an occupational self concept that we make sense of the occupational structure and anticipate what lies ahead of us.

I will be suggesting here that it is precisely because humans react to and reinterpret situations that declining employment opportunities do not necessarily result in traumatic transitions in the short term. Thus, an understanding of subjective interpretation is essential to any sociological analysis since it enables us to explain reactions to changing social structures. In the short term at least, young peoples' reactions may minimize the effects of declining employment opportunities.

In Defence of the Socialization Model

If the traditional socialization model retains its validity in a period which offers few opportunities to young people, then we must discover to what extent occupational entry is still explainable by aspirations. That is, if occupational self concepts are useful in explaining subsequent labour market behaviour, it must be shown that young peoples' aspirations can help in the interpretation of their labour market biographies. It is also necessary to demonstrate that their aspirations are not simply reflections of opportunities available to them in the labour market, and that they are not simply adjusted to fit the available opportunities. In other words, it must be shown that aspirations are defended and pursued in the face of difficulties in attainment.

In the Leicester study young people were asked about the sorts of jobs they aspired to just before they reached the minimum school leaving age. Their aspirations could be seen as realistic in that the distribution of occupations aspired to bore a close relationship to the local occupational structure. This would seem to support Roberts' theory.

Many studies have shown that the occupational aspirations of young people are largely determined by the opportunities available in the local labour market (Carter, 1975; Raby and Walford, 1981). This again would appear to lend weight to Roberts' theory. But while the occupational aspirations of members of the Leicester sample bore a close resemblance to the structure of the local labour market, due to rapid change, jobs which would have been available in the local labour market a few years previously are not necessarily still available to new entrants. Although the majority of respondents said that they expected to achieve their aspirations, many in fact failed to achieve them. Comparing the jobs young people entered with the jobs they had aspired to, we find that the majority, (62 per cent, thirty-four) were in occupations other than those to which they had originally aspired.

Of those accepting a job other than that which they had originally aspired to, 35 per cent (fourteen) accepted the alternative because of problems securing the type of work they wanted, such as difficulties in finding vacancies, finding they lacked the necessary qualifications, or discovering they were too young. A further 25 per cent (ten) abandoned their original aspirations on finding alternative employment. This would be because they found a job which sounded interesting or which was thought to have better prospects, or simply because they lost interest in their original aspiration.

In so far as young people are unlikely to hope for the unattainable, their aspirations can be said to be a product of objective conditions. And the opportunities which are available in the local labour market will have an effect on how far aspirations can be fulfilled. As a result, it may seem appropriate to talk of an 'opportunity structure' model. Yet as I have suggested, the opportunity structure model neglects the effects of human action on labour market biographies. As a result, we are left with a very passive, 'oversocialized' (Wrong, 1961) concept of youth. On the other hand, the socialization model emphasizes the constraints imposed by structure, yet is able to present agency as a dependent variable. One of the strengths of the socialization model is in its ability, through the self concept, to give us a greater understanding of the importance of interpretation and of the cognitive resistance which prevents passive acceptance of a situation.

I am not suggesting that levels of aspiration can in any way affect the availability of jobs. But aspirations do affect the school leavers' willingness to accept a particular job, and once in the job, how satisfied they are with it. Overall, about half of those who had worked, 51 per cent (twenty-eight), gave a negative reason for accepting their job, saying that as jobs were in short supply they could not afford to be choosy, or that they just took it as a temporary measure whilst seeking something more in line with their tastes. Yet failure to achieve an objective, especially within such a short period of time, does not necesarily result in passive acceptance of the situation. In fact, 40 per cent (sixteen) of those who have failed to achieve their ambitions, so far have not abandoned hope of achieving them. Some of them, while accepting the first job offered, are still searching for the type of work they really want. In this chapter I will examine the ways in which these people react to the declining demand for youth labour.

Declining Opportunities and Image Maintenance Strategies

As we have seen, it used to be suggested (for example Ashton and Field, 1976) that prior to leaving school young people came to develop fairly accurate ideas about the level of job they would get. Consequently the transition was fairly smooth as the occupations they entered broadly confirmed their prior expectations. Yet today, many young people fail to achieve their aspirations due to declining opportunities. As such, their aspirations are out of line with the jobs they are likely to enter.

Others have argued (Gurney, 1979; Hutson, 1962) that the entry into work often causes young people considerable trauma and frustration as they struggle to reconcile past images with reality. However, evidence from the Leicester study shows that declining employment prospects for youth has not, in the short-term, resulted in the rough transition that would be predicted as young people are forced to reconcile occupational self concepts with changing opportunity structures. In response to the situation they find themselves in, many of the young people in the Leicester study adopted a variety of image maintenance strategies to enable the retention of a self concept which had been developed under different structural conditions. In other words, their aspirations were not simply modified to take account of existing opportunities, but continued to be pursued.

Work and Image Maintenance

A variety of strategies are adopted by young people to protect their occupational self concepts against the threats posed by declining opportunities. Goffman (1961) has referred to this process as 'role distancing'. He suggests that 'role distancing' is a defensive strategy which is adopted by individuals in roles they feel are beneath them. One 'role distancing' strategy which is adopted by those in a different type of work to that to which they had aspired, is to see the current work they do as being a temporary situation until they find the type of work they want. The young person who adopts this strategy realizes that current levels of unemployment mean that the type of work they want may be in short supply. By accepting different type of work they see themselves as biding their time until the economy picks up.

This sort of strategy is illustrated by the case of Gary. Gary had a long term ambition to work in the building trade as either a 'brickie' or a 'chippie'. Yet since leaving school he had been unable to find such work despite a three-month search. Eventually he accepted a job in a factory as a packer. However, he continued to regard this job as a temporary 'fill-in' while continuing to look for an opening in the building trade. Gary expected to find the kind of work he wanted once winter, which he knew to be a slack period, was over.

Young people who regard their current work as a stop-gap feel no commitment to remain in such work. I would suggest that this may be one of the reasons for the continuation of relatively high levels of job abandonment among young people in times of high youth unemployment. When jobs for young people were more plentiful, dissatisfied young workers were able to make a successful job change. Nowadays, those disillusioned young people who leave a job, are less likely to enter another straight away. Of the fifty-six people in the Leicester study who had worked since leaving school, nine had changed jobs within the first nine months, and a further nine had left their jobs and had as yet been unable to find another, (four of the eighteen who had left a job were made redundant, and two were sacked). Of the forty-six who were still working when interviewed, twelve (26 per cent) said that they would only remain in their job until something better came up. It is this group of young people who are maintaining their aspirations whilst temporarily accepting an alternative job.

Education Training and Image Maintenance

Another strategy which some young people adopt, is to continue their education or training in order to postpone their entry into the world of work. Some young people remain in education in order to retain aspirations they would be unlikely to fulfil if they left at 16. Where this is true, remaining in education can be seen as a strategy to maintain the occupational self concept. This is particularly true of those with high occupational aspirations, even if they had obtained disappointing examination results. In the Leicester sample, this type of strategy was particularly popular among girls, who displayed a more favourable attitude towards the school than did the boys.[1]

Tracey is very keen on sports and desperately wants to get work as a PE teacher. She realizes that she will need to get 'A' levels, and then go to college for three years. In the fifth-form Tracey only managed to get a handful of average grade CSEs. She left school and went full-time to the local further education college to get the qualifications necessary for college entry. After a year at the college, to her disappointment, she had only passed two 'O' levels, yet still decided to go back and resit the following year. Tracey still expects to get the qualifications which will enable her to get into college, although she realizes that her ability in sport is not matched in the other subjects she must take.

Of the twenty-six members of the sample who continued their education after the minimum age, nine people indicated that if employment prospects were better they would not have remained in education. Although only two of these young people actually looked for work during the summer vacation, nine admitted that they casually looked for work, and had they seen a suitable vacancy they would have gone for the job in preference to remaining in education. It is this group of young people, whose continued presence in education is a consequence of the current level of youth unemployment, who can be regarded as operating image maintenance strategies.

Occupational self concepts are therefore important to an understanding of the increase in participation in post 16 education. Young people become more willing to remain in education when a lack of 'suitable' vacancies in the local labour market makes them uncertain about their prospects. However, those who have a positive predisposition towards the educational system (these being mainly female), feel that extending their education will pay off in terms of eventual achievement of their aspirations. There is evidence to suggest (Raffe, 1984) that the qualifications gained through extended education may benefit the girls in terms of the jobs they eventually get. Yet remaining at school for an extra year may disadvantage boys due to employers' preference for younger school leavers in many skilled occupations. Consequently this sort of strategy may involve more risk for boys.

High levels of youth unemployment have prompted governments in many countries to set up training schemes specifically aimed at unemployed youngsters. In Britain a variety of special measures have been used since 1975 culminating in the present Youth Training Scheme. While there is a growing body of literature on the effects of these schemes, much of it concentrates on their effect upon youth wages and the attitude of young people to the schemes. While analysis of this type is important, it tends to neglect the ways in which young people themselves attempt to use the schemes to their own advantage. The contradiction is that the young people who join schemes may regard them as slave labour, yet join one as a way of trying to resist the dead end jobs on offer, and of trying to fulfil their aspirations. Just as youngsters may use continued education as an image maintenance strategy, so these schemes are often used by young people as a means of protecting their occupational self images (Furlong, 1983).

Dawn was a reluctant recruit to the Youth Training Scheme, who discovered that the route into hairdressing apprenticeships is increasingly through YTS.

> Last year I'd have said that I'm not going to go on a scheme, it's just cheap labour. But when it came down to it, it was either do hairdressing on a scheme, or go in a shop or factory. I still think it's slave labour, but it'll get me into hairdressing.

Twenty-three people in the Leicester sample had spent some time on the Youth Training Scheme, and of these, the majority, 87 per cent (twenty), said that they joined as they thought the basic training provided would pave their way into the particular job to which they had aspired.

Schemes are often used as an image maintenance strategy by those who aspire to the skilled trades. Of those currently on a scheme, the majority, 67 per cent (fourteen), expected to find work on leaving in the type of trade they had learnt on the scheme. Indeed, most of those who had joined a scheme were those who had originally aspired towards short-career jobs, (such as the skilled trades), and the majority of those currently on schemes still expected the same sort of work they had aspired to when they left school. Indeed, two people in the Leicester study had left permanent jobs to join schemes in order to maintain their aspirations. Young people who attempt to maintain their occupational self images by staying in education or by entering the Youth Training Scheme may, eventually, achieve their objectives. For some, the strategies they adopt may be successful. However, many will fail in their strategies. For these, the investment they have made in an occupational self image which they are subsequently forced to abandon, is likely to result in their experiencing severe difficulties in adjustment.

Unemployment and Image Maintenance

Paradoxically, high levels of youth unemployment can make the transition from school to work less traumatic for some by enabling the young person to maintain and reinforce an otherwise unsupportable self image, at least in the short-term. Thus for some young people, remaining unemployed can be seen as a strategy which enables the maintenance of their occupational self concepts.

It has been suggested (Ashton and Field, 1976) that in times of relatively full employment, being out of work is often a traumatic experience. It can often lead to the abandonment of occupational self images as the young people involved come to see themselves as failures. However, in times of high unemployment, young people are more able to retain a belief in their capabilities, seeing unemployment as temporarily thwarting their aspirations, but nevertheless retaining a belief in their eventual attainment. It has been found that unemployed school leavers do not experience a drop in their level of self-esteem (Gurney, 1980). Rather, their self-esteem remains static, and it is those who find work whose self-esteem gets a boost. This seems to be due to the increasing 'normality' of youth unemployment in parts of the country where unemployment has become commonplace.

Prior to leaving school a majority of the young people in the Leicester study 62 per cent (sixty-two) felt that youth unemployment was largely a consequence of the personal inadequacies of the unemployed. Yet when they gained personal experience of unemployment, the majority of those who had been unemployed, (76 per cent, sixteen) came to see youth unemployment as being a feature of the overall job shortage and saw it as beyond their control. It has been suggested (Gurney, 1979) that someone who is unemployed is unlikely to see their current status as being the result of personal factors if there is a factor in the environment they can hang the blame on.

As a result of their being able to place the blame for their unemployment outside of their personal realm of influence, there was little change in their occupational self images.[2] In fact the majority of those who were unemployed were still looking for their ideal choice of occupation. Wayne left school with four 'O' levels and wanted an engineering apprenticeship. Although the careers officer has tried to get him to look at other types of career, and has tried to persuade him to join a Youth Training Scheme, Wayne prefers to hold out for the type of work he wants:

> I know if I take another job I'll get stuck in it and it'll be too late to get a trade.

Although Wayne has been out of work for six months, he is still confident that he will get an apprenticeship eventually. He feels that it is wiser for him to be unemployed in the short-term than to end up in a job he does not want.

In her recent study of Birmingham school leavers, Jones (1985) discovered that young people with the greatest confidence in obtaining the sort of job they wanted tended to persist in their attempts to find that job, whilst those with lower levels of confidence were more likely to accept the less desirable alternative (see aso MacKay and Reid, 1972). In this context, some youth unemployment has been characterized as self-inflicted (Roberts *et al*, 1982) in that some youngsters prefer to remain unemployed and retain their occupational self-image, rather than to enter unskilled jobs when they feel themselves to be capable of better. As *Coffield et al* (1983) observed in their study, young people were not worried simply by the prospect of continued unemployment, but by the quality of jobs which they were offered.

Those who hold out for the type of work they want, may find that their strategy pays off. Yet many will eventually discover that their prospects of gaining any form of employment have declined. Coming to terms with this failure may well be a traumatic experience.

Anomie and Declining Opportunities

In advancing an 'opportunity structure' model Roberts (1968) has suggested that a young person's prior orientations are of little importance in that the vast majority of young people adapt their prior aspirations fairly unproblematically upon entering the labour market. Similarly, Festinger (1962) suggested that people do not generally maintain aspirations they cannot realize, but reduce 'cognitive dissonance' by abandoning them. As I have shown, preliminary evidence from the Leicester study shows that this is not the case. Young people are not the passive recipients of structural dictates, an in the short-term at least will resist pressures to abandon their aspirations. Rapid structural change within many local labour markets has led to a situation whereby in a period of uncertainty, people hold onto what have become 'inappropriate', values, (a situation which Durkheim (1951) would regard as 'anomic'); that is, values which are not reducible to current opportunity structures. In the Leicester study many young people are unlikely to attain their aspirations due to declining opportunities for youth within the local labour market.

It would seem that in an anomic situation young people's reactions are rather different. A combination of strong occupational self-images which developed under different structural conditions (opportunity structures), and a feeling of uncertainty about what the future holds, means that prior orientations are retained and self-images remain intact. Ashton and Field (1976) suggested that a high rate of unemployment in one locality over an extended period of time is likely to bring about a corresponding adjustment in the perspectives young people hold. Yet Hayes and Nutman (1981, p. 54) suggest that in areas of high youth unemployment, an individual may be able to sustain an 'assumptive world commensurate with his or her self-image', as unemployment carries less stigma when it is commonplace.

There is some evidence that young peoples' occupational aspirations are lower in places with high levels of youth unemployment. (Ashton and Maguire *et al.*, 1986), such as in Sunderland where the labour market opportunities for young people have been in serious decline for many years. Yet in such areas, economic changes have had over a decade to bring about changes in subjective orientations. That is, whilst young peoples' occupational self concepts may have been restructured, this restructuring has taken place through experiences within a local labour market which has offered few opportunities over extended periods of time. As a result of this, the young person incorporates into their self-image a realization of the prevailing structural conditions. Thus, the occupational self concept undergoes changes primarily as a result of their experiences in the home and school, rather than as a result of direct experiences of the opportunities available in the local market.

In areas such as Leicester, where the change have been more rapid, a young person is less likely to abandon a self concept which has been structured under different economic circumstances. The occupational self concept is an integral part of a person's identity and is not subjectively abandoned but undergoes slow modification through experiences within the labour market. Ashton and Field (1976) suspected that failure by young people to achieve the level of career they expected at school would be traumatic. Yet in the Leicester study there seems to be an absence of trauma among young people, even though large numbers have failed to achieve their aspirations and even though many are dissatisfied with their current jobs. This, as I have demonstrated, is mainly achieved through the adoption of image maintenance strategies which are developed in response to a threatened self concept. In the short-term such strategies help explain behaviour such as remaining in education. or giving up a job. In some instances these strategies may bring about the desired ends, yet when a strategy fails, the consequent changes to the self-image and the adoption of a new assumptive world may be very traumatic for the person concerned.

Conclusion

The last few years have seen a sharp rise in the incidence of unemployment among school leavers. When levels of unemployment among young people suddenly rise, it is not just those who cannot find work who are affected. Many others fail to find the type of job that they could realistically expect in different circumstances. Others, anticipating the difficulties they will face in the labour market, manage to postpone their entry into the job market by remaining in education or by joining government sponsored training schemes.

An increase in levels of youth unemployment over a relatively short period of time will have little effect upon young peoples' occupational self concepts. Their occupational self concepts are the result of a socialization process which has been built on and reinforced over many years prior to labor market entry. Indeed, the occupational self concept is an integral part of the young person's overall self-image and of the way they see the world. It is because the self concept is not simply a subjective construct, but is the result of long-term experiences within the family, school and peer group, that change in the short-term is unlikely. Indeed, young people go to many lengths to protect their self concepts.

As a young person's occupational self concept is developed through experiences within the family, school and peer group, it typically comes to incorporate a fairly realistic appraisal of the types of opportunities which have been open to members of their particular class and sex within the local labour market.

Just as occupational self concepts are built up through experiences, so change in the self concept is a result of new experiences. Therefore, in the long-term, high levels of unemployment will lead to a lowering of aspirations. When high levels of youth unemployment persist in an area over time, the young person's experiences lead to the development of an occupation self concept which takes account of the limited opportunities which are available within the local labour market.

In order to understand the ways in which young people make the transition from school and come to terms with the declining demand for youth labour, we need a synthesis of the 'socialization' model and the 'opportunity structure' model. Both models contain some truth, but the notion of the self concept as contained in the 'socialization' model enables an appreciation of the ways in which the opportunity structures are cognized, and through cognition, affect future action. It also allows an appreciation of the material base of cognition, and can show how changes in material circumstances may bring about changes in our cognition.

However, one of the main shortcomings of the socialization model is that it fails to show that an accurate impression of what lies in store for young people is not simply the consequence of powerful socialization. Rather, the accuracy of preconceptions tended to be a result of the stability of labour market structures in a particular era which made prediction less uncertain.

The opportunity structure model solves this problem by showing how the scope for human action is a variable constrained by structure. Structure is not a fixed variable, but its strength fluctuates. As such, the power of structure and thence the scope for action may show marked variation in different time periods as well as in different geographical locations.

Acknowledgements:

I would like to thank all the members of the Labour Market Studies group at the University of Leicester for their helpful comments on aspects of this paper. I am especially grateful to David Ashton and Malcolm Maguire, who both read the manuscript in its entirety and made many invaluable suggestions. However, any mistakes or misunderstandings are my own.

Notes

1 School attitude was measured by scaled responses to the following statements:
I will be glad to get away from school.
There are some things I expect I will miss about school when I leave.
I get bord with school because it's always the same.
2 It should be noted that at the time they were interviewed, all the unemployed were short-term, in that the longest period it was possible to have been unemployed was nine months. Recent work by Willis (1985) suggests that in this respect the long-term unemployed may differ from the short-term unemployed.

References

ASHTON, D.N. and FIELD, D. (1976) *Young Workers*, London, Hutchinson.
ASHTON, D.N. and MAGUIRE, M.J. *et al*,(1986) *Young Adults in the Labour Market*. London, Department of Employment Research Paper, no. 55
CARTER, M.P. (1975) 'Teenage workers: A second chance at 18?' in BRANNEN, P. (Ed.) *Entering the World of Work*, London, HMSO.
COFFIELD, F. BORRILL, C. and MARSHALL, S. (1983). 'How young people survive being unemployed', *New Society*, June, pp. 332–4.
COOLEY, C.H. (1922) *Human Nature and the Social Order*, New York, Scribner.
DURKHEIM, E. (1951) *Suicide: A Study in Sociology*, Glencoe, Free Press.

FESTINGER, L. (1962) *A Theory of Cognitive Dissonance*, London, Tavistock.

FURLONG, A. (1983) 'Facing up to reality', *Youth in Society*, December, pp. 24–5.

GINZBERG, E. GINSBURG, S.W. AXELRAD, S. and HERMA, J.L. (1951) *Occupatonal Choice*, New York, Columbia University Press.

GOFFMAN, E. (1961) *Encounters*, New York and Indianapolis, Bobbs Merrill Co. Inc.

GURNEY, R.M. (1979) 'Aspects of school leaver adaptation to unemployment', unpublished PhD thesis, University of Melbourne.

GURNEY, R.M. (1980) 'Does unemployment affect the self-esteem of school leavers?' *Australian Journal of Psychology*, 32, 3, pp. 175–82.

HAYES, J., and NUTMAN, P. (1981) *Understanding the Unemployed: The Psychological Effects of Unemployment*, London, Tavistock.

HUTSON, P.W. (1962) 'Vocational choices: 1930 and 1961', *Vocational Guidance Quarterly*, 10 pp. 218–22.

JONES, P. (1985) 'Qualifications and labour market outcomes', *British Journal of Guidance and Counselling*, 26, 3, pp. 275–291.

MACKAY, D.I. and REID, G.L. (1972) 'Redundancy unemployment and manpower policy', *Economic Journal*, 82, pp. 1256–72.

MILLER, D.C. and FORM, W.H. (1951) *Industrial Sociology*, New York, Harper.

RABY, L. and WALFORD, G. (1981) 'Career related attitudes and their determinants for middle and lower stream pupils'. *Research in Education*, 25, pp. 19–35.

RAFFE, D. (1984) 'The transition from school to work and the recession. Evidence from the Scottish School-Leavers Surveys, 1977–1983', *British Journal of the Sociology of Education*, 5, 3, pp. 247–65.

ROBERTS, K. (1968) 'The entry into employment: An approach towards a general theory', *Sociological Review*, 16, 2, pp. 165–84.

ROBERTS, K. (1977) 'The social conditions, consequences and limitations of careers guidance', *British Journal of Guidance and Counselling*, 5, 1, pp. 1–9.

ROBERTS, K. (1984) *School Leavers and Their Prospects: Youth in the Labour Market in the 1980s*, Milton Keynes, Open University Press.

ROBERTS, K. DUGGAN, J. and NOBLE, M. (1982) 'Out of school youth in high unemployment areas: An empirical investigation', *British Journal of Guidance and Counselling*, 10, 1, pp. 1–11.

WILLIS, P. (1977) *Learning to Labour*, Farnborough, Saxon House.

WILLIS, P. (1985) *The Social Condition of Young People in Wolverhampton in 1984*, Wolverhampton, Wolverhampton Borough Council.

WRONG, D.H. (1961) 'The oversocialized conception of man in modern sociology', *American Sociological Review*, 26, 2, pp. 153–93.

4   Inner City Decline and Regeneration: Young People and the Labour Market in London's Docklands

Andrew Church and Pat Ainley.

Introduction

Two of the main concerns of recent sociological research into youth unemployment have been to assess the responses of young people to both the rapidly changing labour market and also the plethora of policy initiatives designed to affect the transition from school. The relative stability of the 1950s and 1960s, in terms of labour market change, meant that sociologists had developed a reasonable understanding of the transition from school and the labour market behaviour of young people. Recent upheavals in the youth labour market and rapid increases in youth unemployment have necessitated the collection of new data and a reassessment of previous interpretations. Much of the current research has been conducted in youth unemployment blackspots, often inner city areas, where the problems facing young people are greatest.

London docklands, despite its location in the relatively prosperous south east, has been subjected to the worst ravages of economic decline and industrial restructuring. This has left behind an area on the doorstep of the City of London and the affluent West End, that on the basis of any indicator, is experiencing economic and social problems comparable to the inner areas of Britain's other conurbations. Since 1981 the area has also been subject to the Conservative government's most energetic inner city regeneration programme, in the form of the London Docklands Development Corporation (LDDC). The LDDC is broadly charged with the physical, economic and social regeneration of the area. It has planning approval powers and applies its own funds of 60–80 million pounds per annum to the provision of infrastructure, industrial support and environmental improvements. Further extensive powers in relation to land acquisition and incentives such as the Enterprise Zone have been used to attract 1182 million pounds of private investment to the area between 1981 and 1986. This had led to yet further changes in the industrial structure of the local enconomy.

Therefore, young people in London docklands have been faced with rapid and confusing chages in the local labour market in which they seek work. Data from a survey of 150 individuals who attended the only comprehensive school in the docklands, based on the Isle of Dogs, indicates that the responses of young people to this changing labour market are far from simple or predictable.

Previous Studies of the Transition from School

In the post-war period, a series of studies since Ferguson and Cunnison's follow-up of all the 14 year-old boys leaving Glasgow's schools in 1947 have clearly shown the place of this transition in the working-class life cycle. These studies were undertaken by industrial sociologists, occupational psychologists and others concerned with careers guidance, rather than by educational sociologists who were largely concerned with what went on within schools rather than what happened to pupils once they left. As Bazalgette (1978) wrote of his Coventry study,

> It was evident that there were two transitions in which young men and women were engaged simultaneously. The most obvious was ... the transition from school to work ... The change of role here was from the pupil role to the role of employee. The other transition underlay that organizational one. This was the transition from childhood to adulthood ... This is, of course, a long drawn-out transition in present-day Britain, unmarked by any ritual indicating change of status or responsibility. The lack of ritual ... has consequences for different aspects of life: the key one ... is the act of leaving school which becomes in the young person's mind, the ritual changeover point from being a child to becoming an adult (p. 47).

The overall picture was clear: the occupational aspirations of working-class pupils were found to be depressingly and uniformly limited, influenced as they were by what Jahoda (1952) called the 'climate of opinion', consisting of 'more or less diffuse currents of feeling against (or in favour of) certain kinds of jobs'. 'In general, the investigation ... confirmed the popularity of the skilled trades — mechanic, electrician and carpenter — among the boys, and shop work, typing, hairdressing and nursing among the girls' (Wilson, 1952). The general picture which emerges from a study by Liversidge is similarly:

> one of startlingly accurate appraisal of life chances by the children, and a shrewd appreciation of the social and economic implications of their placing within the educational system. They know at what age they will marry, the best type of job they can get, and the best

wage they can hope to earn in that job. Having accepted the role they are to play in life, they rarely venture out of it even in fantasy (Liversidge, 1962, p. 74).

Carter, in his classic 1962 account of the relations between 'Home, School and Work' in Sheffield, found that fantasy and ideal choices 'were dismissed from the mind ... without regret, disappointment or impatience' (p. 136) because 'the particular occupations were not a vital matter to a large number of children ... What was important was the status which being a worker conferred' (pp. 150 and 122). This was not the idea of progress through a career entertained by the school. High rates of unemployment did not alter and perhaps further confirmed this disjunction between school values and those of home and work, for, as Markall wrote in 1982, 'any perspective which places emphasis on commitment, discipline and other work-related "skills" is more than irrelevant; it actually inverts and challeges those characteristics and attitudes which sustain many working class youngsters in wage labour'. For, like Carter, Ashton and Field (1976) reported '... contrary to a fairly widely accepted belief expressed in the literature, most young people did not experience severe problems of adjustment in the course of their transition from school to work' (p. 11; also Roberts, 1971, p. 134).

Once in work, 'young workers' were discovered to follow a predictable pattern of behaviour ranging from their 'initially euphoric reaction' to subsequent disillusionment and resentment at the authority imposed upon them (Keil *et al.*, 1966). Industrial sociologists accepted unstable and dislocated employment as normal for young workers, a pattern of job changing or sampling that declined towards the end of adolescence (Miller and Form, 1964). Employers anticipated this high turnover in juvenile labour, consequently provision for young workers came low on their list of priorities. Wilmott (1966) indicated that his *Adolescent Boys in East London* were most 'discontented' aged 17 and 18 when 'They care less than formerly what their parents think, but they have not yet acquired a girlfriend whose opinion of them matters. When they do acquire one and move towards a family of their own, they become once again subject to the social controls of the local community and the national society' (p. 162). As a young informant put it many years later, 'They change jobs very quickly; have periods of temporary unemployment; get another job; can't stand it and leave ... It all ends when you get married, then you have to keep the job you're in, hate it or not' (Corrigan, 1979, p. 92).

The 1970s ushered in a period of economic decline and recession that resulted in the disappearance of a stable youth labour market in Britain and a rise in the youth unemployment rate. But given the long established patterns of the transition from school to work it could not be assumed that changes in the transition process would be a simple reflection of alterations in the labour market. Therefore, several studies, some of which also provide chapters for this book, have examined in detail the changes in the aspirations and work patterns of young people. Also as seen, most earlier studies were characteristically concerned only with male school leavers rather than young women. The sample from the comprehensive school in London docklands is comprised of seventy-five males and seventy-five females. The results indicate the importance of studying gender divisions. The work histories of the sample exhibit traditional gender differences but there is evidence that they are starting to alter marginally, possibly to the advantage of males and the disadvantage of females.

Recent National Policies: The Role of the MSC

A more complete understanding of the transition process from school to work was made possible by studies that attempted to integrate the previously separated concerns of schooling and the transition to work. Willis's (1977) study, of individuals from a secondary modern school in a working class locality analyzed the link between school and the transition in a rigorous way for the first time. It is ironic that just when the two separate strands of studies of what happens to pupils within schools and what happens to them when they leave were at last brought together, a new state agency was created precisely to deal with the labour problems arising from deepening unemployment. The MSC understood the 'transition' from school to work to represent two culturally distinct worlds, together with ideas of more 'relevant' and less academic schooling to erode this separation, and effected a sea-change in their use. What had seemed previously the terms of progressive critique of existing education became justifications for a new economic realism. The Manpower Services Commission accepted school culture, on one side as an influence from which pupils have to be institutionally desocialized, ignoring that evidence of educational sociology which questioned how far working-class pupils made a more than bodily transition into schools in the first instance. The world of work, on the other, was presented as the unproblematic and natural arena in which an individual finds his (or her) self-fulfilment and achieves 'vocational maturity' as the final stage of an evolutionary psychological development. This conception of 'transition' resuscitates Kitchen's (1944) notion of a 'culture shock' being involved for pupils' passage from school to work. It incorporates American theories of occupational choice that posit freely acting individuals selecting rationally from the available alternatives, grafting upon this basic economic model a sociology of roles and a psychology of developmental states (see Ainley, 1986). From the beginning the MSC implied, as did the 'Great Debate', that it was schools that presented the problem:

In recent years the social environment of a number of schools, with more emphasis on personal development and less on formal instruction, has been diverging from that still encountered in most work situations ... The contrast is more marked where changes in industrial processes have reduced the scope for individual action and initiative (Training Services Agency, 1975, p. 15).

How far the MSC has been successful in its attempt at a major modification of the transition from school in which the state increasingly forecloses upon young people's options as part of an overall restructuring of the entire workforce to meet the demands of recapitalization, has been the subject of much confusion and hype. Beneath the fine words in the glossy brochures, the delivery of YTS especially has always been an unparalleled rush and shambles. MSC's computerization of its counting system in 1984/85 makes comparison with 1983/84 particularly difficult; however it is clear that the total number on YTS peaked in October 1984 at 312,832, just 4000 more than the maximum achieved by YOP two years earlier and 3 per cent more than on the first year of YTS one year previously (Youthaid, 1985, p. 10 and 13). Of those who joined schemes *The Guardian* reported in April 1984 that one in four dropped out within six months and of 123,000 entrants unaccounted for in the first year, the MSC admitted it did not know how many had left, where they had gone or how many had been counted twice because they had moved from one scheme to another. As for the placement rate into employment, which Lord Young declared the criterion for success for the scheme, in 1985, according to MSC's own figures, it dropped below half to 48 per cent just as YOP's placement rates fell as the programme expanded. For, although announcing itself as radically different from any of its temporary predecessors, being both permanent and universal, YTS is directly continuous with the discredited YOP. Although designed and marketed as a foundation for employed and unemployed alike, YTS is used by most managing agents for unemployed youth only, like YOP. In its first year the number of employed trainees anticipated was revised downwards from 33 per cent to 5 per cent and now the latest proposals for the two-year scheme guarantees a place only to the unemployed.

Frith (1980) states that '... the long term strategy of the MSC is the development of a state run secondary labour market for young workless and temporarily unemployed adults' (p. 40). From the chaotic organization of the projects at local level, it is doubtful whether there is any 'long term strategy' at all; rather it seems the desperate response to an uncontrolled and unforeseen situation. It may be that the series of *ad hoc* reactions may eventually add up to have the effect predicted by Frith, particularly as the MSC pulls together the existing programmes into what increasingly looks like a progression from TVEI, starting for some at 14, through 'guaranteed training' on YTS for the rest with YWS as its second year, followed by the Community Programme, now being expanded to offer a 'job guarantee' to 250,000 up to the age of 26. This links with the Fowler Review's apparently arbitrary decision that the majority of claimants below 25 are not fully independent and will therefore only be entitled to a lower rate of 'income support' (Department of Education and Service Green Paper, Vol II, para 2, 7, 3). Finally there is graduation to the Adult Programme, where MSC, through its involvement in the city action teams, touts small business as the solution to unemployment. The dependence of youth upon their families and upon state agencies is being extended, but this prolongation of social childhood contradicts with what Frith sees as another aim of the initiative, which is to maintain labour discipline in the absence of real work. Just as the current extension of YTS to two years negates its original aim to replace time-serving apprenticeships. YTS as a permanent response to mass youth unemployment is persistently undermined by the continued aggravation of that unemployment. The MSC's annual report for 1985 shows unemployment now moving up the age-range to affect those over 18 as badly as school leavers. Increasingly the processes already apparent during the first years of YTS will further erode the original consensual aims agreed with the TUC as the scheme, together with the MSC's other programmes and initiatives, becomes subordinated to the government's overall political strategy. In essence, as Finn (1984) has summarized,

> This involves using the YTS as part of an attack on the financial autonomy of local authorities; the privatization of public services; 'freeing' employers from legislative constraints; marginalising trade union involvement; undermining comprehensive education and pricing the young back into work.

As to the contents of schemes, it has not escaped notice that of the three main components of YTS — instruction in 'broad-based practical skills', 'work experience' and 'social life skills' — 'It is strange that while a few years ago school leavers without qualifications of any kind had no difficulty in getting jobs, many of them are now deemed to need "work experience" before they can be regarded as employable' (Showler and Sinfield, 1980, p. 117). However few have also noted how — revealingly — SLS courses in FE colleges have developed from the existing provision for special school leavers. Indeed the MSC's *Instructional Guide to Social and Life Skills* presumes an identity between the small number of special school leavers who have always found difficulty functioning in normal life and who have been helped by colleges to do so and the unemployed youth now drafted into YTS. 'Many people', it says, 'lack some of the basic day-to-day skills which most of us take for granted. Life skills refer to all those abilities, bits of informaion, know-how and decision-making which we need to get by in life' (1983, p. 1). Attitudes and habits are treated like skills, the lack of which in individuals being responsible for their unemployment. Though — paradoxically — if Matthew's (1963) claim that most of his sample of educationally subnormal boys could more easily be placed in employment holds true, it is special school leavers who are better adapted to the demands of modern industry than their more normal contemporaries. The assumption, shared also by the Labour party's programme for education *Learning for Life*, is that 'All young people need to be equipped to cope with the adult world'. The extension of school/college which is proposed is not recognized as a further prolongation of a dependent state of non-adulthood and exclusion from productive employment. As the CCCS (1982) critics of *Learning for Life* argue, 'This might not matter if real benefits were to accrue, such as still attend the prolonged dependence (and licensed freedom) of the full-time university or college student' (pp. 30–2), but the 'work relevant' courses, which sound so similar to the MSC's are hardly intended to confer upon the mass of the young population the benefits presently enjoyed by a minority of students. Rather they are a preparation for a lifetime of flexible and adaptable labour.

'Britain needs a flexible, adaptable workforce to cope with the uncertainties that cloud the future … Individuals will need to be able to adapt to the changing demands of industry, a process which is not once and for all but continuing' (Training Services Agency 1981, p. 164). Adaptability being, as Sarup (1978) remarks 'a synonym for unskilled labour' (p. 164). This demand for 'flexibility and adaptability' corresponds with a major reorganization of employment strategies by large firms, collapsed round a core group of permanent employees and with a large periphery on 'hire and fire' and short-term contracts, agency 'temps', outsources, self-employed and subcontractors that can be expanded or contracted according to demand (see Atkinson, 1984). Logically and fully developed, the MSC's response to this 'demand flexible environment' is a radical and comprehensive application of labour rationalization and restructuring of the entire workforce beginning with its youngest entrants. Following a 1980 report of the Central Policy Review Staff, in place of training for particular tasks, there was a reclassification of the skills needed for a modernized economy as 'competencies' required for eleven occupational training families. But such was the demand for general training adaptable to many occupations (or rather the lack of demand for specialized craft skills which are being replaced by new technology) that this division was still not broad enough. In the two-year scheme which Lord Young now speaks of as 'the successor to YTS', core competencies will be built into prevocational courses that begin with a general introduction to the world of work. Trainees then move more or less quickly through a range of job tasters into other 'experiential learning situations' where work experience

demands of different working environments. Since the work is not specialized, the skills which it requires can be transferred to other areas, having
been demonstrated in practical tests and accredited as part of a profile.

The Labour Market in London Docklands

Assessing the impact of these measures on the experiences, behaviour and
attitudes of young people and the transition from school has become a
major research area. Also, it is apparent that the recent changes in the
nature of the labour market have also resulted in major changes in the
lives of young people, regardless of the existing policy measures. Rising
youth unemployment and the disappearance of many job opportunities for
young people have meant that the labour market experiences of young
people have changed dramatically. Pahl (1984) and others have suggested
that one response by adults to changes in the labour market has been the
emergence of divisions between those in and those out of work to create a
new permanent divide between those employed and the rest. Therefore,
it could be argued that a clear unemployed sub-class may emerge amongst
the young, creating a group whose aspirations are low and are resigned to
a youth of near permanent unemployment. While there is much evidence
outlining the existence of this unemployed sub-class in many inner areas
of the northern conurbations and other locations such as the Isle of
Sheppey, it is necessary to avoid seeing this description of a youth labour
market as typical of all labour markets.

The following account is based on data collected on selected groups of
school leavers from a comprehensive school in London's docklands over
the period 1981–86. The data clearly shows that in this inner city area
rapid changes in the local labour market have not produced an
unemployed sub-class of young people. Also the aspirations of this group
of young people have changed but not in a predictable way and the
various policy initiatives of the MSC have had only a minor impact on the
experiences of young people in docklands.

London docklands provides a useful case study since the changes in
the labour market are quite varied, similar in nature to both declining
and better-off parts of Britain. Overall, the labour market facing these
150 school leavers was a contrasting one. The Isle of Dogs is located in the
London Borough of Tower Hamlets and it is within this Borough, the
City and the West End that local young people work and seek
employment. Tower Hamlets as a whole lost 34,000 jobs (29 per cent of
the total) between 1971 and 1981 (Censuses of Employment). As with
London as a whole, most of this loss was concentrated within the
manufacturing sector which lost 52 per cent of total jobs in the
corresponding period, whereas service sector employment actually grew by
1.5 per cent (Censuses of Employment, 1971 and 1981). Within the

service sector there were some marked contrasts: transport and communication as a sector declined by 44 per cent and distribution by 22 per cent, while financial services grew by 80 per cent from 9891 jobs in 1971 to 17,780 in 1981.

The more local docklands economy, of which the Isle of Dogs is a part, has been even harder hit. In the three years between 1978 and 1981 the docklands lost 27 per cent of 37,000 jobs. This loss was a result of dock closure, registered dock employment fell from 25,000 in 1960 to 4100 in 1981, and the decline of local manufacturing and dock-related industry. One estimate suggests that for every job lost in the docks three others were lost in related industries. However, this local economy is not just declining but also undergoing a fundamental change in its nature due to the policies pursued by the LDDC (1986) and its Enterprise Zone on the Isle of Dogs. The LDDC claims to have created 8000 new jobs in the docklands during 1981–85. This is a misleading figure since many of these jobs are transfers and some, such as the jobs in the News International plant at Wapping, result in job losses elsewhere. In fact, between 1981 and 1985 the number of jobs in the docklands rose from 27,213 to 28,180, a rise of 3.5 per cent. It is more realistic to say that the LDDC has stemmed the decline rather than created much new employment. However the docklands economy has fundamentally altered from 1981 when 43 per cent of jobs were in manufacturing and 52 per cent in services, plus 7 per cent in construction, to a situation in 1986 in which only 24 per cent of jobs are in manufacturing, 6 per cent in construction and 70 per cent in services (LDDC, 1986). The consequences of this decline and change have been unemployment rates as high as some Northern metropolitan disticts. Male unemployment was 32 per cent in the docklands in 1983 and unemployment among 16 to 24-year-olds on the Isle of Dogs rose from 19 per cent in 1981 to an estimated 34 per cent in 1986 (LDDC, MSC and London Borough of Tower Hamlets, 1986). Thus, the employment outlook for young people on the Isle of dogs has fundamentally altered over a five-year period. Certain sectors of the local economy have grown in recent years, while large scale growth is predicted for LDDC inspired developments, such as the ten million square feet of offices planned for Canary Wharf.

Untypically for an inner city locality, the catchment area served by the school selected for study remained homogeneous and mainly white working-class. In 1981 only 9 per cent of the docklands population lived in a household in which the head was from the new Commonwealth or Pakistan (Census of Population, 1981.) A longitudinal survey was undertaken of a sample of 150 interviewed in groups of thirty, one year after reaching minimum school leaving age from 1981 onwards. Therefore the first group who left in 1981 were interviewed in 1982 and the last two groups who left in 1984 and 1985 were interviewed in a period during 1985 and 1986. In addition, seventy-six of the 1981, 1982 and 1983 groups of leavers were reinterviewed in 1986, along with twenty-four new respondents with similar educational qualifications to those who could no longer be contacted. This gave a total sample for 1986 of 150 ranging in age from 17 to 21. The survey data on parental occupation indicated family backgrounds typical of an area where the local economy for many years was dominated by manufacturing and dock-related industries. Thirty seven per cent of fathers currently worked in skilled manual jobs and a further 17 per cent worked in semi- or unskilled jobs, so that over half of the respondents fathers worked in manual jobs. Only 13 per cent of fathers worked in non-manual jobs. The current occupations of mothers were also indicative of the nature of female work in this area. Forty-two per cent of mothers currently worked in non-manual jobs but over half of these were in personal services which included many working in part-time catering jobs or shop work. Fifteen per cent of respondents came from households where the head was registered as unemployed and a further 15 per cent lived in households where the main income provider was either sick, disabled, retired, deceased or had left home. The longitudinal nature of the survey makes it possible to see how attitudes and labour market behaviour have changed in response to the rapidly changing employment situation and new policy initiatives. Changes in the transition from school in docklands indicate the need for in-depth analysis going beyond existing stereotypes. To clearly illustrate these changes in behaviour and outlook it is necessary to turn to an analysis of aspirations and actual employment trends of young people in the docklands.

Changes in Aspirations

The changes in the employment structure of the docklands and Tower Hamlets might be expected to have significantly altered young people's aspirations for work and led to a general lowering of their sights and even a lack of motivation. Again though, current aspirations compared to those held ten years previously show the danger of jumping to such conclusions. A preliminary 10 per cent survey of all 16 year-old pupils in Tower Hamlets leaving school in 1976, the earliest year for which figures were still available in the Borough's careers office, was indicative of the local pattern of employment before high levels of youth unemployment became established. It showed that for most boys a skilled job or trade was the most popular aspiration expressed in their careers interview while still at school, with office work the equivalent for girls. Listing aspirations in order of popularity, electronics was the year's favourite for boys, while 'office, typing, bank' held steady as the first preference for girls. In the following years also motor mechanic for a time replaced electrician as boys' first choice, unrelated though this was to any change in the actual opportunities for formal employment available, motor mechanics is, however, of some use outside formal employment, allowing someone who has some idea about it to do small repairs for others without being formally employed (Pahl, 1984). The data from the Tower Hamlets careers office 1986 'live register' shows striking similarities with the sample of ten years previously, even though these 696 individuals were no longer at school but were mostly unemployed. In 1986 34 per cent of those on the register expressed an interest in practical work and, as these were predominantly males, this indicates that a skilled, manual job is still the aim of most young men. However very few of them specified a particular trade in which they aspired to work; 4.5 per cent and 2 per cent wanted work in the building or motor vehicle mechanics trades and 2 per cent in a technical trade. Thus, there is a tendency to be less specific about the precise trade desired, which probably reflects diminishing opportunities but this is not necessarily the first step in a lowering of aspirations. In fact it is not that different from the situation in 1976, for two long-standing careers officers in the Borough indicated that each year often produced a different 'craze' for trades from boys they interviewed in school. Peer group communication meant that one year word went round that a motor mechanic was the best trade to enter, while another year painting and decorating for the Borough seemed the most secure and desirable occupation. It was felt by the careers officers that this 'herd instinct', as they called it, was less apparent in the 1980s due to more limited opportunities in any particular trade. The most popular aspiration for girls remained in 1986 as in 1976, junior clerical work: 18.5 per cent of those on the register wished to enter this type of job, 90 per cent of them girls.

The aspirations of the sample of 150 young people on the Isle of Dogs show how intentions change with a more extended labour market experience. The sample was aged from 17 to 21 and is thus not directly comparable with those interviewed in school by the careers office or with those on the office's 'live register'. Aspirations might again have been expected to drop over time as unemployment rose, but in fact this, on average, older group have aspirations that are often higher than those of the youngsters recorded by the careers office. Aspirations are less towards manual work and more towards non-manual. In particular, 17 per cent of respondents aspired to work in jobs that are in socio-economic group (SEG) 5.1 (ancillary workers and artists — intermediate occupations). This includes several seeking welfare work, nursery nursing, design, etc. Aspirations of the 150 respondents as defined by socio-economic group are listed in table 1.

Fifty-eight per cent of respondents aspire to non-manual jobs as opposed to 24 per cent who aspire to manual jobs. Apart from the eighteen respondents in a skilled manual job, only twelve others were interested in pursuing a trade. This not only differs from the 1986 careers office register but also from some of the respondents' earlier aspirations recorded

Table 1:   *Aspirations as defined by Socio-Economic Group (SEG)*

Socio-Economic Group		Number of respondents with aspirations in SEG	Percentage of respondents with aspirations in SEG
4	Professional workers	2	1
5.1	Ancillary workers and artists. Intermediate occupations	26	17
6	Junior non-manual	41	27
7	Personal service workers	19	13
	Total non-manual	88	58
9	Skilled manual	30	20
10	Semi-skilled manual	4	3
11	Unskilled manual	2	1
	Total manual	36	24
12	Own account workers	8	5
16	Members of the armed forces	1	1
	Anything	5	3
	Don't know	11	8
	Inadequately described	1	1

a year after they left school in interviews carried out with the first ninety who were 16 in 1981, 1982 and 1983. A year after leaving school 43 per cent of these ninety respondents aspired to a manual job and 39 per cent aspired to a non-manual job. So rather than lowering their aspirations, some respondents had transferred them to other areas of work upon realizing the limited opportunities in traditional manual work, and others had targetted them towards particular occupations. The maintenance of aspirations in spite of rising unemployment requires some explanation. For those in continual work with well-paying jobs aspirations are easily maintained but this phenomenon was found throughout the sample including individuals for whom unemployment had been a regular occurrence since leaving school. There seem to be three key factors to take into account. Firstly, as is described in the next section, 94 per cent of the sample had been in work at some point since leaving school and it is the experience of working however infrequent and exploitative that helps maintain self-image and therefore aspirations and the belief amongst many of the unemployed that it is possible to eventually obtain what was often referred to as a 'proper job'. The importance of simply being in work for the purposes of self-image lies behind the finding that 41 per cent of the unemployed respondents when asked what kind of work they were looking for replied anything or anything within limits (limits included factors such as not wishing to move house or work for very low pay). They would rather do a job of any sort than be unemployed. Secondly, the Isle of Dogs is a close-knit community and of those who had left home the majority were living in the local area. Peer group communication meant that respondents were often aware of each other's whereabouts even if they were not friends. Therefore, those out of work or in unsatisfying jobs were always aware of similarly qualified individuals who were in good jobs and adjusted their aspirations accordingly. Finally, although the local labour market is very depressed, the City and the West End of London represent relatively buoyant labour markets compared to other urban areas and the perceived, but not necessarily real, job opportunities in these areas also maintain the aspirations of some interviewees.

Recent Patterns of Employment

The already observed shift in aspirations away from manual to non-manual jobs suggests an element of adaptation to the changing labour market and this adaptation is even more pronounced when the type of work done by respondents is examined. Fifty-five per cent of respondents were currently in paid work and the types of jobs they did, as described by SEGs, are shown in table 2. And listed are the types of job by SEG done by respondents in the job in which they spent the longest time. The final column gives the jobs by SEG being done one year after leaving school by the groups who left in 1981, 1982 and 1983.

Table 2: Type of jobs undertaken by respondents as defined by Socio-Economic Group (S.E.G.)

Socio-Economic Group	Current job (Number of respondents whose current job in SEG)	Longest job (Number of respondents whose longest job in SEG)	Number of respondents who left in 1981-1983, whose job one year after leaving school in SEG
6 Junior non-manual	59 (70%)	74 (56%)	16 (31%)
7 Personal service workers	3 (4%)	10 (8%)	5 (10%)
9 Skilled manual	11 (13%)	18 (14%)	9 (18%)
10 Semi-skilled manual	2 (2%)	13 (10%)	10 (20%)
11 Unskilled manual	9 (11%)	15 (12%)	11 (21%)
Total	84 (100%)	130 (100%)	51 (100%)

Percentage figures are based on column totals and not the total number of respondents

It is significant that 74 per cent of current jobs and 64 per cent of longest jobs are in non-manual (SEG 6 and 7) jobs. These compare markedly to the figures for the ninety respondents one year after they left school in 1981–83 when 59 per cent of those in work were in manual jobs and only 41 per cent in non-manual jobs. The traditional concentration of work in manual jobs has weakened. However the traditional gender division exists in that only four of the forty-six girls currently in work were in manual jobs. This gives an indication of the nature of the changes in behaviour and adaptation and suggests they must not be exaggerated. Females have traditionally worked in clerical/secretarial jobs often in local manufacturing and dock-related companies. Despite the decline in these firms, young women have continued to find similar work elsewhere. Males faced with declining opportunities in manual work are responding by working in increasing numbers in non-manual jobs. So the changes that have taken place have been based partly around the reduction of gender divisions in work by only in one direction, with males moving into jobs more often done by females. It is not clear if this is because of an increase in demand or a displacement of females by males. But the fact that this sort of change is occurring raises some important questions. This change could mean that the type of regeneration occurring in the London docklands may in the long run be more beneficial to males rather than females, as males take up new and transferred jobs in the area. More likely though, this take up of non-manual work by males may be a reflection of winder changes in the economy. Atkinson's (1984) claim that recent changes in the nature of work are giving rise to groups of 'core' workers and a longer group of 'peripheral' workers. 'Peripheral' jobs are typified by flexibility, low pay and poor conditions which have been the characteristics of many female jobs in Britain. It is possible that some respondents are obtaining these peripheral jobs that happen to be in non-manual traditionally female occupations. Therefore, this slight change in gender division maybe an initial reflection of this wider shift in the nature of work in Britain.

'The Lower Quartile'

It is possible to detect some changes in both the attitudes and labour market experiences of young people from the Isle of Dogs that suggest an element of adjustment by some individuals. For many respondents the last few years have not been a rewarding experience in relation to work. When all 150 respondents were interviewed in the summer of 1986, 28 per cent were currently unemployed, 55 per cent were in paid work, 15 per cent were in training or education and 2 per cent were not in paid work but not unemployed. But unlike other studies, the data when examined in detail does not provide evidence of a bifurcation between those in jobs and those who are unemployed.

Thirty-eight per cent of the 150 respondents had never experienced a period of unemployment and two-thirds had spent less than 20 per cent of their time since leaving school on the dole. At the other extreme 25 per cent of respondents had been unemployed for over a third of their time since leaving school. This group is referred to as the lower quartile and although this comprises only thirty-eight respondents it is a large enough number on which to draw some basic conclusions. In particular, it is apparent that this lower group are not permanently unemployed. Only two of the thirty-eight respondents had been permanently unemployed since leaving school. Another eight had never worked but had been on a training scheme. But eight had done one job since leaving school, twelve two jobs, three three jobs, two five jobs, two six jobs and one of these thirty-eight had done seven jobs. Therefore over 50 per cent of this group had done at least two jobs and only a third of this group had been unemployed for over half the time since leaving school. In other words, unemployment is not the norm for this group; periods of unemployment, although lengthy are broken up by periods of work and attempts to train. In fact nineteen, exactly 50 per cent, had at some point started a training or educational scheme. This included four individuals who spent a short time back at school after completing the fifth form, eight who started YTS, two who started an apprenticeship and five who had been, or were, on the community programme. However, the average time spent in training was only five months and only three individuals had completed a scheme.

This group was evenly divided by gender comprising twenty females and eighteen males. It also covered all five year groups with seven from the 1985, 1984 and 1983 groups respectively, eight from 1982 and nine from the 1981 group. At the time of interview six of the lower quartile were in paid work, four in training, twenty-six were unemployed and two were not in paid work but no unemployed (one looking after children and one looking after a sick parent).

The periods in work were not always for short periods. The longest job done by the twenty-eight members of the lower quartile who had at some stage been in paid work varied considerably in length. For nine the longest job lasted less than six months (five of these had only left school a year). Whereas for 13 of this group their longest job had lasted over 12 months. The type of jobs done by the lower quartile were not concentrated in any particular occupational group. Eight of the twenty-eight longest jobs were in junior non-manual occupations; five in personal services; seven in skilled manual; five in semi-skilled manual; and three in unskilled manual occupations. All but one of these longest jobs were full-time and none were self employed. But when the twenty-four respondents in the lower quartile who had left their longest job were asked for the main reason why they had left it seemed that many of the jobs were far from ideal. Three had been made redundant, ten left because of pay and conditions, four were dismissed and four left because the job was temporary. Although this is only limited evidence, it could be, that as was suggested earlier, this group are doing the peripheral jobs described by Atkinson (1984) with poor pay and conditions where work is temporary and redundancy is common. The complaints of one 20-year-old girl summarized the experience of many of this group; 'I've had three jobs and they've all been bad, one made me redundant, one paid £45 a week before tax and the other was only temporary ... I just hope I get a proper job sometime'.

One common characteristic of the lower quartile was a lack of qualifications. Twenty-two of the thirty-eight had no qualifications and ten had three or less CSEs, none of which were grade 1. Of the remainder four had three or more CSEs but none were grade 1 and two females had one 'O' level each as well as some CSEs below grade 1. Generally, this group were poorly qualified. However, there were many equally poorly qualified respondents who were not in the lower quartile. Fifty-four (36 per cent) of the whole sample had no qualifications and a further thirty-six (24 per cent) had three CSEs or less (no grade 1s). So ninety respondents were in these two least qualified groups and many have been in nearly permanent employment since leaving school. Forty-four of these ninety were currently in work and this included only two from the lower quartile. A comparison of the characteristics of the lower quartile and the forty-two respondents from the two least qualified groups who are currently in work and not members of the lower quartile reveals no clear differences. Family background measured by parental occupation and intact families is often seen as an influence on young people's labour market history. But the parental occupations of the lower quartile and the least qualified in work were remarkably similar. While material difference between employed and unemployed parents had often made it imperative for some respondents to find work of any sort if their parents were unemployed, and certain employed parents could sustain their offspring longer in anticipation of their finding secure employment, no definite pattern emerges. Also, there seems to be no apparent difference between those from intact families and those from less stable family situations. It is in fact very hard to say what separates the poorly qualified who find work from the lower quartile who have spent a large proportion of their time unemployed. Although family background may still exert an influence in that for the sample as a whole 'contacts' were by far the most used and most successful method of job search. Sixty per cent of the forty-two lowest qualified respondents currently in work had found their job through friends or relatives and a further 20 per cent had used contacts with local firms provided by the former deputy head of the school. So 'contacts' are an important method of job search for the poorly qualified.

The pattern that does appear with some certainty from this albeit small sample is of a lower quartile group for whom the transition from school is a depressingly 'chequered' period (Harris *et al.*, 1987). Long periods of unemployment are common but work or training has not led to a settled pattern of regular work. Very few of this group were working in the informal sector. Three of the twenty-six unemployed members of the lower quartile claimed to have worked in the informal economy but only one had done so on a regular basis. Whether it is just luck that leads equally poorly qualified respondents into long-term jobs is by no means clear. This chequered pattern has not reduced aspirations of the lower quartile and many, like other respondents, have focussed them on particular areas of work. The focussed nature of this groups aspirations is indicated by the fact that only four of this group did not have a specific aspiration and wanted any type of work. Fifteen respondents from the lower quartile aspired to junior non-manual jobs and seven to personal service jobs. Therefore 58 per cent of the lower quartile aspired to particular non-manual jobs indicating a good understanding of the changing labour market. Only six aspired to a skilled manual job and even less, four, aspired to unskilled jobs. Two of this group hoped to be self-employed in the future. The fact that this lower quartile have been able to maintain their aspirations and that the London docklands does not seem to have a permanently unemployed sub-class of young people does not mean that youth unemployment is any less of a problem. At any one time a large number of young people are unemployed in this area and although many are able to find work again, the jobs they are finding are not providing them with the stable employment that the vast majority of the sample claimed to be a desirable goal in their lives.

Reactions to Policy

The responses of young people in the London docklands to a rapidly changing labour market outlined in the previous section owe little to the impact of major policy initiatives such as YTS. Reactions to various training initiatives show large-scale scepticism amongst respondents that the directives are unlikely to make any difference to the local employment situation. Some had the chance to go on YOP schemes when they left school but none were willing to do so. YTS in East London has the lowest take-up rate in the country. At its peak 28.3 per cent of local school leavers were on YTS but this has now fallen to 8 per cent (ILEA careers office figures), compared to one in four nationally. The experiences of the sample reflect this situation: thirty-four respondents (23 per cent) of the total had started YTS or YOP. However, only fourteen (9 per cent) actually completed their scheme. As with most of East London, the Isle of Dogs is almost a YTS free zone.

Those who had not gone on a YTS scheme were asked to give the main reasons for their non-participation. These are summarized in table 3. For many respondents YOP/YTS was not even a distant consideration since they had jobs arranged upon leaving school or were following a course in higher or further education. For those making a conscious decision, sources of information were people they knew or had heard about who had gone on schemes.

'A mate went on it', 'A couple of mates went on it', 'There's this kid in our firm — they've got him 'til September, then they'll probably get another one', 'There was a kid with me who was on YTS and I had to train him. I'd been there about two months before he came; that made me feel right big-headed but they didn't treat him properly. They gave him all the crappy jobs and he wasn't on the cards; he was paid by the government or something. I used to have a laugh with him.'

Other important reasons for not going on YTS were the perceived low status of trainees, summarized in table 3 by replies that saw YTS as both exploitative and demeaning, as well as more predictable criticisms of the low allowances received by trainees. A smaller group felt YTS was a waste of time because it did not necessarily lead to a job and others expressed the desire for what was usually referred to as 'a proper job'. The accepted model for training was that provided by apprenticeship for a trade. 'Proper training' was for a definite craft or skill and the pre-vocational transferable skills of the MSC's occupational training families were not appreciated. Nor were they likely to be whilst they represented in practice a dilution of existing skill levels and thus a degradation of the idea of a trade. Only a new skill, like computing, which did not have a traditional level of craftsmanship with which it could be compared, was

Table 3: Reasons given by respondents for not doing YTS

Reasons for not doing YTS	Number of respondents citing reason	Percentage of respondents who had not done a YTS scheme citing reason
Already had a job	38	33
Doing further/higher education course	19	16
Wanted a proper job	14	12
Low pay	29	25
Disagree with scheme	10	9
Exploitative	20	17
Family objected	2	1
Waste of time/no point	11	10
Just never considered	4	3
Other	12	10
Don't know/can't remember	10	9

Respondents could give multiple responses so column totals are greater than total number of respondents and 100 per cent.

likely to gain any acceptance. The local ITEC, while its scheme was tainted by association with the rest of YTS, so finding it hard to recruit trainees, was able to train the increasing numbers it did get, so that after only six to ten months they could find employment as data entry operators, or, with day-release to further training, in offices or as electronic technicians. Both trainees and trainers knew that this was an adequate preparation and the ITEC staff are presently resisting pressure from the MSC to extend their training to cover the two years of YTS.

Then there was the question of money — the YTS allowance currently being set at £27.30 per week for the first year (raised from £25 in 1983), £35 in the second. 'When the careers office offered me YTS I told them to shove it. £25 a week — it's slave labour. You can't live on that after you've given your mum £10 a week and if you smoke you've got nothing left, so you've got to get a job. The careers office never offered me any YTS 'cos they knew I wouldn't take it. I wouldn't take it 'cos of the money. You might as well stay on the dole and get the same for doing nothing. My parents agree with me; they want me to get another job, but at decent money'. 'I knew about YTS but I wouldn't go on it 'cos it's slave labour 'cos they could employ people but that's just a cheap way of employing them. If you think about it, you get £25 a week for working whereas on the dole you get £16.80 and you don't have to do anything for it. I know they say they'll train you but they can still pay you on a normal wage can't they?'. 'The careers office had them (YTSs) on their boards but I wasn't interested in them 'cos I couldn't take just £25 a week for a year'. As seen, parents endorsed these opinions.

Other training initiatives were often tarred with the same brush whether local or nationally run. Perhaps more striking was the lack of knowledge of many schemes. Only 27 per cent of respondents had heard of the Job Club on the Isle of Dogs and no one had made any use of it. Also, only 27 per cent of those interviewed had heard of the local ITEC which had been operating since 1984. Other courses were slightly better known: 30 per cent had heard of TOPS, now called the Job Training Scheme, and 29 per cent had heard of the Community Programme (CP). Another observation, although based on only small numbers, is that four of the six who were currently on the CP described this as their job rather than the scheme they were currently undertaking. Since they were paid approximately £50 and did not work a full week, the programme was not felt to be as directly exploitative as YTS, this was similar to the psychological benefits reported of YOP, when those taking part were able to view it as the equivalent of a full-time job (Stafford, 1982). However, with the distinction that was created by the special status of trainee on YTS, this was no longer possible.

Twenty-two of the 150 young adults surveyed were currently on a training scheme or educational course but overall training was not viewed in a very complementary way. Of those interviewed 106 said they had not thought of doing a training course (in addition to any course they had already done). The majority of those thinking of doing a training course in the near future were considering mainly academic further or higher education and had often already done a course. Also, 40 per cent of those currently unemployed had not thought of doing any further training or education courses. It is not suprising that respondents had this negative attitude to training. As already stated, interviewees were often aware of each others whereabouts even if they were not friends. Therefore it seemed that the lower quartile particularly were aware that members of their own peer group with few qualifications were obtaining jobs. So there was some logic in hoping to obtain work as well without going on a training course.

It is quite apparent that national training initiatives and certain more local efforts, such as the Job Club, seemed to have had little effect on the labour market experiences or for that matter the job search methods of these young people. A few have already adapted to changed conditions and others hoped they may also be able to do so even when they have experienced long periods of unemployment. Those who have obtained work have started to acquire skills once in work, although these are rarely gained through formal instruction. In this way young people gain skills and experience where training schemes like YTS are not a major consideration for them.

Conclusion

In summary the young people from London's docklands have responded to the rapidly changing local labour market in a not altogether expected way. Aspirations, rather than declining as unemployment rose, have become less specific for the 16–17 age group and become more focussed amongst the older 17–21 age group, most often towards non-manual jobs. Labour market histories also indicate the increasing importance of non-manual work. The proportion of the sample working in non-manual jobs has grown in the last few years. This is mainly due to young males taking up non-manual jobs in increasing numbers as manual job opportunities decline. The influence of various policy measures in this process is minimal. More importantly, despite high local unemployment a permanent unemployed sub-class does not seem to exist. Instead a lower quartile exists who despite periods in work or training are not able to establish themselves in permanent employment, unlike some of their similarly lowly qualified peers. The type of jobs done by this lower quartile are perhaps symptomatic of changes in the nature of work, for many of them have worked in the 'peripheral' jobs certain commentators (Atkinson, 1984) suggest are emerging in the economy of Britain. However, the 'chequered' labour market histories of this group has not seen any lowering of aspirations and like the rest of the sample their aspirations are mainly orientated to non-manual work. This is not to argue that a permanently unemployed sub-class does not exist elsewhere, even in London. Rather particular geographical effects such as the proximity of the area to central London and the changes encouraged by the LDDC have combined in this locality to produce a different but equally pressing youth unemployment problem.

References

AINLEY, P. (1986) *The Effects of Changes in Youth Employment and Unemployment upon Secondary State Education: A Case Study of an Inner London Comprehensive School*, unpublished PhD Thesis, University of London.

ASHTON, D. and FIELD, D. (1976) *Young Workers*, London, Hutchinson.

ATKINSON, J. (1984) Work at the Institute of Manpower Studies reported in *Executive Post*, 190, 15 May.

BAZALGETTE, J. (1978) *School and Work Life, A Study of Transition in the Inner City*, London, Hutchinson.

CARTER, M. (1962) *Home, School and Work, A Study of the Education and Employment of Young People in Britain*, Oxford, Pergamon.

CENTRE for CONTEMPORARY CULTURAL STUDIES (1982) 'Comments on learning for life', *Schooling and Culture*, 12, Autumn.

CORRIGAN, P. (1979) *Schooling the Smash Street Kids*, London, MacMillan.

FERGUSON, T. and CUNNISON, J. (1952) *The Young Wage Earner*, Oxford, Oxford University Press.

FINN, D. (1984) *Draft Submission to the National Labour Movement Enquiry into Youth Unemployment and Training*, unpublished.

FRITH, S. (1980) 'Education, training and the labour process', in COLE, M. and SKELTON, B. (Eds) *Blind Alley: Youth in a Crisis of Capitalism*, London, Hesketh pp. 25–44.

HARRIS, C.C. *et al.* (1987) *Redundancy and Recession in South Wales*, Oxford, Blackwell.

JAHODA, G. (1952) 'Job attitudes and job choice among secondary modern school leavers', *Occupational Psychology*, 26, pp. 125–40 and 206–24.

KEIL, E., RIDDELL, C. and GREEN, B. (1966) 'Youth work, problems and perspectives', *Sociological Review*, 14, 2, pp. 117–37.

KITCHEN, P. (1944) *From Learning to Earning*, London, Faber.

LIVERSIDGE, W. (1962) 'Life chances', *Sociological Review*, 10, 2, pp. 17–34.

LONDON BOROUGH of TOWER HAMLETS (1986) *Quarterly Unemployment Report*, Policy and Resources Committee, 3, 44, unpublished.

LONDON DOCKLANDS DEVELOPMENT CORPORATION (LDDC) (1986) *Central Index of Statistics*, LDDC.

MANPOWER SERVICES COMMISSION (1983) *A New Training Initiative*, Sheffield, MSC.

MARKALL, G. (1982) 'The job creation programme: Some reflections on its passing', in REES T. and ATKINSON, P. (Eds) *Youth Unemployment and State Intervention*, London, Routledge, and Kegan Paul, pp. 82–98.

MATTHEWS, G. (1963) *Post-school Adaptation of Educationally Subnormal Boys*, unpublished MEd thesis, University of Manchester.

MILLER, D. and FORM, W. (1964) *Industrial Sociology*, London, Harper.

PAHL, R. (1984) *Divisions on Labour*, Oxford, Blackwell.

ROBERTS, K. (1971) *From School to Work, A Study of the Youth Employment Service*,

London, David and Charles.

SARUP, M. (1978) *Marxism and Education*, London, Routledge and Kegan Paul.

SHOWLER, B. and SINFIELD, A. (Eds) (1980) *The Workless State, Studies in Unemployment*, Martin and Robinson.

STAFFORD, E. (1982) 'The impact of the youth opportunities programme on young people's prospects and psychological well-being', *British Journal of Guidance and Counselling*, 10, 1, pp. 12–21.

TRAINING SERVICES AGENCY (1975) *Vocational Preparation for Young People, a Discussion Document*, TSA.

TRAINING SERVICES AGENCY (1981) *A New Training Initiative — An Agenda for Action*, TSA.

WILLIS, P. (1977) *Learning to Labour, How Working Class Kids Get Working Class Jobs*, Farnborough, Saxon House.

WILMOTT, P. (1966) *Adolescent Boys in East London*, London, Routledge.

WILSON, M. (1952) 'The vocational preferences of secondary modern school children', *British Journal of Psychology*, 26, pp. 97–112.

YOUTHAID (1985) *The Youth Training Scheme, Youthaid's Evidence to the House of Commons Employment Committe*, London, Youthaid.

5   Coming of Age in South Wales

Susan Hutson and Richard Jenkins

Introduction

In Swansea most young people celebrate their 18th birthday with a party, a pub crawl or perhaps both. The family and the peer group celebrate the date on which society declares that a young person is an adult, a citizen in his or her own right. Not forgetting the role of the state and the peer group in 'coming of age', this chapter will focus on the family and its role in this process in the current social context of high youth unemployment.

At 18, the majority of young people in the United Kingdom still live at home. Much everday life is within, or bound up with, the family. The amount of freedom a young person has is bargained for and decided within each household. The family continues to play an influential part in the transition to adulthood. Recent research shows that parents can, for example, be influential in helping a young person get a job (Jenkins, 1983, pp. 114–28; Lee and Wrench, 1983, pp. 33–5). Parents, or rather mothers, have a large part to play in marriage and the setting up of a new home. In contemporary British society, the move from childhood into adulthood is made, at least in part, with the guidance of parents. More generally, whether or not parents treat their child as an 'adult' will fundamentally affect his or her everday life.

Diana Leonard (1980) has argued that adulthood, especially for young women, is typically bestowed by marriage, and that marriage in Great Britain still depends on a male wage (p. 259). Paul Willis (1984) goes further, saying, 'The wage is still the golden key to a personal household, separate from parents ... (A household which gives) protection from the aggression and exploitation of work, from the patriarchal dependencies of the parental home' (p. 19). Without this wage, what will happen? Will the unemployed in this generation be left in a state of 'suspended animation' between childhood and adulthood, unable through lack of finance to leave home, get married and start their independent, adult lives?

This was one of the main questions informing a pilot study into youth unemployment which we carried out in Swansea in 1985 (Jenkins and Hutson, 1986). Subsequently we obtained funding from the Joseph Rowntree Memorial Trust for a two-year project concerned with the issue of youth unemployment and family relationships, starting in September 1985. This chapter draws upon interview material from both projects. Research has been carried out on two council housing estates — one, fairly affluent, in West Swansea, the other, more deprived, in Port Talbot — and with a group of families living in owner-occupation in West Swansea. Because we were typically looking at families where the sons or daughters were still at home, it can be argued that we have missed the families who have experienced the most severe intergenerational conflict. This should be borne in mind when reading the discussion which follows.

We found that most of these unmarried young people, living at home, considered themselves to be adult. Their parents also considered many of them to be adults. When asked why, some referred to age — we were mainly concerned with young people over 18-years-old — but most referred to independence: independence of mind and action, and responsibility in their attitudes and behaviour. The language which is used implies that the transition from childhood to adulthood is in large part a moral transition — a change in the individual's ability to make certain kinds of deisions — and that a bargain, and an agreed definition of adulthood, is struck between parents and children.

In this negotiation, this transactional process, we found that the mothers play a crucial part. Fathers tend to be shadowy figures. In our society it is primarily the mother who has responsibility for bringing up the children. The mother is seen, and sees herself, as helping her children into the next stage of life. At the same time as easing their children into adulthood, mothers also play a crucial role in managing the 'problem' of youth unemployment at the level of the household. Mothers often see themselves as responsible for their children well into their adult lives. A young person, not going out to work, will in many cases spend more time at home, often in the company of the mother. It is the mother who will cope with or delegate the extra cooking and housework involved. In most families it is the mother who asks for, and is responsible for collecting, the young person's contribution to the housekeeping, whether the young person is working or not. Our findings indicate that the young employed and the young unemployed do not inhabit different worlds. This is a result of the low wages and instability of the youth labour market, as has also been noted by Allatt and Yeandle (1985).

Money, Unemployment and Adult Status

For most of the people we talked to, a job means money. Being unemployed means not having enough money. For example, having a job means going to a disco once or twice a week; being unemployed means going once a fortnight when the benefit cheque comes in.

The giving of 'keep' by young people to their mothers, the management of their benefit over the two weeks, is, however, about more than everyday budgeting. It is about the learning of values and the practice of 'right' behaviour. The lending and giving of money to children is seen to be part of good parenting. These quotes — one about a 'bad manager', one about a 'good manager' — illustrate clearly that parents are concerned about more than the strictly economic issues involved:

> It's his clothes and his social life. He gives me something and I take it off him. But he gets it back by the end of the fortnight. But you have to, to give him a sense of responsibility, don't you? ... I buy all his clothes and its 'lend me a pound here and there Mum', but I never get it back. He gives me his £20 and he thinks he's paid me back ... Before Christmas he had no money to buy Christmas presents so I bought some for him ... he must owe me about £200 altogether. (Mrs Roberts, son David, 20 years)

> If something is £25 I will pay half. She always pays back. She's very good. She borrows off Dad. She offers to pay back, but he doesn't take it ... For example we paid for Ruth and Brian, Dennis and his wife to go out and have a meal ... If I didn't work Ruth wouldn't have so much ... She doesn't want for nothing. She knows she can ask her father. Last week she had a new jacket. She couldn't afford it. Father said: 'Get it ... I'll pay'. (Mrs Jones, daughter Ruth, 18 years)

Why is the management of the benefit so important to both parents and young people? There are three likely reasons. In the first place, one must recognize the importance of econmic constraints. There is a strict limit — often tightly defined for these families — to the amount of strain the overall domestic budget can bear. Second, being able to manage one's benefit shows some ability to cope in the outside world. Third, to manage one's own money was also to be independent (to a degree) from one's parents. Many of these young people, if they could afford it, preferred not to ask their parents for money, or to pay back loans promptly.

Ten years ago a first job, a first wage, would have provided the basis for independence and for adult behaviour. Today, unemployment or supplementary benefit just about manages to serve this function for many young women and men. Young people drawing benefit are usually receiving more money than when they were at school. It seems that adult status of a sort can be achieved by leaving school and drawing social security, however meagre this may be. In the words of an 18-year-old young woman, a student at the local technical college: 'At one stage I was really pissed off ... not drawing benefit or anything.'

Parents commonly face a dilemma in their financial dealings with their older children. On the one hand, they do not wish their offspring to be materially deprived — or, at least, too deprived — as a result of their unemployment. Thus sometimes they only take a token amount of house-keeping money (nevertheless, the majority of the young people contributed ten pounds a week to the household budget). Many of the mothers we spoke to bought, or helped in buying, clothes. Some gave or lent their children small sums. Gifts at Christmas and birthdays — of either money or goods — are an important mechanism for transferring resources within the family in a non-problematic and legitimate fashion. Sometimes loans did not need to be paid back, although this was not necessarily admitted at the time of the advance. The degree of parental subsidy is obvious in the quotes about the 'good' and 'bad' manager above.

On the other hand, many of the parents interviewed did not want life to be too comfortable for their children either. A minority thought that financial austerity would be the best spur in pushing their, in these cases, sons to go out and look for work. As Mr Jenkins said, speaking of his 20-year old son, Philip: 'I keep him a bit hungry'. Many parents also felt that it was important that their children should learn the 'real' value of money. The young man or woman is encouraged to learn the independent and 'sensible' way to manage their personal finances as one of the major practical accomplishments bound up with becoming and being an adult. The regular contribution of 'keep' is an important part of this lesson. The restriction of the size and frequency of loans by both sides of the transaction is an attempt to foster and maintain the young person's independence. This moral dilemma facing some parents — and there can be no doubt that this is how it is perceived — of how to provide for their unemployed young adult children in an acceptable manner, while also teaching them values and maintaining their independence, will be echoed in subsequent sections of this chapter.

Domestic Bargaining

The elder of two young women, both of whom were unemployed, living with their father, summed up the themes of this section when she said that:

> As long as I do my bit, I can come and go as I please ... Before, when I did nothing, relations were bad. Now I do my bit, it's okay.

This quotation illustrates that a bargain is being struck within the household: good behaviour on the part of the young adult is being exchanged for a measure of greater independence. In other cases, parents felt that an unspoken contract was not being observed by the son or daughter. What is interesting is the frequency with which domestic work was mentioned as forming one side of these contracts. For the parents of both young men and young women, domestic work done and not done involved not simply work, but also 'right' behaviour, independence and even adulthood.

In several cases we encountered, either underlying tension or explicit conflict between children and their parents about the young person's not getting a job actually erupted — or so it appears — over domestic tasks which had been neglected:

> I say, 'You can do so and so while I'm out — washing up or something in the garden'. When I get home often he hasn't done anything. Then I'm angry — over a dirty saucepan or something. (Mrs Beynon, son Richard, 20 years)

Willingness to help in the house, however small the task — to do the dishes etc. — was often seen as symbolic of 'right' behaviour and 'right' attitudes in a wider sphere than the household. In the same way, just 'going to the Job Centre' or 'looking regularly in the paper' was taken as evidence of the young person's willingness to work, of their acceptance of the conventional work ethic. This can be illustrated by the following quotation:

> I talk to some mothers and they say that their sons have been round every building firm in Swansea. Now Stephen doesn't do that. Down the marina, there's lots of building jobs down there. He could call in. Someone could say, 'Call back next week'. If they haven't, you've still tried. (Mrs Farrell, son Stephen Jackson, 20 years)

It appears that what is important is not so much what is done but what is *seen* to be done. In the symbolic economy of the household and family relationships, appearances can count for a great deal. As the basis and subject of an, often implicit, intergenerational contract, they constitute a vital dimension of the social construction of each family's reality.

Young Adults and 'Spoiling'

Diana Leonard put the Swansea of the 1960s on the map with her description of the spoiling of its young people (Leonard, 1980). She paints a picture of warm, close relationships, particularly between mothers and their indulged, lazy offspring. The picture does not appear to have much changed. Times may be leaner and belts pulled tighter, but twenty years later we were struck, as interviewers, by the apparent warmth of feeling between most mothers and their 'adult' children. Some mothers and children mentioned liking each others' company and there were many other manifestations of emotional closeness and affection.

We were also frequently struck by the way in which mothers, many of whom held part-time jobs, rushed around doing most of the cleaning and cooking. A shift-working husband often made cooking complicated. A casserole might be prepared hot for a husband at midday, then served up cold to an unemployed daughter and her boyfriend returning from work at tea time. In some households, little use was made of unemployed children who were in bed all morning and out all evening. Against this statement, of course, we must record the boy, the youngest of a large family and the last to remain at home, who did much of the housework and cooking for his father after his mother died. Although varied, this pattern agrees with Lydia Morris's findings that male unemployment brings little or no alteration to patterns of domestic labour in the household (Morris, 1985). The wife or mother continues to bear the brunt of housework in most families. The children, be they male or female, typically infringe only in a small way upon their mother's sphere of responsibility, and only assume a small share of her burden.

Our material shows that unemployment can often create or exacerbate conflict between parents and their children. On the other hand, however, it may also bring a degree of greater closeness in its wake. In many cases, the relationship is, by and large, not felt to be altered. The two following quotations illustrate the two extremes of the spectrum of possibilities:

> Mother, she doesn't like it at all but she knows I'm looking for a job. We argue all the time, like … It's being in the house, like, I'm just under her feet. I'm in a miserable mood. She's in a miserable mood. Sometimes she rings my father and he comes over and gets me and I go and stay there for a week. It gives her a break. (Peter Davies, 18 years)

> I help mum in the mornings. I clean upstairs — making the beds, cleaning the bathroom. Mum does the downstairs. At 11 am, I pick up mum from her cleaning job at the University. We have a cup of coffee and a chat. Then we do the dinner. My brother and sister come home from school for dinner … (Michelle Hughes, 18 years)

The job of being a mother is not simple, in this respect as in other things. The conflict between the desire to cushion unemployed children from hardship, on the one hand, and 'keeping them hungry', on the other has already been mentioned. There is also, however, the conflict between giving children independence and 'keeping an eye'.

It was evident that most parents were deliberately giving their children greater independence, relaxing the controls of adolescence as they got older. Coming in at night was not often mentioned as a topic for conflict and several boys and girls regularly spent nights away from home. Job-hunting was often left, sometimes reluctantly, to the young person. As one mother said:

He wasn't applying. He was just bowling along. His friends seemed to be in a similar situation. There was just a limit to what we could do. You can back him up but he said: 'I know what I'm doing'. We had to leave it to him. (Mrs Jenkins, son Philip, 19 years)

Parents are well aware of the 'normal' stages of life. They also know that independence must be nurtured.

On the other hand, several were aware of the dangers involved in the assumption of adulthood. Interestingly, it is probably young men who are most seen to be at risk, not young women. The dangers of drugs and an 'alternative' life style were seen by parents to threaten their sons. Some young men themselves mentioned the threat. Mrs Farrell, below, expresses well the dilemma between allowing children more independence and keeping an eye on them. Although she thought that Stephen was better turned out and better company when he was living away from home, she said,

I didn't like it at all because I was worried. We live in a difficult age with drugs for instance. I feel you don't have any control over them ... these board and lodging cases ... they're there together, not to feel left out — they're more inclined to be in moral danger .../ /... I'd like to see him living independently but coming home a couple of nights a week. So you can see everything's okay. A mother's got her feelings at the end of the day whatever they've done. (Mrs Farrell, son Stephen Jackson, 20 years)

Why do mothers spoil their children? Diana Leonard suggests that it is through the unpaid labour of the mother that she retains the company of married children and their care in old age. From our material one could suggest that, as well as love and affection, there is some feeling on the part of mothers that 'spoiling' can help to keep an unemployed son or daughter at home. At home a young person is 'safe' and, for the time being at least, set on the acceptable path through life. Philip's mother, already worried by his 'surfie' lifestyle — a distinctive local sub-culture — and lack of interest in finding a job, felt that it was important to keep relations good at home otherwise Philip might leave. If he did, she and her husband would lose completely whatever small control they had over him and his future completely. Ruth Jones' mother also was careful not to have major rows in case her daughter should use this as an excuse for leaving home and living with her boyfriend. If she left home her mother knew she would never manage to save up and get married.

Allatt and Yeandle (1986) talk about the 'concept of fairness', an unwritten contract between the young worker and his or her employer. The parents in our sample seemed to be more concerned with the unspoken contract which we suggest exists between themselves and their children. While a job, with its attendant financial independence and responsibility, may not be available to many — or even most — young people at present, a degree of adulthood within the family may be conceded. The bargaining between parents and children around the assumption of adult status is an ongoing process. As such, it is fragile and may be fraught with difficulties. The fact that both parents and children persevere in the face of these difficulties is eloquent testimony to the importance of the issue.

An Alternative Lifestyle

A way a life in which a job is not important, in which the acquisition of consumer goods has less importance as a spur to conformity, was felt to be a threat by some parents and young people. Everyone in West Swansea knew about 'surfies' and drugs. Situated as it is close to the Gower Peninsula, many local boys go surfing from their early teens. We encountered at least three boys who surfed, and by this we mean going out three or four times a week throughout the year. School children in West Swansea, and their parents, know that some 'surfies' take drugs. We did not, however, ask directly about drugs. Two of the young men who we interviewed admitted to minor convictions for possessing cannabis. Although none appeared to be using drugs regularly, it is, of course, impossible to make a judgment in this respect with any confidence.

What is important, however, is that this alternative style of life is *seen* as a threat by some parents — interestingly, all parents of boys. One aspect of this life-style was to lie in bed all day and not to look for a job. Drug taking and trouble with the police were also thought to be part and parcel of it. One mother was anxious when her son turned the normal work day routine on its head:

> There was a time when he was going to bed in the early hours of the morning and got up very late in the morning. He was turning night into day. We had to speak to him about that — it got better when he had to go to tech. (Mrs Powell, son Kirk, 19 years)

To many of the parents and young people in our sample, the 'normal' — and ideal — progression through the life cycle means putting down a deposit on a house (finances permitting), getting married and having children (although the ideal order of these events does vary). Progression is firmly based on material accumulation. That the desire for material possessions acts as an important spur in accepting or seeking a job is recognised by several parents. As one father said, talking about his son:

> The fellow next door's got a Capri. The guy down the road's got a Capri. They're running about. (If only you'd think) 'I've got no-

thing. I want a Capri you know'. Then you'd start doing something. You'd start growing up.

The best protection for this ideal way of life against threatening alternatives was to keep children at home; homes where employment was valued
and material possessions highly prized.

Paul Willis (1984) hints at the emergence of an alternative life style in
a context of high youth unemployment. Claire Wallace, in her work in the
Isle of Sheppey (1986), argues that young people are eventually tied into a
capitalist system by the need for consumer durables, particularly when
children are born. Jenkins (1983), writing about Belfast in the late 1970s,
has also argued that 'households are important means of locking workers
— both male and female — into waged labour' (p. 133). Several of our
informants felt that young women were more tightly tied into the consumer durable market: they needed more money to buy clothes, make-up,
etc. This they felt was a reason why they were more prepared than their
male peers to take part-time jobs or extra evening work. Several parents
noted the way in which a steady girlfriend could pull a young man back
into 'respectable' society:

> If you have a regular girlfriend you drink less, go out with boys
> less. You are less likely to get into trouble.

One 20-year-old boy noted, with interest, that he thought that girls
tended to work harder in school and be more successful in getting jobs.
He describes them as fitting more successfully and quickly into adult
society:

> ... I think it's because (boys are) lazy in school that they're lazy
> outside school. (Girls) they're more interested (in going to tech). I
> know this is going to sound funny but they grow up more quickly.
> Suddenly, they come out of school and they shape up a bit and
> have a good time but we just carry on, plodding along.

The role of the girl in the developmental process by 'settling down the lad'
is clear and has also been documented by Jenkins (*ibid.*) for the young
people of 'Ballyhightown' housing estate in Belfast (pp. 80–3).

In mentioning the threat of the alternative life style we do how, however, want to overemphasize it. In actual fact, only a small number of boys and
fewer girls were thought by their parents to be in direct danger. But it *was*
seen to be a vague threat lurking beyond the threshold of comfortable
domesticity by a significant number of the parents. Just as many, however,
never mentioned it. What is perhaps surprising is the number of young
people who retain a strong commitment to the mainstream values of con-
sumerist accumulation despite their long term unemployment. Clearly, a
lifetime's socialization by the family, the education system, peer groups and
the mass media is not going to be easily undermined by what may be

perceived as only a short hiccup in the expected pattern of life. The fact that it may *not* be a hiccup, that 'something' may *not* 'come up', is possibly too bleak a prospect to live with.

Unemployment, Life Cycle and Gender

The young men who we interviewed tended to spend more time with, and gain more emotional and financial support from, their peer groups than the young women. They also *appeared* to be less wedded to the ideals of a consumer society. A generation ago, if Diana Leonard, for example, is to be believed, mothers were concerned about their daughter's sexuality. Now it is their sons' potential abandonment of mainstream values which seems to be more of a concern for them. These two 'problematic' characteristics of young men may be related to the fact that there were more unemployed males in the areas under study. By comparison, some young women tended to be relatively socially isolated, not meeting other girls through work, and this is also perceived as a 'problem'.

Girls tended to do more housework, but some boys also did a considerable amount. Most young people, either male or female, in fact did very little 'round the house'. The common-sensical picture of the unemployed girl absorbed into the domestic round of the family is not confirmed by our material. At this age, such a domestic commitment seemed to depend more on the family circumstances — for example the death or absence of the mother, or the illness of parents — than the gender of the young person.

It was surprising both how many parents appeared to treat their adult sons and daughters in a similar way, and how many notions of gender equality had filtered through to these families. Mothers talked of their children as individuals, their individual personalities seen to be determining their present circumstances more than their gender. Parents appeared to be just as concerned about the unemployment of a daughter as a son. Few of the young women saw their immediate goal as marriage; all appeared to want jobs. For example, one girl, actually engaged to be married, was determined to get into the army, 'to make a name for myself'. She also wanted to learn to drive and to earn enough money to buy a Suzuki jeep. She knew that if she stayed in Swansea neither of these ambitions would be fulfilled. Another girl refused to get engaged until she had a job because she wanted to start saving on equal terms with her employed boyfriend.

Almost everyone we talked to felt that young women liked greater independence in their relationships with the opposite sex today. This was symbolized by girls paying for themselves on social occasions. Most of those who did not agree with this state of affairs felt some need to apologize for being 'old fashioned'.

Despite these emerging notions of equality, an issue was mentioned several times which may have important implications for the life cycle. There was some agreement that young men needed money to take women out. A few felt that unemployment directly hindered their relationships with their girlfriends:

> It's a strain moneywise. Not being able to afford things I want or take her where she wants to go ... She tends to want to pay a lot, which is embarrassing for me. I just feel ashamed ... Her mother and father knowing I'm unemployed. That's also been a strain. You can imagine a girl brings a boy home and he's not working. There's no real future. It's not that they interfere directly. (I asked him whether they own their own house and whether this makes a difference.) 'Yes, it's class, isn't it? It shouldn't be but it is. They want to know what you do. (David Roberts, 20 years)

The fact that the majority of parents and their sons did not feel that unemployment significantly affected the sphere of romance and relationships, and that most young men were not yet interested in marriage, may merely hide a very different reality, although the topic was often couched in terms of changing sexual values, living together, rather than of marriage. The postponement of marriage due to unemployment is only hinted at in our material. If this is happening, it will be seen more clearly in five to ten years time. All we can say for the moment is that many of these young people did not *want* to get engaged, get married, live with somebody, become parents or even leave home. Not *yet*.

Particularity and Individualism

Again and again we came up against variations, the particular. In some families conflict was considerable; in others, there appeared to be little or no conflict. In one family the young person's unemployment was central; in another it appeared to be hardly noticed. Some unemployed young people led a full social life, others were isolated. One boy felt unable to ask a girl out because of lack of money; another saw more of his girlfriend because he was not working.

As an example of this variability, there is the case of one family in which the unemployment of two sons brought about markedly different consequences and reactions. Simon Miles (19 years) was not really seen as unemployed; he was 'taking some time out'. A committed Christian like his parents, Simon contributed to the family budget and was seen to be 'working towards an objective, becoming a social worker'. His elder brother, Peter, at 21, was seen to be a different person entirely. By his own admission he was 'the odd one out' in the family inasmuch as he was not a Christian, smoked, drank and engaged in other 'nocturnal pursuits', to use his mother's words. He was seen as a net drain on the family budget and viewed very differently from his brother despite the fact that he had spent most of his time since leaving school in work. His mother said:

> We do worry, particularly about Peter getting and keeping a job. It does obviously affect the relationship. It puts pressure on our finances as well as his ... And the feeling of someone hanging around not doing anything that seems worth-while during the day.

The situation within this family should alert us to the fact that, because of the importance of the history of relationships within each family or household, it is likely to be difficult to generalize about family relationships or the effect of unemployment on such relationships.

Mothers epitomize another strong theme in the interview material, inasmuch as they often see their children's unemployment as the result of their character as individuals. One mother, for example, thought that her daughter, still at school, would be unlikely to be unemployed because she was more 'go getting' than her elder brother. This was illustrated by the Saturday jobs she now did. The weight of the national and local situation melted into insignificance against the personality of one girl. These mothers were mostly too busy managing, caring for and pushing their children, to raise their eyes to wider economic and political questions.

This way of explaining the present situation in terms of the particular personal characteristics of those involved is the 'individualism' that Jenkins (1983) has discussed with repect to the young people of Ballyhightown, a world view which is 'one of the dominant cultural principles of our society' (p. 131). In the context of explanations for youth unemployment, individualism has also been documented in a recent Australian study (Watson, 1985), and in a study of young people in the North-East of England (Coffield *et al.*, 1986). While unemployment *in general* may be explained as due to the failures of the 'system', *Individual* unemployment is likely to be seen as the result of personal inadequacies: poor education, not enough experience, lack of effort, character deficiencies, or whatever. This contradiction — if indeed a contradiction it be — has been noted in other similar research also (Breakwell, 1985, p. 496).

The progress through life is seen by our respondents, particularly the parents, as a unique journey undertaken by an individual. Different children are seen to take different paths, partly because of the different events that overtake them but also, more especially, because of their different personalities. The personalties of young adults have been observed by their parents (and others) and followed from early childhood. Moreover, this personality is often linked to that of a parent or a grandparent. Listening to parents talking about their children and unemployment, it was clear that they were talking about personalities — and personalities operating in a moral universe — rather than social forces.

It would, however, be misleading to suggest that this ideology of individualism operates in a straightforward fashion. Nor is there much evidence from our data that either parents or young people actually experience the disjuncture between general/systems-level explanations, on the one hand, and particular/individualistic explanations on the other, as a contradiction. While individualistic understandings may prevail, this does not necessarily mean that individuals are *blamed*.

Conclusions

For Diana Leonard, adulthood comes with the full male wage, marriage and the setting up of a separate household. Paul Willis sees unemployment, the lack of a wage, as holding this generation in suspended animation, somewhere between youth and adulthood. We wish to dissent from both of these understandings of the transition from youth to adulthood in contemporary Britain. Many aspects of adulthood are given before marriage — by the state, the peer group and, especially, the family — and, as a consequence, a great deal of independence is gained before marriage. This may reflect the fact that, nationally speaking, young people are marrying later. Cohabitation also appears to be growing in acceptability and frequency (Central Statistical Office, 1986, p. 13). This trend towards later marriage, the extent of which for our sample cannot yet be estimated, may well be related to hardening economic conditions. The inter-connections between later marriage, greater sexual freedom, and increased equality of the sexes, even if only at the rhetorical level, are obvious but complex.

Adulthood was often thought to be conferred on young men when they got their first job, their first wage. Be this as it may, it appears that social security benefit, however meagre, may also give some degree of independence from parents and its management can allow the young person to exhibit adult capabilities. With youth wages being typically low and jobs insecure, the difference between a wage and social security benefit has diminished somewhat. The latter may now serve something of the same symbolic function — albeit in a reduced, less positive fashion — as the wage packet.

Within the family, adulthood is seen to have a strong moral content. This emphasis on morality, also documented by Allatt and Yeandle, may in our research be a function of the fact that we talked with parents as well as young adults. We consider that without taking account of popular morality — a sense of the rights and wrongs of the situation — the effects of unemployment cannot be understood. Unemployment is, in part, about managing, learning values, exhibiting right behaviour. So is the assumption of adult status. Domestic labour within the house is a common currency which may be exchanged for independence. Surprisingly perhaps, right inside the family, hardly a public arena, what is important is not what is done but what is seen to be done.

For these three reasons — that many aspects of adulthood are given before marriage; that social security benefit provides — in the relatively sheltered context of the parental home — some kind of economic base; and that adulthood has a strong moral content, young people in South Wales still appear to come of age, to achieve their social majority, despite increasing and widespread youth unemployment. A discordant note is struck, however, by the testimony of a few young men who felt that their unemployment is unacceptable to potential future in-laws. A lack of interest in marriage in the near future among the unemployed young people we interviewed may be directly related to their economic position, and may lead to late marriage. It may also be — and we are inclined to take this possibility seriously — best understood as part of a longer-term national trend towards later marriage and more cohabitation. Time alone will tell.

Because we are looking at a period of transition, which is felt by both parents and their sons and daughters to have a strong moral dimension, dilemmas of choice and conscience are only to be expected. First, we found a conflict between, on the one hand, attempting to cushion one's offspring against the hardship of unemployment and, on the other, not wanting to make things *too* comfortable for them, at the expense of teaching them the proper value of money. Second, there is also the contradiction between giving young people their independence whilst, at the same time, 'keeping an eye'. It is not, perhaps, surprising that some mothers blamed their son's or daughter's unemployment on their own mishandling of these values.

Finally, this chapter has tended to minimize the differences of experience between the sexes; this view is in sympathy with our awareness of the increasing relative independence of young women. This is in reflection of the overall situation which we discovered in Swansea and Port Talbot. It came as a considerable surprise, given our initial starting point, which took it somewhat for granted that gender differences would be more marked in this respect. It is not, however, that gender differences are insignificant, simply that they appeared to be less significant, in terms of our focus of interest, than we had expected. Ironically, young men are seen to be in greater moral danger — from an alternative life style — than young women. Only one mother that we spoke to appeared to see her daughter's sexuality as a problem.

With these young people moving on through the life cycle, protected and managed by their mothers, interpreting their own experiences within a largely individualistic explanatory framework, it is perhaps not surprising that the social and political fabric of society has been so little ruffled by historically high levels of youth unemployment. Young people continue — despite all the odds which are stacked against them — to achieve adult status. Although it would be stretching credulity too far to argue that they can achieve *full* adult status or *full* social membership as long as they are unemployed, neither is it the case that they are left in limbo, abandoned to a purgatorial appendix of the life cycle. Despite youth (and adult) unemployment, life — of a sort — goes on.

References

ALLATT, P. and YEANDLE, S. (1985) *Family Structure and Youth Unemployment in an Area of Persistent Decline*, Report to the Leverhulme Trust, London.

ALLATT, P. and YEANDLE, S. (1986) 'It's not fair, is it? Youth unemployment family relations and the social contract', in ALLEN, S. *et al.* (Eds), *The Experience of Unemployment*, London, Macmillan, pp. 98–115.

BREAKWELL, G.M. (1985). 'Young people in and out of work', in ROBERTS, B. FINNEGAN, R. and GALLIE, D. (Eds), *New Approaches to Economic Life*, Manchester, Manchester University Press, pp. 490–501.

COFFIELD, F., BORRILL, C. and MARSHALL, S. (1986) *Growing Up at the Margins: Young People in the North East*, Milton Keynes, Open University Press.

CENTRAL STATISTICAL OFFICE (1986), *Key Facts 86*, London, HMSO.

JENKINS, R. (1983) *Lads, Citizens and Ordinary Kids: Working-class Youth Life-styles in Belfast*, London, Routledge and Kegan Paul.

JENKINS, R. and HUTSON, S. (1986) 'Young people, unemployment and the family: report of a pilot project', *Occasional Paper No. 14*, School of Social Studies, University College, Swansea.

LEE, G. and WRENCH, J. (1983), *Skill Seekers: Black Youth, Apprenticeships and Disadvantage*, Leicester, National Youth Bureau.

LEONARD, D. (1980), *Sex and Generation: A Study of Courtship and Weddings*, London, Tavistock.

MORRIS, L.D. (1985), 'Renegotiation of the domestic division of labour in the context of male redundancy', in ROBERTS, B. FINNEGAN, R. and GALLIE, D. (Eds), *New Approaches to Economic Life*, Manchester, Manchester University Press, pp. 400–16.

WALLACE, C. (1986), 'From girls and boys to women and men: The social production of gender roles in the transition from school to (un)employment', in WALKER, S. and BARTON, L. (Eds) *Youth Unemployment and Schooling*, Milton Keynes, Open University Press, pp. 92–117.

WATSON, I. (1985) *Double Depression: Schooling, Unemployment and Family Life in the Eighties*, Sydney, George Allen and Unwin.

WILLIS, P. (1984) 'Youth unemployment: Thinking the unthinkable', *Youth and Policy*, 2, 4, pp. 17–24 and 33–6.

6 From Generation to Generation: The Effects of Employment and Unemployment Upon the Domestic Life Cycle of Young Adults.

Claire Wallace

Introduction

Few of those who have written in the sociology of youth have considered the role of the domestic life cycle explicitly. Of those who have, the majority have been inspired by feminist perspectives and have confined their studies to girls.

However, there is evidence that the life cycle affects young men too. Some who have looked at delinquent careers for example, concluded that the transition to marriage and parenthood caused young men to 'settle down' and become more conforming citizens (Parker, 1977). Similarly, it has been found that 'settling down' influenced labour market behaviour and leisure patterns (Carter, 1975; Jenkins, 1983).

Why has there been this neglect of the domestic cycle in looking at young people? One explanation would be that there has been a focus upon education, the transition to working life and youth culture — all areas of popular concern in the post-war era. Homes were relevant only as transmitters of values, and then only via the father's job. Another explanation might be that there have been few longitudinal studies which have taken such a dynamic into account. The focus has been upon the immediate post-school period. A further explanation is perhaps the androcentric bias in studies of youth with male researchers doing studies of male respondents. Studies have thus reflected perceptions of the marginality of the domestic sphere. Recent feminist writers, however, have indicated that far from being marginal, the domestic sphere is crucial to an understanding of contemporary capitalism (Gamarnikow *et al.*, 1983).

More recently, the relationship between youth, employment and the life cycle has attracted more popular attention because the young unemployed of the 1970s have grown up, carrying unemployment with them into early adulthood. Although only a small proportion of teenagers today have regular jobs, the majority are now absorbed into short college courses or Youth Training Schemes. The 'problem' of unemployment is now found amongst those between 20 and 34, an increasing proportion of whom are unemployed[1]. As a substantial proportion of those under 25 have joined a marginalized population of the 'sub-employed', so the hitherto normal paths for transition from one domestic household to another, established in the 1950s and 1960s during times of full employment, are no longer possible. What new patterns are emerging?

The Study

In order to answer this question, I undertook a study of eighty-four 21-year-olds on the Isle of Sheppey. These were part of a sample first interviewed when they were 16 in 1979 and then again in 1980. They were last interviewed in 1984, when I asked them about their employment and domestic careers. The sample consisted of forty-four young men and forty young women. This was a cross-sectional sample, and so the people in it had pursued a variety of post-school career. Some had held regular jobs, some had been unemployed for long periods and many had been on government schemes of some kind. All except for two girls had had some work experience by the time they were 21, however transitory this was.

Respondents were asked a set of questions from a structured questionnaire, which were later coded and analyzed using Minitab. Respondents were also encouraged to express their ideas freely and the interviews were tape recorded in order to record these accurately. The tape recordings were later transcribed and indexed. In this way, there was both a quantitative and a qualitative record of each interview.

The Isle of Sheppey was chosen as the locus for the research because it had suffered high unemployment since 1959, when the naval dockyard had closed. At the time of the survey there was some employment in 'heavy labour' for men, in the steel mill and the port. For women there was work in some of the small garment manufacturing or electrical assembly firms. Most school leavers, however, found jobs with small employers and in the service sector on the fringes of the 'formal' labour market. This pattern of employment in the local labour market meant that the population of the island was skewed towards the manual working class. Some of the parents of my sample were commuters, attracted to the Island by the relatively cheap housing more than by any cultural or scenic interest, for Sheppey did not resemble the rest of Kent in this respect. It is an industrial island. There was one large comprehensive school on the island from which this sample was drawn in 1979.

In addition to this survey of young people, other research into the local labour market, the housing market and household work strategies had been undertaken over a period of five years[2].

Although this is too small a sample from which to derive statistical generalizations, the combination of qualitative and quantitative methods means that they can be used to generate speculative categories as a basis for further research.

First, however, a baseline is needed in order to ascertain how patterns of transition have changed. In order to create this I have pieced together the 'normal' patterns of transition to work and family as it was established in the post-war period, from a variety of sources. Having described this, I shall then go on to consider how this might have changed before looking at patterns of work and transition in my own sample.

The Work Careers of Young People in Times of Full Employment

These have been well documented (Clarke, 1978). In general, studies taking place before the mid-1970s indicated that the majority of school leavers left at the minimum age, being tempted out of school by high wages available to youth in the post-war period (Roberts, 1984). Those who stayed on at school to gain further qualifications and higher education were more likely to come from middle class homes and to be destined to become the new middle classes themselves. Of the rest, Ashton and Field (1976) provide a clear typology, although a number of others have also been developed. First, there were those heading for 'long-term' or more middle class careers through primary labour markets and occupationally based training, finishing in the Registrar General's social class 2. Second, there were the 'short-term' career orientation for those going into skilled manual or white collar work, normally classified as social class 3. Finally, there were the 'career less' destined for social classes 4 and 5.

This kind of typology could be applied quite neatly to male school leavers but was more problematical in the case of female school leavers whose aspirations and career opportunities were depressed by the expectation of marriage and motherhood and on account of their more limited opportunities in the labour market.

I have not the space here to enter all the arguments relevant to this process, as I am interested at present in the way in which employment careers fitted with the domestic careers of different social groups. However, many of these ideas are more fully developed in Wallace (1987).

The Domestic Careers of Young People in Times of Full Employment

The family has been subject to continual change throughout the twentieth century (Eversley and Bonnerjea, 1982). However, a picture of patterns of family transition during the so-called 'affluent' 1950s and 1960s can be pieced together from previous surveys[3].

It would appear that although age of marriage has fallen throughout the twentieth century, the 'homeless penniless' marriage which is now considered normal was made possible by a period of affluence and full employment (Leonard, 1980).

Leonard goes on to explain that the 'normal' pattern implied that getting married and obtaining a home of one's own was the only means by which young people in Swansea were able to exert their social, psychological and financial independence from the natal home. Until they married they lived with parents as juniors within the home:

> Enormous value is placed on attaining adult status, of being married, having a home of one's own, and the weight of socialisation which is directed towards the goal of marriage and getting a home of one's own affects the attitude towards the whole period in between leaving school and getting married (*ibid*, p. 61).

Thus, marriage and parenthood were of central importance in the lives of young adults.

These patterns differed between social classes. Those with more middle class occupations married at a later age than the working class. Hence an OPCS survey found 10 per cent of those in social classes 1 and 2 married in their teens as against 41 per cent in social classes 4 and 5 (Dunnell, 1976). This was because professional and managerial occupations required a period in higher education and training which might involve moving around the country. Middle class children therefore left home, got married and bought homes later. Those in routine white collar and manual jobs on the other hand were likely to stay with parents until they got married. This was reflected in aspirations and patterns of long-term planning. Hence, the middle class were able to defer marriage, parenthood and home building until they had the resources to do so, confident in the expectation of rising salaries. Working class couples on the other hand were less likely to achieve a range of consumer goods which made deferring families in this way irrelevant.

There were similar social class differences in the transition to parenthood too. Working class young people were more likely to be sexually experienced at an earlier age than the middle class, and there was what Schofield (1973) has termed a 'contraceptive gap' between the initiation of sexual activity and regular use of contraceptives. Moreover, middle class young adults were likely to use abortion as a form of birth control, whereas working class girls were not (Dunnell, 1976; Schofield, 1973). This meant that working class girls were more 'at risk' from unwanted pregnancies and that such unwanted pregnancies were likely to result in an early wedding. As Schofield (1973) concluded:

This research has shown that forced marriage is still the most likely consequence of pre-marital pregnancy for a working class girl (p. 152).

Jenkins (1983) has made the connections between the tendency toward planning and modes of family formation more explicitly. Those in less secure financial and employment circumstances in his sample were less likely to 'plan' families and more likely to be forced into marriage through an early accidental pregnancy and these findings are confirmed by Jones *et al.* (1981).

A note of moral censure often creeps into the accounts of those who consider the so-called 'problem' of early marriage and pregnancy which is thought to affect the undereducated and deviant working class young girl in particular. There are calls, for example, for more education for these 'irresponsible' young mothers-to-be. However, these different patterns of family formation can be explained by the economic and social circumstances in which different social groups find themselves.

This also has implications for housing careers as delayed marriage and childbirth were associated with becoming an owner occupier. The OPCS study found that of those who expected to own their own homes, 12 per cent married in their teens and 3 per cent of them were pregnant. However, of those who expected to find rented housing, 23 per cent married in their teens and 10 per cent were pregnant. Ineichin (1977 and 1981) has made a more detailed study of this aspect of young people's behaviour and found that early unplanned pregnancies were associated with early marriage and consequent exclusion from owner occupied accommodation, which in turn led to what he termed the 'vortex of disadvantage'. The implication then, is that patterns of family formation could operate to advantage or disadvantage the family later in life.

A Proposed Model

Many commentators imply that unplanned pregnancy and early marriage are a 'problem' amongst working class girls, but less so amongst middle class and 'respectable' working class girls who defer family formation. Sexual behaviour, like so many other aspects of working class youth's behaviour is thus rendered problematical. However, if we now relate domestic careers to employment careers, such patterns become more explicable and even appear as logical strategies. The proposed model is set out diagrammatically in figure 1.

Marriage and child rearing amongst social classes 4 and 5 would in fact correspond with the peak earnings potential in most unskilled manual jobs — for men this is in their twenties and thirties. Until recently, this group have been excluded from owner occupied housing and so there was

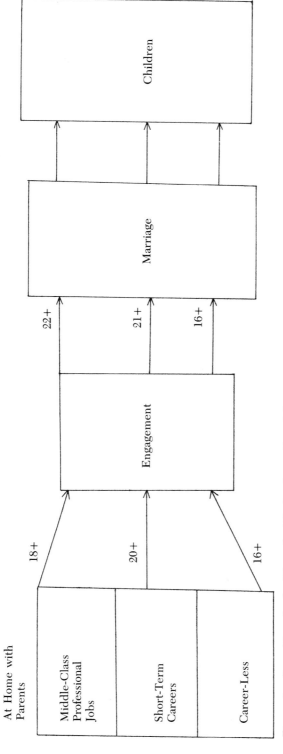

Figure 1: Transitions in the life cycle: The 'traditional' model

little reason to save for a home. On the contrary, accumulating domestic responsibilities would be more likely to secure council accommodation for young couples. Moreover, the early financial independence provided by unskilled work for minimum age school leavers means that they were able to embark upon domestic careers at an earlier age.

For those in social class 3 on the other hand — the skilled manual and white collar workers whose jobs required a few years of training on less money — marriage may have been postponed until after apprenticeship or office training had been completed; that is, until their early 20s. In this time, savings and items for the 'bottom drawer' of a home could have been accumulated, perhaps over the period of an engagement. Hence, this social category would emphasize sexual respectability and continence in order that short term careers would not be jeopardized. This would lead to benefits later on, and hence 'planning' is a concept with different meanings for different social groups.

For those with long-term careers (social classes 1 and 2), often preceded by a period at college or in higher education, marriage clearly has to be postponed until after training has been completed (although many couples may cohabit beforehand) and this will not be before their mid-twenties. Planning towards housing and towards a long-term career, with high financial rewards farther away in time, is clearly necessary for this kind of occupational career to be continued. House buying and childbirth are thus postponed.

In this way it can be seen that patterns of family formation, the housing market and early careers in the labour market all interact to produce different 'ideal typical' models for different social groups. It could be hypothesized that the sexual morality of different social groups also fits this pattern, and represent a constellation of values which relate to class culture and life styles more generally. Hence, lower middle and upper working class families would emphasize sexual continence as being part of an ethos of respectability, but this may be less important amongst the unskilled working class.[4] With the social construction of sexuality familiar to us in a patriarchal society (women defensive, men offensive) (Cowie and Lees, 1981), it is young women's sexual behaviour which is particularly controlled in this context since it is this which will determine a daughter's ultimate destination in the class structure. Early sexual experience could lead to downward social mobility. Hence, it can be seen that there is a connection between control of feminine behaviour and the social reproduction of a class society.

Thus, the domestic life cycle operates in a different way for male and for female young adults. For young women, it is thought to dominate every other aspect of their lives, since the husband's job will normally take precedence over theirs once they are married (Sharpe, 1976; McRobbie, 1978; McRobbie and Garber, 1976). On the other hand, it is argued that the preoccupations of young men lie more in the labour market since this affects their life chances more directly. It can be seen, however, that class dominates the relationships of young adults of both genders and this in turn helps to determine sexual behaviour. The life cycle, class and occupation affect both young men and young women, albeit in different ways, and the gender-biased way of dichotomizing young adults had perhaps blinded us to seeing the interaction of the public and private spheres in this respect (Wallace, 1986). The domestic life cycle is tied to employment and housing careers, and this differs between social groups. The model I am proposing has a different emphasis to that suggested by Ineichin and others. Rather than individual actions determining future life chances, these are structured by labour market opportunities existing outside of the individual. Young adults are forced to adapt their life cycle to external exigencies. Individual moral agency is subordinated to this.

The model outlined above is a hypothetical one based upon 'ideal typical' categories derived from other research. This should provide the 'base line' from which to measure change.

The Life Cycle and Social Change

Given the way in which the life cycle transitions intermesh with social conditions, we would expect them to change accordingly.

First, there are changes in the family itself. There has been a tendency towards younger marriage and first pregnancy and a compression of the child bearing years generally. Improvements in contraceptive technology and women returning to work have no doubt encouraged this.[5]

Second, there have been changes in employment. Full employment and affluence have been replaced by youth unemployment and poverty. With married women more likely to work and young men more likely to be out of work, are we going to see any changes in family forms or in family values (Evason, 1985; Study Commission on the Family, 1982)? Certainly, the school-work-marriage-children transition previously observed for different social groups will now be available to only a few. Others will have new patterns of employment with long periods out of work, periods on Youth Training Schemes and periods in and out of the informal sector (Wallace, 1985; Finn, 1984; Griffin, 1985). Indeed, there is evidence that younger households respond differently to unemployment than older ones (Binns and Mars, 1984).[6] Perhaps young newly established households are the ones most likely to show evidence of change?

Third, it has been argued that domestic cycles are dependent at least partly upon housing provision. With the increased emphasis on owner occupation and the residualization of other tenures, will family formation be affected?

Fourth, it is arguable that family formation may be determined less and less by the labour market and more and more by state policy as families depend upon state income maintenance for their subsistence rather than wages from employment. As the Fowler Review of social security attempts to redefine youth to cover a broader age spectrum, how will this affect the transition from one domestic status to another?

The changes outlined above may lead us to re-evaluate the family dynamic on empirical grounds, as the social and economic bases of traditional family patterns are changed. However, we might also wish to re-evaluate these on theoretical grounds as the gender-biased approaches which have examined men in terms of employment and women in terms of the domestic sphere no longer appear to be appropriate. Also, by looking at the family life cycle it should be possible to link otherwise compartmentalized aspects of social life — such as employment, housing and domestic career — to show the relationships between them. In this way we can illuminate the interrelationships between individual life strategies and broader social and economic processes. Indeed, the importance of the relationship between these different kinds of transition is being increasingly recognized (Roberts, 1985).

Empirical Section

New Work Careers

It has been argued that social class is no longer the only determinant of the career paths of school leavers: access to employment is now a crucial intervening variable (*ibid*). The reproduction of the middle class is achieved increasingly through higher education and those seven in my sample who were in higher education have been excluded from the analysis since they have not yet entered the labour market. Hence, my account concentrates upon those who did not pass through higher education — in other words, it does not include the conventional middle class. Rather than differentiating the sample by occupation — since many did not have a conventionally defined occupation — I have differentiated it according to 'employment career': that is, the length of time in or out of work.

Table 1 shows the three categories of employment career. The first category are the 'regularly unemployed', or all those who had been unemployed for more than a year since leaving school. These were counted as a separate category, since extensive research has indicated that adaptation to employment depends upon the length of time out of work (Warr, 1983; Jahoda, 1982). Many of these had been unemployed for about half of their five years in the labour market. The second category consists of those who had been unemployed for less than a year altogether — the 'occasionally unemployed' — these, like the previous category, may have pursued a

Table 1: *Employment careers*

	Percentage
Regularly unemployed	34
Occasionally unemployed	17
Regularly employed	49
TOTAL NUMBER	74

(There were ten respondents who could not be classified easily)

variety of jobs and government schemes and had experienced periods in and out of casual and informal work, but they had been unemployed for shorter periods of time than the first group. The final category consists of those who had been continuously employed in one or more jobs. These constituted the 'regularly employed'. Only the last category had followed conventional routes (established in the 1950s and 1960s) into work. It is noteworthy, that everyone had some experience of work but that for half the sample their experience was irregular. These together could be said to constitute the 'sub-employed', category identified as significant elsewhere (Harris *et al.*, 1987). Hence in many parts of this chapter they have been counted together with the long-term unemployed in order to contrast them more easily with the regularly employed.

I have not included social class in this analysis since it was difficult to assign a social class to some of these respondents, given their irregular employment careers.

Altogether, of those who had entered the labour market, roughly one-third had spent much of their time out of work, one-half had been regularly employed and another category had been unemployed for less than a year as they moved between jobs or between schemes. A complicated employment career broken by periods of unemployment was the norm as less than one third had been regularly employed in just one job and this was mostly because they had joined the army!

But what consequences do these changes hold for domestic careers?

New Domestic Careers

Young adults lived in a variety of domestic situations. I have divided the domestic status' of young people into four main categories depending upon their position on two dimensions: the degree of dependence or independence from the natal home and whether they lived as couples or as single people. The results are presented in table 2.

The first category is that of the 'dependent single person' — that is, young people who continued to live at home with their parents. There were twice as many young men in this category as young women. Secondly

Table 2: Domestic careers by sex

	Male	Female	Total	Percentage
Dependent singles	17	9	26	35
Independent singles	6	8	14	19
Independent couples: cohabiting	7	5	12	16
Independent couples: married	3	14	17	23
Dependent couples	4	1	5	7

Note: This excludes seven who had never entered the labour market, two who had gone to college later and one who was in a special home.

there were the 'independent single' people. These constituted 19 per cent of the sample (not including those away at college) and included those in the army or in nurse training, as well as those living in flats and bedsits. Thirdly there were the 'independent couples', 39 per cent altogether, or those who were either married or cohabiting but living away from home in a separate unit. These could be said to have made the transition from the home of origin to that of destination. There were twelve young adults cohabiting and seventeen who were married, so traditional marriage was certainly not the only way of establishing a household. Moreover, most of the married couples had cohabited before getting married, so that cohabitation was often a transitional stage between the family of origin and that of destination. The fourth category were the 'dependent couples' (7 per cent), a small but significant category. Again, many of the independent couples had begun as dependent couples. The dependent couples were those who were either married or cohabiting but continued to be dependent upon families for accommodation. They tended to live at different relative's houses at different points of the week as they could not afford a place of their own. This category also includes two young adults — a male and a female — who had children but continued to live with their own parents rather than with the other parent of their child.

Altogether, then, there was a variety of domestic states which involved various degrees of dependency upon the natal home, and various kinds of home of destination. Only 23 per cent had got married by the time they were 21, although the majority had by that time left home. This is in contrast to the findings of Leonard (1980) and others writing in previous decades who found that the majority of young people in similar socioeconomic groups as these left home only in order to get married.

There was therefore a considerable variety and flexibility in family forms. The problem with this cross sectional information is that it does not tell us about longitudinal domestic careers. I will attempt to build a model of domestic careers later, but first let us look at the way in which employment careers affected domestic careers.

Domestic Careers and Employment Careers

In this section I have created a composite variable of household employment status to cover the entire household, for those who were either
cohabiting or married.[7] Elsewhere, I have broken these down more fully
according to the employment of both spouses (Wallace, 1987). Table 3
indicates the intersection of domestic and employment careers. The first
category of interest in this table is the 'single independent'. It can be seen
that the majority of these had been employed. It would appear that the
majority of young people who left home were regularly employed,
although these cells are very small. There were interesting contrasts
between young men and young women in this respect. The young men
had most often left home in order to join the army or the navy, or if they
were unemployed, it was due to family arguments which appeared to be a
direct result of their lack of employment. Girls, by contrast often sought
their own flats or bedsits without becoming part of a couple and many of
the dependent single girls expressed a desire to do this too.

> CW: And why did you leave home?
> Debby: Well, really, I just kind of wanted a place of my own really
>   (pause). It's more or less the last year that I was thinking of
>   it, I got the idea into my head, and I thought, right, that's
>   what I'm going to do, and after that, I couldn't think about
>   anything else.

This is understandable if we take into consideration the role of male
and female offspring within the home. Male youth were not expected to
contribute towards domestic work but could come and go as they pleased
whilst they lived at home. As many informed me, they would have to be
mad to leave. Where else could they have their clothes washed and ironed
and food provided for between £10 and £15 per week? Girls on the
other hand experienced the natal home differently. Their behaviour was

Table 3: Domestic career by household employment career

Domestic Career	Household Employment Career		
	Sub-employed	Regularly-employed	Total
Single dependent	13	13	26
Single independent	5	9	14
Couple independent (c)	6	8	14
Couple independent (m)	2	16	18
Couple dependent	5	–	5
TOTAL	31	46	77

Note: Occasionally unemployed and regularly unemployed have been combined for
the purpose of this table.

much more closely controlled by parents and they were also expected to contribute towards domestic work. For them there was some incentive to live independently as it was more fulfilling to be able to do domestic work in their own home rather than for their parents. However, on the whole they managed to have their own flats and bedsits whilst remaining on good terms with parents. The kind of self-confidence needed to make plans of this kind was often acquired through having earned a living already for five years as these two young women illustrate:

> *Sharon:* And I wouldn't mind sharing a house with a few girls as long as I had a room to myself, and as long as I knew the girls like.
>
> *Anne:* Yeh, and I think its nice that a girl can set herself up in her own place without having to be married sort of thing.
>
> *Sharon:* Yes, I like that place, like that place in West Ally. It was one of these great big houses all cut up into different rooms. They shared the kitchen and bathroom and that, but it was really nice that was, I'd love to live there. And most girls, you know, cos they're used to sharing anyway because they've either shared with their sister or their brother or their mum. You know, so people don't mind sharing things that way.
>
> *Anne:* But if I could get enough money, a decent wage and that, I'd like to buy me own place, get a mortgage and buy a flat of me own, cos then you wouldn't have to rely on a bloke, would you? Cos I think these days people depend on men too much to give them things. See, you get into a routine, you depend on them and then when they leave you it all goes to them.

Thus, for girls, living independently was seen as an ideal — one which they could fulfil with the right job and enough money — whereas for boys it was forced upon them by circumstances. This determined independence on the part of the girls was often justified in terms of their experiences of divorce between their parents or unemployed or fickle boyfriends. Under these circumstances, men just could not be relied upon as breadwinners.

Turning now to couples, it can be seen that those with regular jobs tended to get married, whilst those without jobs continued cohabiting. The exception was one young man who had been long term unemployed but married as soon as he had a regular job. There were several reasons for this. Firstly, young adults did not like to get married unless they could do so properly, with a real wedding and the accoutrements of a real home — and perhaps even their own house. They could not acquire these things without a regular job and so they tended to postpone getting married until such things were available.

CW: Do you think that people should get married when they are unemployed?

Marie: If one's a wage earner, yes, but if he's unemployed, what chance has the chap got of actually getting a house? Or even if you rent a flat and you go up to them and say 'Oh, I'm unemployed' they don't want to know ... As for buying, they'd laugh in your face if you tried to buy a house. Then there's furniture to buy and everything else.

CW: So you wouldn't do it?

Marie: No, well its silly. You start off on the wrong foot. You've got to have a good bank balance, I think, to get married, so you can get the things you want, your house together.

The second reason was that parents did not approve of their daughters marrying an unemployed man and discouraged them from doing so. This caused problems for the young couples in this position and one solution was to cohabit:

Sarah: You see, the way my mum saw it, was that she never had a bad life when she got married, but when she had visions of Martin like not ever being employed, and she didn't want to see her daughter in that situation where she's with someone who's not employed. And you see he's got no financial background. None at all. None. And in her eyes she could see us really struggling to bring up a child and have a place of our own like, and he'd be unemployed all the time. When I was pregnant that's when it looked like he wasn't ever going to get a job, didn't it? And then he got a job and she was over the moon and started talking to him again.

The third reason was that the young men themselves felt that in order to be heads of the household they also had to be breadwinners, as Sarah's cohabiting partner. Martin, explains:

Martin: Well we will be getting married next year, but no, I wouldn't get married if I were unemployed.

CW: Why is that?

Martin: Well, as far as I'm concerned, marriage isn't just a question of popping down the registry office, get a piece of paper and that's it, sort of thing. Well, you're on the dole that's all you can afford to do.

CW: And you want a proper wedding?

Martin: The proper thing.

    CW: In a Church?

    Martin: Oh yeh, yeh, so we can be proper man and wife. (He then goes on to relate stories of magnificent weddings and receptions laid on by relatives).

Cohabiting was also thought to provide a way of getting to know a potential partner without the kind of irrevocable commitment necessitated by marriage. In this way, it provided an ideal prelude to marriage.

    Andy: They keep saying that married life changes yer. They start arguing more. Women especially, they think they've got yer.

    Tracy (Andy's cohabiting partner):   Yeh, it's more hard to get out.

    Andy: Hard to get out.... What's the point of getting married to someone if you haven't lived with them? You don't know what they're like do yer?

In practice however, cohabitation was usually a permanent arrangement which often led to marriage.

Finally, the dependent couples all had considerable experience of unemployment with four out of five having had long-term experience of unemployment. These were young men and women who wished to lead joint lives, but due to lack of employment were forced to remain dependent upon different parents and relatives. This often caused considerable tension and hence those who were long-term unemployed and cohabiting independently had begun like this but left after family disagreements:

    Andy: We was living at her mum's house and it was getting on top of us. We decided to get a place. After we got engaged we decided to buy a place if I got a job. But I didn't get a job, so I just stayed at her mum's house and I just wanted to get out after Christmas.

The experience of another young couple was a follows:

    Martin: You see, we were seeing each other every day anyway. Yeh, you see, we were staying round her mum's house, up her sister's, up her aunt's, we were just all over the place. so we thought we might as well live together. It was two days there, two days up mum's, two day's round her sister's. We were all planned out all week. Plus then of course we got Ruth (their daughter) so obviously we had to be together.

Hence, it can be seen that employment careers played a very important part in domestic careers.

However, movement from one domestic status to another did not only involve moving in with a partner, it often meant children too. Thirteen young adults had had children and the majority were living with the parent of their child. Table 4 indicates the distribution of children.

Young women who had children mostly got married, although they might have cohabited until then. Children were thus a way of bringing forward a marriage which was planned in any case.

> *Marie:* As soon as we had this place (the house where they had been cohabiting) it was obvious we were going to get married eventually anyway. We just married a bit sooner than we had to really.

Indeed, unmarried motherhood was considered as an acceptable alternative for many of those unemployed couples who were likely to embark upon it (although the 'respectable' regularly working respondents were far more censorious.) Tracy and Andy, an unemployed cohabiting couple, explained their plans like this:

> *CW:* Would you get married before you had children?
>
> *Tracy:* Oh I don't see as how it makes much difference really. I mean me brother's not married and he's got two children and they're in his name as well.
>
> *Andy:* Yeh, well it's O.K. if you've got a decent job.
>
> *Tracy:* We'd like to really —
>
> *Andy:* Oh, I'd like to.
>
> *Tracy:* Yeh, get married first, but we haven't got the money to get married.
>
> *CW:* But what if you had children?
>
> *Tracy:* I don't know, we'd think about it. It would all depend if we had enough money. You see we're happy now really.

Some waited until the child was born to see how they would manage with their new partners, arguing that an unplanned pregnancy should not precipitate a 'shotgun' marriage. Abortions were nearly universally disapproved of, and very few said they would use this as a form of family planning. However, these pregnancies were not necessarily 'unplanned' so much as 'allowed to happen' often so that the young couple could enjoy more independence.

> *Martin:* He got engaged on the Saturday and found out she was pregnant on the Wednesday! That happened to us. We got engaged first and then found out she was pregnant the same week. But with an engagement you see, it makes it a little

Table 4: Domestic careers of those with children

Single dependents	2
Cohabiting	2
Married	9

> more respectable don't it? We discussed all this anyway, we discussed it. We decided that if she'd fallen pregnant at what? 16, 17, we wouldn't of had it because it would have spoilt our lives sort of thing.
>
> CW: Yes.
>
> Martin: See, we thought if she fell pregnant when she was 19, and we decided that well, at that age we could accept it sort of thing. We discussed quite a few things like that, the future and everything.

For a young woman without a regular job it was often the only way of having any independent status either outside or inside the natal home. This point is disputed. Campbell (1984) and Willis (1984a and 1984b) found in their research that unemployed girls were likely to become pregnant, as this provided them with a source of status, and in some circumstances, a better chance of local authority housing. Griffin (1985), on the other hand, has argued that girls did not see motherhood as an alternative status to unemployment, but rather as a long-term inevitability, one which was not necessarily welcomed. However, the conclusions of these studies are based upon ethnographic data. Systematic information using larger samples is still awaited. It was evident from my respondents that this was not an actively planned alternative to unemployment, but rather that they turned to this domestic career when others appeared to be out of reach:

> CW: Are you trying for a baby then?
>
> Tracy: Well its not so much that we have actually been trying but I was on the pill before Christmas and I just stopped taking it. Well, after Christmas I suppose we started trying.
>
> CW: Do you think if you found a job, you'd change your mind?
>
> Tracy: Oh, I don't think so. No, there again, I suppose if I had a good career, job you know that was leading me somewhere I probably would've changed my mind. I would've put that first. But I wouldn't change it if I had just an ordinary job. You know, the sort of thing that's not leading anywhere. Round in circles.

Like Griffin's young women, those on Sheppey did not necessarily have a glamourized view of motherhood. Indeed when they were 16-years-old many were very critical of marriage, motherhood and domestic careers. Some still felt this way at 21. Nevertheless, many of those who had been outspoken opponents of domestic career for women in 1980 had children and husbands by the time they were 21. What had happened? One explanation is that the possibility of a good job and some independence of life style would have perhaps provided an alternative. However, this alternative was beginning to seem more and more unrealistic or remote as they grew older. In this respect, motherhood seemed to offer more status than a low status job or than unemployment, but less status than a 'good' job. It would appear that marriage and motherhood 'caught up' with girls, despite some initial resistance, rather than being an actively espoused status. This ambivalence perhaps reflects the kind of status which full-time wives and mothers hold in our society — elevated as an 'ideal' pursuit on the one hand and seen as 'lower status' on the other. Moreover, many girls held examples of their own mothers — struggling on low incomes, divorced or downtrodden — as negative role models in their minds.

Such accidental pregnancies as did happen were less a result of irresponsibility so much as a result of an uncertain economic future. There was really no point in planning a family when there was no certainty of a job and the solution was either not to have children, or to allow them to happen.

CW: Would you have children if you were unemployed?
Martin: (Laughter) We got one!
CW: But did it influence your decision at all?
Martin: Well, it stops you from making any plans you see, it completely stops you from planning ahead. You just think day by day. You just try and survive. You can't plan anything.

Two respondents, however, had children but never lived with the partners. One girl (whose son was taken into care) lived with her mother, and one young man claimed that family responsibilities might hinder his career as a rock star! This underlines the fact that children were considered a woman's responsibility once they had arrived on the scene. They determined her life prospects from then on. For young men, there may have been moral sanctions against them abandoning the mother, but the decision to take responsibility for them was a choice.

Certainly, the Isle of Sheppey was no different from the rest of Britain in terms of attitudes to unmarried parenting. The number of illegitimate children has tripled to 17 per cent of all births between 1961 and 1984 (Social Trends, 1985) and children are more likely to be registered in the father's name as part of some kind of non-married stable relationship. The fact that these forms of familial transition were becoming normal rather than deviant and stigmatized was reflected in the attitudes of my respondents.

Where the girl needed assistance, this was normally provided by the girl's mother. Nearly all the girls who had children before they were living with their partners lived at home with their mother, and those who broke up with partners also depended upon 'mum' for help. 'Mum' was particularly important as a stable figure, because as many young adults had experienced divorce in their own families, 'dad' was often an absent partner. 'Mums', and later 'nans', were therefore the bedrock of the domestic world and the mother-daughter bond was one of the strongest (Binns and Mars, 1984). It is possible, therefore, that where the man's economic status is undermined, so is his status within the couple and girls had to turn to their mothers for economic and social support. This would reflect the patterns observed in black families (Stack, 1974). However, two of the girls who became pregnant soon after leaving school by young men of whom the parents did not approve, were refused support and ostracized by their parents, so the relationship was not always a harmonious one.

If we now relate employment status to childrearing, (table 5) the results are interesting although the cell sizes are perhaps too small to draw any conclusive results.

When the sample as a whole were asked their attitudes to marriage, children and unemployment, slightly more (47 per cent) said they would not marry if they were unemployed, than those who would (35 per cent). However, a large majority (72 per cent) said they would have children as against the 16 per cent who said they would not have children whilst they were unemployed. Hence, unemployment would appear to inhibit 'normal' family transitions in principle. However, in practice, table 5 shows that those with irregular employment careers were just as likely to have had children by the time they were 21, particularly amongst the girls. This would confirm the idea that the unemployed tended to 'drift' into parenthood for lack of any positive alternatives, although they would not necessarily plan to have children on the 'dole'. Indeed, both employed and unemployed respondents held strong opinions on the question of children and unemployment:

CW: And would you have children if you were unemployed?
Ian (unemployed 'dependent couple'): No.
CW: Why is that?
Ian: I mean you've got enough on you plate to find yourself a job without an extra mouth to feed.
Mandy: And it's not really fair on the child anyway, is it?
Ian: Plus, I'd have to be mum all day with her at work!

Table 5: Employment careers and children by sex

	Male	*Female*	*All*
Regularly employed	50%	33%	38%
Sub-employed	50%	44%	46%
Other	–	22%	15%
TOTAL	4	9	13

('Other' refers to girls who had children before embarking upon an employment career)

And this employed couple confirmed this:

CW: Would you have children when Stephen (her husband) was
        unemployed?
Marie: No, it wouldn't be fair.
CW: Not fair on who?
Marie: Not fair on us and not fair on the children cos you don't get a lot
        of money when you're unemployed considering the amount of
        stuff a baby needs.

Hence, one of the reasons why the long-term unemployed couples
were so vague about their family plans was because ideally they would
have preferred to have waited until they had a job and a home. However,
they also realized that this might be a remote possibility.

This point was made more clearly when I asked respondents what
they hoped to do in the future. Regularly employed and regularly unemployed couples all hoped for a very 'conventional' future with a family,
children, a regular job for the head of household and a home of their own:
As two of the regularly unemployed expressed it:

CW: And what do you think you will be doing when you are 50?
Ian: (thinks): Well I suppose I'd have my own house, car, couple of
        kids, sort of thing, not be unemployed I hope, not changing
        my car every year for a new model, nothing like that, just an
        ordinary, average Mr. Jones really.

CW: What do you think you will be doing in five year's time?
Andy   (pause): I reckon if I had a decent job I'd want a nice house and a
        decent job then I'd start saving up, something to look forward to.
        Otherwise you haven't got much to look forward to have you?
        Yeh, yeh, when you come back in five years time I'll have me
        house, I'll have a decent job, a little kid to cause me lots of
        trouble. I should think we'll be married by that time too.

Those who were already married with houses were planning their
second and third houses in the future and planned their childbearing
strategies around these housing strategies:

CW: And what are you planning to do next?
Elaine: Yeh, well, I'm going to stay here you see for about five years
        and then we're going to have children, but we want to get
        our house sorted out before that.

Domestic Careers, Employment Careers and Tenure

I have indicated that domestic and employment careers were associated
with housing opportunities. How was this reflected in this sample? Table 6

Table 6: Tenure by household employment career

H-Employment Career	Tenure				
	Owner occupier	Local Authority	Private rented	Tied	Parents
Sub-employed	1	3	6	–	18
Regularly employed	14	1	7	11	13
TOTAL	15	4	13	11	31

indicates the interaction of tenure and the employment status of the household.

There is a clear association between having a regular job and becoming an owner occupier. Local authority accommodation (becoming increasingly scarce) or the private sector was the only alternative for those without regular jobs. Those with regular jobs may begin in the privately rented sector before getting their own homes, but most people saved for their own home by staying with their parents until they had found a house. This link between owner occupation and employment status was well recognized by respondents themselves:

> *Richard*: ... if you get married before you've got a job you're not going to have much of a wedding day are you? You're not even going to have much of a good life after that. Or if you're in a council house, for example, if you're in a council house and you've got food and that, you've got to find the money to support the marriage. There's food, there's electrical items, there's gas and there's rent. And you have to save up for a house. And where would you get the money from? An' it might be a little while before you move into the house, so you've got to think of that. You've got to get your mortgage together. How would you do it if you were unemployed?

In general it was the man's job which was thought to determine the prospects of the household in this respect, since men were more likely to remain continually in work and they earned more. However, in practice, those households who managed to purchase homes were ones with two regular earners, implying that the female partner's earnings were crucial too:

> *Marie*: If we'd had this place and was living here when he got unemployed, that's different. But if I was pregnant and living apart and he was unemployed, then no, I wouldn't have got married. We would just have carried along together as we were until he found a job, but I always said to him I'd never get married until we had a house anyway.

Indeed, those who were able to buy property were already considering their second home. Two were buying land to build their own houses. They tended to see their futures in terms of a progressional housing career involving a move every five years or so. They hoped to improve their life style by aiming for a better house, in a better area, with a bigger garden and other assets. Employment was just a means to this end. Thus one girl told me:

CW: What do you think you'll be doing in five year's time?

Marie: I don't think we'll be living here. I'd like a nice semi with a garage. I can see that actually. Eventually we're going to have to sell up to better ourselves. Because we can't do any more with this place. We've had the walls knocked down and the bathroom done and we could always get a third bedroom and it would be worth £19,000 and we only paid £14,000. But we couldn't go any higher you know, because of the road it's in. All we can do now is better ourselves.

Not surprisingly, tenure was also associated with domestic career. Table 7 indicates that all of those who became owner occupiers were independent couples, whilst single young people were more likely to be found in the privately rented sector or still at home. This may have been partly due to the need for two incomes but it was also due to the fact that a family of ones own was ideally associated with a home of one's own.

This emphasis upon owner occupation as part of a life strategy was partly a consequence of the local housing market: there were more owner occupiers in this locality than in Great Britain as a whole. However, I would suggest that with the present government's policy, this might be a pattern which other areas are moving towards. The extension of mortgages to younger people, to cohabitees and to working class couples during the 1970s may have made this more of a possibility for those who are regularly employed. Thus, employment careers were more important than social class in this respect. Owner occupation has been absorbed into the ideology of the family in the 1980s.

Table 7: Domestic career by tenure

Domestic Career	Tenure				
	Owner occupier	Local authority	Private rented	Tied	Parents
Dependent singles	–	–	–	–	26
Independent singles	–	1	6	7	–
Independent couples	15	3	7	4	–
Dependent couples	–	–	–	–	5

New Domestic and Employment Careers: A New Model

Bringing together new patterns of employment, new patterns of tenure and new attitudes towards family formation, it is now possible to construct a new model of family transition. The tables so far give us a cross-sectional view of the lives of 21-year-olds, but little idea of the process of family formation, for this takes place over a period of time. Each young adult may pass through several of the stages mentioned so far. The new patterns of family transition are set out below (see figure 2).

Whilst figure 1 showed fairly simple and predictable transitions to the first stage of the life cycle, this is not so in the 1980s. Figure 2 illustrates the complex and multi-stage nature of such transitions with a number of intervening stages between family of origin and that of destination. These stages can be taken in a number of different orders, with some moving from home to family of destination, some cohabiting or having children first, some preferring to live in single person's accommodation, either after an argument with parents or by preference.

However, within this complexity, a number of ideal typical strategies can be mapped out. These are based upon access to employment rather than upon social class alone (at least in classes 3, 4 and 5) as it was in the

Figure 2: Transitions in the life cycle: The 1980s

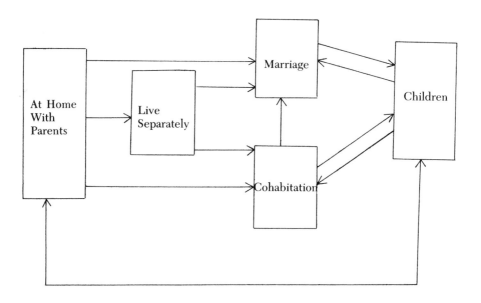

first model. No doubt if a larger cross section of the population had been included differences between middle-class and other groups of young adults may have emerged.

Employed Man

The regularly employed young man would most probably remain at home until he was at least 20 years old. If he meets a partner, and is in a good job, he will get engaged and save for a house before moving there with her either as a cohabitee, or more usually getting married first. He plans to have children once his house has been organized and he has all the goods he wants. If he has a less lucrative job, he may find a flat on getting married and later moves to a council house or remains in privately rented accommodation.

Unemployed Man

The unemployed man will probably stay at home until he is 20 year of age or more, unless he argues with his parents. If he meets a partner, he will spend time with her at his parents' house or at her parents' house, until the situation becomes intolerable and the couple move into a privately rented flat. Here they will cohabit until the women falls pregnant, then may get married. If he gets a job he may get married, and if the job lasts long enough they may buy a house too. Otherwise, they will look forward to a council house, which they are more likely to obtain once children are on the way.

Unemployed Women

The unemployed woman will live at home until she is between 18 and 20 years of age unless she argues with her parents. If she meets a man she likes and he has a job, she will marry him and move away, or move away and cohabit with him first. If he does not have a job, he may move in with her parents, or she with his until the situation becomes intolerable. If they both have no job, they will probably continue to cohabit either in council accommodation or more probably in the privately rented sector until she falls pregnant. Then they will get a place on their own and may get married.

Employed Women

The employed woman will stay at home until aged between 18 and 20 and then may find a shared flat and live separately. On the other hand, if she meets a man she likes and he has a job, they will get engaged, buy a house and get married, although they might cohabit whilst waiting to get married. She will plan to have children once they have everything in their house. If he does not have a job, then she will have to decide if she can keep them both on her money (which would be less than a man's). If she cannot, then he will live with her parents, or she with his, until the situation becomes intolerable and they move into privately rented accommodation. If he gets a job they will get married and save for a house.

This model is an 'ideal typical' representation of young people in the sample in terms of their housing, domestic and employment careers.[8]

Conclusions

The research has demonstrated the utility of using a longitudinal perspective in looking at domestic or employment careers rather than a status at any given point in time. It was the accumulation of opportunities and disadvantages contingent upon a given history which determined life chances in the long-term. Furthermore, it has illustrated the importance of looking at the effects of unemployment in early adulthood as well as immediate post-school careers.

Whilst the survey was only small scale, it demonstrates some of the interconnections between domestic, employment and housing careers, and the ways in which these have changed during the 1980s. Thus, the 'ideal typical' model of domestic and employment careers in the 1950s and 1960s was based upon social class, or the kind of employment entered by young adults. By the 1980s the likelihood of being unemployd for any length of time was becoming as important as the occupational level of the household. A new 'ideal typical' model was formulated which took this, and gender difference into account. These models could be tested more thoroughly on larger samples.

Moreover, it is evident that in the 1980s there were a variety of different stages between the family of origin and that of destination and a variety of orders in which these stages could be undertaken. This greater flexibility allowed young adults to be able to pursue a domestic career which might have been denied them by the prevailing morality of previous decades. For example, the widespread practice of cohabitation could be used as a prelude to marriage, or as a way of getting young adults out of an impasse: they could not get married whilst they had no job and there were no jobs. So they cohabited. There has been a dramatic increase in the rate of cohabitation during the 1970s, although previous surveys may have underestimated this due to the phrasing of questions ('Are you married, single, divorced or widowed?') (Dunnell, 1976). Nevertheless, a higher proportion of young people in this unemployment-prone community cohabited than the 24 per cent cited by the General Household Survey for this age group nationally (Social Trends, 1985) suggesting that this is one form of adaptation to unemployment.

The way in which couples had children was similarly related to employment. Despite the apparent tolerance of 'unconventional' arrangements there was an underlying conservatism. 'Unconventional' family forms mirrored the conventional ones in most respects and it was widely believed that marriage and children should really only be embaked upon with at least one full-time earner — usually the man. Realities were out of phase with expectations in this respect, for around one-third of the sample had already been out of work for long periods of time and this pattern was likely to continue. Hence, this would also confirm Fagin and Little's (1984) conclusion that unemployment amongst young adults is likely to lead to family formation being postponed — at least in principle.

These results would indicate that new forms of social division are emerging. The middle-class professional couples are not represented in my sample, but amongst the last three socioeconomic groups, divisions are based less upon differences between skilled, white collar work and other manual jobs (such differences are perhaps being eroded anyway by deskilling and new technology) than upon differences between the mainly employed and mainly unemployed. Disadvantages accrue to those who were mainly unemployed and advantages accrue to those who were regularly employed. Those who were condemned to living most of their lives to date on declining state benefits simply had to adapt their aspirations and circumstances to this. This is perhaps not so much evidence of deviance so much as adaptation. This social polarization was reinforced through housing policies which served to benefit owner occupiers but not those in other sectors. The regularly employed in all social classes increasingly had access to this accommodation, whereas the regularly unemployed were excluded. This did not prevent them from wishing for a home of their own.

The patterns indicated in this study, along with the increasing difficulty of access to housing, would suggest that one consequence may be. increasing numbers of three generational households and shared living accommodation as young couples and mothers with babies continue to live with older relatives rather than moving out.

This would confirm studies which have argued that unemployment has a differential impact at different stages of the life cycle (Fagin and Little, 1984; Binns and Mars, 1984).

Finally, the present Conservative government is committed to strengthening the family and transferring responsibility for unemployed young adults to the natal home. The Fowler Review has proposed that young people under 25 years of age, whether single or in couples, should receive less benefit than the over 25s. Moreover, the regulations are designed to discourage young people under 25 from living away from home if they are unemployed (Youthaid, 1985).

It can be seen that when these proposals become policy, they may tend to further undermine the 'traditional' forms of family transition in social classes 3, 4 and 5 rather than reinforcing the family. In such homes, children are expected to be economically independent and have formed their own families by this time. It would appear that the 'non-traditional' family forms of couples being dependent upon parents and young women not being supported by their children's father may become more common. The economic and social dependency between families of origin and new households may become reinforced, particularly that between mothers and daughters, which may in turn lead to less stability in relationships between couples. Without a secure economic future — or something to plan for — such proposals are unlikely to deter young people from embarking upon some form of transition — but these may not be of the 'traditional' kind. There was already considerable subsidization of dependent teenagers by parents, but this was only possible in the prosperous families. Those where the parents too were out of work were in great hardship. These proposals then, may well serve to further divide the regularly employed from the mainly unemployed at the very time when there are substantially more permanently unemployed young adults.

1   *Unemployment By Age Range: Great Britain October 1984*

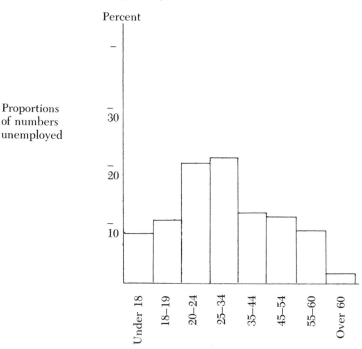

Age ranges

Source: Employment Gazette

What will happen to young households in the future? It would appear from these results that amongst young adults in social classes 3, 4 and 5, planned family formation of the 'conventional' marriage-home-children type will be increasingly deferred or diluted. It will be deferred amongst the employed until they can obtain owner occupied accommodation. It will be deferred — perhaps indefinitely — amongst the unemployed due to lack of employment and income. The Fowler proposals to cut benefits for those under 25 is likely to exacerbate this trend. Unplanned family formation, on the other hand, may increase as prospects look increasingly hopeless for young couples. Moreover, stability in relationships could decline as the possibility of becoming a breadwinner becomes increasingly remote amongst the long-term unemployed and leads to these 'traditional' roles being undermined. Some might welcome the emergence of new 'non nuclear' family forms, although I doubt if this was what was intended by a return to traditional Victorian values!

Notes

1   Unemployment By Age Range: Great Britain October 1984
2   Other publications arising from this research which are relevant to this chapter are listed under Pahl and/or Wallace in the references.
3   The main studies to have been carried out in this field are: The Family Formation Survey (Dunnell, 1976) which covered a random sample of 6589 women between the ages of 16 and 49; the longitudinal survey conducted by Schofield (1973) who interviewed 376 young people at the ages of 18 and 25; the study of fifty weddings in Swansea conducted by Leonard in 1967. Whilst the OPCS survey provides detailed data across a representative range of the population, the surveys of Leonard and Schofield, whilst less representative and wide-ranging, provide a source of more general interpretative comment.
4   This confirms the conclusions of the report of Kinsey *et al.* in the 1940's who found that working-class males were more sexually active at a younger age than their middle-class counterparts. There were no equivalent class dimensions amongst women.
5   However, others suggest that the 1950's were untypical years for family formation as the ideology of motherhood and domesticity was particularly heavily emphasized at this time (Rindfuss and Morgan, 1984). These authors argue that if we look at a longer time-span in the USA, we find that there is increasingly a tendency for young people to postpone having the first child.
6   Research into adults has indicated that unemployment does not tend to precipitate new ideologies of domestic status, or a new division of labour within the household: the man remains a breadwinner/head albeit an unemployed one (Pahl, 1984). However, recent research by Binns and Mars (1984) indicates that younger house-olders (under 25) are apparently more flexible in their approach to domestic roles. Whether this is a new trend or a temporary adaptation will remain to be seen. It would appear that women are still primarily in charge of domestic affairs in younger households.
7   The households were reclassified according to the occupation of the dominant partner — almost invariably the male household head. This was not on grounds of unreflective sexism, but rather because households generally adapted their plans

and status to the occupation of the male earner (or non-earner). Hence, following Erikson (1984) I have classified households according to the dominant partner in this respect. Elsewhere, I have broken down the sample according to the different employment status of male and female partners and this provided another interesting dimension to the study which I have not pursued in this paper (see Wallace, 1987).

8 Here I have concentrated upon the effects of employment career upon the domestic life cycle. I consider the reverse effect — the effects of the domestic life cycle upon attitudes to work elsewhere (Wallace, 1986 and 1987). Acquiring children and a spouse in fact operated as an important labour discipline amongst this age group.

References

ASHTON, D.N. and FIELD, D. (1976) *Young Workers*, London, Hutchinson.

BINNS, D. and MARS, G. (1984) 'Family, community and unemployment: A study in change, *Sociological Review*, 32, 4, pp. 662–95.

CAMPBELL, B. (1984) *Wigan Pier Revisited*, London, Virago Press.

CARTER, M.P. (1975) 'Teenage workers: A second chance at eighteen?' in BRANNEN, P., (Ed.) *Entering the World of Work. Some Sociological Perspectives*, Department of Employment, London, HMSO.

CLARKE, L. (1978) *The Transition from School to Work: A Critical Review of the Literature*, Report No. 49, Department of Education and Science, ESD2.

COWIE, L., and LEES, S., (1981) 'Slags or drags', *Feminist Review*, 9, pp. 17–31.

DUNNELL, K. (1976) *Family Formation*, OPCS, London, HMSO.

ERIKSON, R. (1984) 'Social class of men, women and families', *Sociology*, 18, 4, pp. 500–14.

EVASON, E. (1985) *On The Edge: A Study of Poverty and Long Term Unemployment in Northern Ireland*, London, Child Poverty Action Group.

EVERSLEY, D. and BONNERJEA, L. (1982) 'Social change and indicators of diversity' in RAPPOPORT, R.N. *et al.* (Eds) *op. cit.* pp. 75–94.

FAGIN, L, and LITTLE, M. (1984) *The Forsaken Families*, Harmondsworth, Penguin.

FINN, D., (1984) 'Leaving school and growing up: Work experience in a juvenile labour market' in BATES, I. *et al. Schooling for the Dole?* London, Macmillan, pp. 17–64.

GAMARNIKOW, E. *et al.* (Eds) (1983) *The Public and the Private*, London, Heinemann.

GRIFFIN, C. (1985) *Typical Girls?* London, Routledge and Kegan Paul.

HARRIS, C.C. *et al.* (1987) *Redundancy and Recession in South Wales*, Oxford, Blackwell.

INEICHEN, B. (1977) 'Youthful marriage: The vortex of disadvantage' in PEEL, J., and CHESTER, R., (Eds) *Equalities and Inequalities in Family Life*, London, Academic Press, pp. 53–69.

INEICHEN, B. (1981) 'The housing decisions of young people', *British Journal of Sociology*, 32, 2, pp. 252–8

JAHODA, M. (1982) *Employment and Unemployment: A Social Psychological Analysis*, Cambridge, Cambridge University Press.

JENKINS, R. (1983) *Lads, Citizens and Ordinary Kids: Working Class Youth Life-Styles in Belfast*, London, Routledge and Kegan Paul.

JONES, P. *et al.* (1981) *Out of School: A Case Study of the Role of Government Schemes at a Time of Growing Unemployment*, MSC Special Programmes Occasional Paper No. 4. Sheffield, MSC.

LEONARD, D. (1980) *Sex and Generation: A Study of Courtship and Weddings*, London, Tavistock.

McROBBIE, A. (1978) 'Working class girls and the culture of femininity' in WOMEN'S

Studies Group Centre for Contemporary Cultural Studies *Women Take Issue*, London, Hutchinsons.

McRobbie, A. and Garber, J. (1976) 'Girls and subcultures: An exploration' in Hall, S. and Jefferson, T., *Resistance Through Rituals*, London, Hutchinson, pp. 209–22.

Pahl, R.E. (1984) *Divisions of Labour*. Oxford, Blackwell.

Pahl, R.E. and Wallace, C.D. (1985) 'Forms of work and privatization on the Isle of Sheppey' in Roberts, B., Finnegan, R. and Gallie, D. (Eds) *New Approaches to Economic Life*, Manchester, Manchester University Press, pp. 368–386.

Parker, H. (1976) 'Boys will be men: Brief adolescence in a down town neighbourhood' in Mungham, G. and Pearson G. (Eds) *Working Class Youth Cultures*. London, Routledge and Kegan Paul, pp. 138–158.

Rindfuss, P.R. and Morgan, S.P. (1984) 'The transition to motherhood: Intersections of structural and temporal dimensions', *American Sociological Review*. 49, 3, pp. 359–71.

Roberts, K. (1984) *School Leavers and their Prospects*, Milton Keynes, Open University Press.

Roberts, K. (1985) *ESRC young people in society/16–19 initiative: A sociological view of the issues*, mimeo, University of Liverpool/ESRC.

Schofield, M. (1973) *The Sexual Behaviour of Young Adults*, London, Allen Lane.

Sharpe, S. (1976) *Just Like A Girl*, Harmondsworth, Penguin.

Social Trends (1985) Central Statistical Office, London, HMSO.

Stack, C. (1974) 'Sex roles and survival strategies in an urban black community' in Rosaldo, M.Z. and Lamphere, L. (Eds) *Women, Culture and Society*, Palo Alto, CA, Stanford University Press, pp. 113–128.

Study Commission on the Family (1982) *Values and the changing family*, London, Study Commission on the Family.

Wallace, C.D. (1985) 'School, work and unemployment: Social and cultural reproduction on the Isle of Sheppey', unpublished PhD thesis, University of Kent, Faculty of Social Sciences.

Wallace, C.D., (1986) 'From boys and girls to women and men: The transition from school to (un)employment' in Barton, L. and Walker, S. (Eds) *Youth, Unemployment, and Schooling*, Milton Keynes, Open University Press, pp. 92–117.

Wallace, C.D., (1987) *For Richer, For Poorer*, London, Tavistock.

Wallace, C.D. and Pahl, R.E., (1985) 'Polarization, unemployment and all forms of work' in Allen, S., Purcell, K., Waton, A., and Wood, S., (Eds) *The Experience of Unemployment*, London, Macmillan, pp. 116–133.

Warr, P., (1983) 'Work, jobs and unemployment' *Bulletin of the British Psychological Society*, 36, pp. 305–11.

Willis, P., (1984a) 'Youth unemployment 1: A new state', *New Society*, 29 March, pp. 475–7.

Willis, P. (1984b) 'Youth unemployment 2: Ways of living', *New Society*, 5 April, pp. 13–15.

Youthaid (1985) *The Fowler Review: Effects on Young People*, London, Youthaid.

Acknowledgement

I am grateful to the Rowntree Memorial Trust for supporting this research and the ESRC for providing the studentship which formed the basis for all my subsequent work. I would also like to thank George Giarchi of Plymouth Polytechnic for his guidance and support and Vlastimil Malinek for help with presentation.

7 Youth Training, Life Chances and Orientations to Work: A Case Study of the Youth Training Scheme.

David Lee, Dennis Marsden, Mike Hardey and Penny Rickman in Collaboration with Ken Masters

Introduction

Ever since it was introduced, the Youth Training Scheme (YTS) has been extensively monitored, evaluated and researched, both by the Manpower Services Commission and in similar measure by its critics. A notable feature of much of this work, however, has been a pre-occupation with what is in effect book-keeping, the focus being largely confined to the immediate objectives of current youth training policy itself. Unfortunately, there have been frequent changes and developments in the relatively short time that the Scheme has been in existence so that the research is constantly 'aiming at a moving target' and the results have all too frequently been overtaken by events before they appear.

This chapter reports upon a three-year case study of YTS with rather different intentions, seeing the Scheme as a phenomenon of wider social and economic change in Britain — with especial reference, of course, to the situation of school leavers. By taking a longer and wider perspective than usual, we have attempted to show some of the cumulative and perhaps unintended effects of successive policy initiatives. We have also sought to put YTS into the context of what is usually called in mainstream British sociology 'stratification research'. We take this to mean the study of the (unequal) distribution of life chances in contemporary society as well as the social perceptions associated with it.

Concern with inequality and stratification is a particularly logical and natural way to broaden the horizons of research on youth training. There is, after all, a compensatory element in YTS itself, based on an implicit version of human capital theory and designed to promote greater equality of opportunity for trainees of different gender and levels of attainment through the enhancement of their marketable skills. In practice, as we shall see below, trainees in our survey (though rarely fully aware of it) were confronted by a maze of very unequal opportunities. But the relevance of the Scheme's manifest objectives for the study of contemporary life chances seems clear enough.

Furthermore, the ethos of YTS, with its emphasis on individualism and self-help through direct work experience could have major implications for young peoples' perceptions and *consciousness* of inequality, a possibility which has received much attention from its radical critics. In practice, the position is likely to be much more complicated. Young people do not accept YTS passively. They and their families often use and manipulate it in various ways which require careful research. Nevertheless, it is important to try as far as possible to observe any changes in social consciousness which YTS actually does bring about. The issue of how people in general perceive the distribution of rewards, power and privilege and, furthermore, how such social imagery may be changing over time, has been at the forefront of debates about stratification in Britain (Marshall, 1983). Research into the factors affecting the social perceptions of those now entering the adult world will thus be highly pertinent to some key sociological themes.

These, however, are in themselves somewhat general and broad points. They provide perspectives from which to put YTS in a wider context, perhaps, but a single case study of the kind reported here has also to be concerned with a third problem: namely, that the labour market conditions within which YTS is introduced vary widely. Explaining the full significance of this for the study of change and inequality in British society necessitates a brief foray into the literature surrounding the term stratification *per se*.

Stratification, Segmentation and Labour Markets

There is an impressive body of research in the social sciences which has been concerned with the general characteristics of youth labour markets and their responsiveness to the training and employment policies of governments. Recent British work in this genre has repeatedly pointed to the dependence of the majority of young people upon opportunity structures created by very local conditions. This dependence seems to have been greatly intensified by the recession. Admittedly, typical adolescent careers have always varied to some extent on a geographical basis (for example, Lee, 1973). But numerous studies have shown that with the declining demand for youth labour in the seventies and eighties, the majority of young people have become very reliant on what the local community and especially the local youth labour market can offer. (Hockley, 1984; Spilsbury, 1985; Roberts *et al.*, 1986). A graphic illustration of this point is the recent finding of Ashton and Maguire (1986) that '... the chances of the sons of middle class fathers in Sunderland finding employment were less than those of sons of lower working class families in St. Albans' (p. 2).

Such findings tend to run counter to an assumption which is commonly made in British sociology: that systematic differences in life chances are mainly transmitted to the young through the effects of 'social class background'. This is a way of referring to a cluster of influences associated with the occupational position of the parental household together with the values and cultural capital which are acquired there. But, as Ashton and Maguire themselves suggest, in today's youth labour market explanations of the 'chances of obtaining employment and type of employment obtained ... [which are] ... based on social class origins are unsatisfactory ... [because] ... the character of the local labour market affects employment chances, independent of personal attributes and social background'.

It is, in our view, highly doubtful that class differentials, even as conventionally undersood and studied in research on 'social class background', can be dismissed as a causal component in life chances quite as readily as the above quotation implies. Nevertheless, as we see it, Ashton and Maguire do highlight an important aspect of inequality and distributional conflict in present day Britain, revealing by implication the inadequacy of the conceptual language through which sociologists have been attempting to study it.

Much of the problem can be traced back to the metaphor of stratification itself. Borrowed from geomorphology, it depicts society as a whole divided into layers or strata. When used, as it often is, in conjunction with terms like working/middle-*class* and *class*-stratification there is scope for much confusion. Worse, the local social structure, in so far as it is recognized at all, is presumed to be merely a reflection or refraction of the larger unit.

But is contemporary society like this? As we have seen it is necessary to take locality into account in describing the market situation of young people. But local labour markets are themselves internally divided into areas of exclusion and non-competition. More generally, it seems clear that the manner in which all people (and not merely the young) are linked, through their market situation, to the underlying structures of power and privilege is highly diverse, varying both between and within markets. Arguably, then, the stratification metaphor fails to do justice to the complexities of inequality. It needs to be replaced, or at the very least supplemented, by a concept which can handle the diversity. Such a concept we suggest is already available in principle from within recent theories of labour market *segmentation*.

As we understand it, the term segmentation is a very general term denoting the existence of groups of workers who are not in wage competition with each other the labour market does not 'clear' in the manner predicted by orthodox economic theory because of the existence of institutional, political, or normative barriers to so-called natural market forces. These barriers can, and often do, include the exclusive devices operated by workers themselves against the substitution of the cheap labour of, say, women or, more relevantly in this case, young people. The prevalence of such non-competing groups in actual labour markets has been well observed and documented over the years.

But labour market segmentation theory developed not merely as a device for *describing* variations in labour market conditions which were inconsistent with the assumptions of orthodox economics. It was also a way of *analyzing* the consequences which this variation had for class relations in the wider society. To be sure, the validity of this very simple insight was obscured because the original versions of it were unnecessarily functionalist and conspiratorial (Blackburn and Mann, 1979, esp. pp. 29–33). Labour market structure may, as some writers suggested, at times have been deliberately engineered by capital (ists) in order to inhibit labour unrest and prevent social tension. But it is not necessary to assume this in order to make use of the basic point. 'Segmentation' at its simplest is a working hypothesis that the existence of mutually exclusive non-competing groups at the micro level in the labour market has macro consequences for the class structure. This is because it fosters a multiplicity of divisions of interest and experience among the working population and their dependent households. In turn these obscure the underlying power structure of society and personalize perceptions of inequality and distributive justice. Britain today remains a class society in the sense understood in classical sociology. The fact that empirical research finds people to be as dependent as ever upon their *market* situation is sufficient testimony to that. But it is, we would argue, more accurately described as one which is segmented rather than stratified.

To be of further use, however, the term segmentation itself needs to be refined and qualified. Some forms of segmentation influence the behaviour of markets because they are already deeply institutionalized in the wider community. Among them we should include not only the divisions attributable to 'social class background' but also the effects of gender and race. Other forms of segmentation, however, result from the processes of the labour market itself, though their effect may well include the intensification of pre-existing divisions. Thus, following Ryan (1981, p. 4.) we have found it helpful to distinguish between pre-market and in-market segmentation. On the supply side of the labour market, *pre-market* segmentation 'denotes the differentiation of opportunities to enhance one's productive potential ... before commencing employment'; such a usage makes it possible in principle to control the labour market effects of upbringing, attitude and knowledge. As we explain in a later section, however, in our own work we extended the notion of pre-market segmentation to the demand side of the labour market as well. *In-market* segmentation denotes 'the subsequent and further differentiation of opportunities *within* the market' (our emphasis) the most relevant example being variations in training opportunity.

The failure systematically to consider in-market inequalities constitutes a major weakness in much sociological writing in Britain. Instead effort has more usually been spent in trying to demonstrate, usually by means of single shot surveys, that types of social imagery can be linked to the work and status situations of whole occupational groups. We are not suggesting that such work is useless or should not be done. On the contrary, it has itself tended to conclude that strata have become more internally varied or fragmentary over time and individuals increasingly 'privatized' or 'instrumental' in their attitudes. The problem, as Marshall has pointed out in an extensive and searching review, is that 'such conclusions do not follow unambiguously from the data currently offered'. What is required instead is 'intensive, longitudinal ethnography' (Marshall, 1983, pp. 290–2). We understand Marshall's comment as a call not simply for ethnography *per se*: rather it is a recognition that there has been insufficient work in general on the *microsociology* of inequality. In particular it would seem to be profitable to know far more about the minutiae of in-market events through which the class situation of the majority of individuals seeking employment are determined.

Hence the need for in-depth case studies of significant segments and localities. We shall now try to show, therefore, how we applied this perspective to our own research on the Youth Training Scheme.

YTS in Southwich

We begin by describing briefly the background and design of our research. Since January 1983 the Leverhulme Youth Project at the University of Essex has been conducting a case study of the impact of YTS within an expanding town in southeast England which, in order to protect our respondents, we will call Southwich. Some 200 trainees from the town, sampled from the 1984 entry to the Scheme were interviewed during the Spring of their YTS year and again in Spring of 1986. Over the same period we have endeavoured as far as possible to keep a record of the destinations and fortunes of the entire 1984 cohort of school leavers from which the YTS sample came. In addition, observational and interview data have been collected on the 'trainers': the individuals and institutions and employers involved in the Scheme. At the time of writing analysis of the material, much of it qualitative, is still incomplete and we present here, in a very summary form, only such evidence as helps to expound our overall approach.

Some account of how Southwich came to be the subject of a case study is called for. Much of the critical literature on YTS has concentrated upon its irrelevance to the extensive areas of deprivation in Britain of the eighties: how could a training scheme, however suited to the needs of industry for human capital, overcome the severe absence of jobs in areas of industrial decline or among ethnic minorities in the inner cities? The best that could be hoped for would be that in time the young would form, in the apt words of one *Guardian* correspondent, 'a well trained dole queue'. Elsewhere in the country, though, especially in the south east, the operation of the Scheme may be much closer to the stated intentions behind it. It is important to recall that YTS is officially billed as first and foremost a permanent reform of training, and only secondarily if at all as an unemployment measure. Relatively favourable employment conditions ought therefore to give scope for the training element to dominate. In particular it should allow the policy of handing back training to private rather than public organizations, a key element in the reform, to flourish. Thus, it was felt that a case study of a town in the south east like Southwich would be more than justified and could contribute to the literature on the growing divisions between different localities and between individuals within localities.

Admittedly, the town does not altogether conform to the stereotype of the affluent south east. Its adult unemployment rate during the period of our research has stood at about 11.5 per cent which is somewhat below the national average, but above that for two other somewhat larger towns close by which contained more manufacturing industry. We soon uncovered at first hand what we had already suspected: the existence of areas of well concealed but very real deprivation. This, however, is the case throughout the otherwise affluent south east. The isolated position of those who are unemployed or deprived, in the midst of wealthier people and parts is important in itself.

The situation of the rest of the community stems in large part from Southwich's geographical position. This enables it is to function as a service and shopping centre for a wide area, much of it agricultural in character, and the local council has actively cultivated the expansion of major retail outlets, in the old town centre and in new out-of-town shopping complexes. The movement of firms and administrative units out of inner London has been encouraged but the bulk of employers so attracted have been in the services sector, particularly in banking and finance. Relatively cheap housing prices have fostered the growth of a small but wealthy commuter population (though for young people, journey times and costs make commuting prohibitive). The result of these trends was already visible in an intercensal comparison published recently by the County Planning Office. This showed that by 1981 employment in services had expanded well above the national average, sufficient to offset a net decline in manufacturing jobs. Further expansion of population and service employment during the past five or six years have accentuated this development. A situation in which services provide the livelihood of the bulk of the population of a community is, of course, of interest from the point of view of recent debates in both British politics and British sociology. Thus, we concluded that the main socio-economic features of the town were such as to add usefully to what Roberts *et al.* (1986) call 'a new generation' of youth labour market studies in which the focus is upon the widely varying consequences of broad trends for young people in particular localities (pp. 6–8).

The retailing, distribution and administrative organisations which now dominate the town's labour market set their mark on the development of YTS, creating a relatively large potential demand for young, especially female, trainees. The Regional MSC Office claimed at the time that the rate at which YTS had been developed in the county was one of the most rapid in the country and that it remained among the 'leaders' in terms of the quantity, quality and range of Schemes offered. Southwich shared in the rapid expansion. By the time our fieldwork began in mid-Autumn 1984, YTS had assumed major importance. Entrants to the Scheme already constituted nearly half of the previous summers' leavers and the number went on rising well into 1985. More importantly, some 80 per cent of the places were Mode A places provided almost exclusively by private sector employers and training organisations. On the other hand the availability of real jobs for 16 year olds, particularly for girls, declined just as rapidly as in the rest of the country.

Our investigations showed that employer based YTS had created a *surrogate* youth labour market in which, much as one might expect, ties of mutual dependence with the actual labour market were developing. This outcome, we would argue, can be expected in any relatively prosperous area which is dominated by private YTS schemes. YTS had also largely reproduced the segmentation of the actual labour market in the sense that there were non-competing groups of young people recruited to YTS and a clear if complex hierarchy of schemes, occupations and placements. We shall now discuss this segmentation in relation to both the supply and the demand for trainee labour using the distinction already discussed between its pre-market and in-market forms.

The Surrogate Labour Market

Pre-Market Segmentation of the Supply of Labour

In this section we outline briefly some general considerations regarding the supply of recruits to YTS based upon the statistical, questionnaire and interview evidence we collected from a large cross section of school leavers in the town — though the details will be omitted in order to keep the chapter to a reasonable length. There are two points to be made. First, Southwich school leavers already showed on entry to the labour market a high level of general work commitment, individualism and competitiveness. Secondly, though the supply of trainees appeared to be relatively homogenous in this respect, it was highly segmented along lines of prior education, social background and above all gender.

Motivations and orientations to work were studied by means of both formal and informal techniques. Our written questionnaires contained a short set of Likert-type attitude statements based upon longer attitude scales devised by the Sheffield MRC Research Team. (For an overview see Banks and Ullah, 1986) The statements elicited from the trainees and school leavers strongly individualistic responses and patterns of agreement and disagreement indicating firm commitment to working in employment. Unemployment was *not* preferred to having a job even where the statements offered unpleasant working conditions and wages. Our more informal probings not only supported this finding but suggested why it should be the case. They largely confirmed what has been shown in earlier research, namely that leaving school, and in particular leaving behind the position of classroom pupil, is welcomed by many leavers as a sign of imminent adulthood. And that obtaining paid employment is perceived by them as both a necessary and sufficient condition of actually being an adult (Stafford, Jackson and Banks, 1980; Jahoda, 1982).

Of those who found themselves accepting YTS places, a small minority — we estimate about 10 per cent — did so with some element of deferred gratification in their decision preferring the prospects offered by their particular YTS Scheme to the relatively dead-end jobs they might have taken up. The majority, however, entered YTS as second best, something better than being merely unemployed. Once in a placement, there appeared to be a need to talk of it as if it *were* employment, contrasting 'me job' with 'going back to school' for off the job training. From this vantage point, the trainees can look down upon the unemployed YTS refuser. In the words of a typical hostile comment: 'At least I did something but that sort, you know, ... (i.e., unemployed school leavers) ... you saw them at school. Just lazy.' (Construction Trainee)

Nevertheless, the YTS intake in Southwich was far from homogenous. Data obtained from the Education Authority on school leaving exam results showed that roughly a third of the intake possessed at least some 'O' levels and that about five per cent actually had five or more 'O' levels (or CSE grade Is). The remainder had at best CSE passes (below grade 1 only) but we found that schemes discriminated in recruitment between those who appeared to be just below GCE standard in attainment and the rest. About 10 per cent of the intake had no leaving qualifications at all, mostly recruited into Mode B.

The segment of 'better qualified' youngsters leaving school were highly sought after both by YTS Schemes and by the minority of employers recruiting direct into full-time jobs. Consequently they experienced little difficulty in entering into their chosen areas of work and indeed our data show that they tended to be concentrated into a limited range of organizations and occupations. These were mainly ones such as the larger engineering firms with a tradition of systematic training, or banking and insurance with a reputation of giving access to an internal promotion structure of some sort. The less qualified YTS entrants tended to end up either in occupations such as retailing where systematic training has been until now somewhat cursory and the Scheme, in so far as it was effective, relatively innovatory; or in occupations with a large amount of small firm employment; or where, as in the building trade, such internal labour markets as do exist are of the craft kind and subject to considerable instability.

It soon became evident too that schemes were seeking youngsters taking 'O' levels less for the content of the qualification, than as an ascriptive indicator of potential as a 'good trainee'. Possibly, this ascriptive use of individuals' educational biographies goes further. In Southwich the state schools are themselves socially graded in a manner related to their intake at 11 plus and their social catchment. YTS recruited from all schools but it became evident to us that which school a trainee had attended was a consideration in addition to formal credential level and as in the case of the few leavers from selective schools could even override them.

'Social background', especially as measured by paternal occupation, emerged as another ascriptive feature which, albeit indirectly, entered the selection process, segmenting the supply of trainees within the locality — Ashton and Maguire notwithstanding. Although some of our data on this issue were badly affected by non-response, we established that about a third of Southwich trainees came from homes where the father did a non-manual job. The necessary inclusion of mothers' occupation heightens the picture of a sizeable middle class drawn into or even availing themselves of YTS. The explanation for this has to do with the social composition of the town itself. Like many smallish southern Towns, the workforce contains a relatively high proportion of professional and white collar workers in comparison with other places in Britain (see the examples given by Roberts *et al.* 1986, p. 13). The effect was exacerbated by the fact that school leaving rates in the Town were found to be comparatively *high*. A substantial number of youngsters were thus underperforming in relation to what might be expected from a knowledge of their social background. Yet our data show that the YTS recruitment process had produced a situation in which youngsters from non-manual homes had been disproportionately selected for training in a limited range of occupations and, to a lesser extent particular Schemes. We expect further analysis to show the processes through which this had arisen.

The segmenting effects of parental background were important, however, for another reason. We have strong indications from our qualitative data that familial and neighbourhood connections were important to some trainees in giving privileged access to certain types of training and placement opportunities. Such openings were particularly important in differentiating between youngsters whose educational record was otherwise very similar and for the most part undistinguished. One obvious example occurs where firms prefer to recruit from the relatives and friends of existing employees creating what Manwaring (1984) has called an extended internal labour market. But we also found evidence that in certain trades, notably in building and retail and domestic services such as decorating and plumbing, parents and neighbours were actively creating openings for young people in their communal network. Household and communal ties thus constitute an additional crosscutting and often somewhat intangible source of pre-market segmentation.

Finally, as other investigations have repeatedly found, there is a major axis of pre-market segmentation among school leavers based upon gender. Like them we found little evidence in our surveys that traditional gender boundaries between occupations were being breached by the advent of YTS. Schemes themselves tended to specialize in male or female occupations, and their places were in turn occupied appropriately by boy or girl trainees. We heard of only two girl YTS engineering apprentices, neither of them among our interviewees. While the first, we learned, had done well, the second expressed a wish to leave and have a family. In the reverse direction, there *were* examples of boys on 'girls' schemes', but they were not doing work placements in the same way as girls. For example, boys on the top clerical schemes were not usually secretaries but were more likely to be doing computing work, or on their way to progress as managers. On the fringe of a clerical scheme, one boy was offered the chance to move into a craft skill: glazing. Further down the hierarchy boys on retail schemes were placed firmly in the menswear departments, DIY, electrical, computing or camera shops. Scarcely any boys entered the care schemes which were so sought after by girls, sometimes even girls with good academic credentials as well as the lower achieving girls trying to follow on from child care schemes at school.

The implication of this section then is that the supply of trainees to the YTS surrogate labour market is subject to a process of segmentation that reflects well known sets of pre-market influences. Before going on to consider how far the working of YTS itself amplifies or depresses the resultant differences in life chances between individuals we shall examine the extent of pre-market segmentation in the *demand* for trainees.

Pre-Market Segmentation of Demand

In the surrogate labour market the place of employers directly looking for employees has been largely taken over by private training organisations of various kinds. But YTS has, nevertheless, under active guidance from the MSC, been grafted onto the pre-existing labour market and training structure: partly through the efforts of the larger firms and older training agencies which already organised apprenticeship or adult training; partly through the efforts of new training entrepreneurs; and partly through the actions of families and informal networks at the margins. Particular YTS schemes and placements set out with built in advantages or disadvantages of reputation and prestige derived from their pre-YTS function whereas others were relative newcomers. In effect there was a hierarchy of YTS schemes based on the credibility of the 'opportunities' they were offering.

Of course, in judging the prestige and credibility of schemes we should distinguish between conventional occupational rankings and those which young people themselves would apply. For example, some school leavers deliberately opt for low skill or unpleasant labouring, care or retail work which on any external view offers few rewards or job prospects. However for this part of the discussion it will be helpful to keep in mind mainly conventional criteria of life chances in terms of job prospects and training. This can then be related to whether the agents and surrogate employers appeared to be in a buyers' or sellers' market for suitable school leavers.

The top schemes and placements were largely reserved for boys, being made up of the relics of apprenticeship. This was notably the case where, as in engineering, catering, construction and road transport, the old Industrial Training Boards retain their training functions and are even able to override MSC policy. In so far as these quasi-apprenticeships gave access to the internal labour markets of large or well established firms the sponsors were able to demand 'O' levels and to insist upon traditional day or block release in further education. Top clerical placements in banking and insurance also offered some openings more evenly distributed between the sexes, again with FE credentials and a clerical credential route. Similar considerations applied to the so called 'large company' schemes in retailing and distribution. In general, though what was noticeable was the relatively small number of such openings via YTS and the very competitive selection procedures through which they were able to recruit. In addition to these but slightly down the hierarchy were other sought after traditional routes resurrected through YTS, with FE training and technical board credentials, in catering, vehicle maintenance and construction, again often under the auspices of the old training boards.

At the bottom of the hierarchy were the public sector schemes. They included the main Mode B1 for the unemployed in the Town, a legacy of YOPS still run through the Youth Service by the LEA. However, the position of this scheme in the hierarchy differed interestingly by gender. The boys recruited to it were mostly unemployed with poor school leaving records. They were instructed in the rudiments of manual trades such as bricklaying. When interviewed they reported initial scepticism about the ability of the Scheme to prepare them for a real job at the end. For girls, however, the Scheme offered the opportunity of a back-door entry into care work ahead of the statutory recruitment age of 18 and thus prized by the trainees. At the very bottom of the hierarchy are to be found bridging courses and carefully selected and sheltered placements for children from special schools who were the responsibility of the Authority. The function of such schemes in effect was to take on the problem youngsters who for one reason or another had not been recruited to the competitive sector, and if possible to select some who could survive in menial employment.

In between these two extremes can be found a middle range of some complexity. YTS has developed into areas where previously there had been no training at all or even, sometimes, jobs. Existing large employer schemes, for example in the struggling engineering industry, but also in clerical and retail occupations, were encouraged by the MSC to take on additional trainees, most usually by a process of internal segmentation, placing the less promising trainees out to satellite or 'fringe' positions in nearby subsidiaries or in the surrounding smaller firms. Meanwhile, however, new kinds of trainers have emerged, partly stimulated, partly controlled by MSC. Analogous with and occasionally based upon the old group training schemes, these so called 'umbrella' organizations largely covered clusters of small firms and varied considerably in credibility. At one extreme a local Chamber of Commerce produced a 'model' rationalized clerical and retail scheme, bringing a variety of small commerical organizations under one training umbrella. Among small scattered craft employers of various kinds new collective umbrella schemes were developed through a combination of private entrepreneurial activity and MSC stimulus and regulation — though the scattering of work sponsors in such arrangements seemed to be presenting the local MSC with problems of adequate policing, and trainees with a large element of chance. Enterpreneurial training organizations might be existing adult training establishments serving the residual functions of old defunct ITBs; or alternatively, quite new and often colourful entrepreneurs who had moved in to colonise whole occupational (or even outlying geographical) areas. Still other kinds of Schemes with a more avowedly philanthropic rationale were established by organizations such as churches, youth clubs, voluntary societies and the Co-op. We say avowedly because all Managing Agents tend to profess philanthropic motives, but some deliberately set out to reach the more disadvantaged to the extent where they may subsidize their Schemes; whereas others on the fringe of the occupational structure and YTS had the disadvantaged thrust upon them by the economics of the Scheme which at the time required a balance of a certain number of placements.

Finally, as we have already noted, very small firms and self employed tradespersons, over quite a wide range of occupations and types of work, including some, we suspected, close to the black economy, were able to create training places through YTS usually for their own, or a friend or neighbour's, progeny. Our interviews indicate that the familial dimension to the development of YTS was important in our area and growing.

Thus, far from being equivalent, YTS schemes in the Southwich area presented a range of very unequal opportunities in terms of type of work placement, the specificity or generality of training, access to the real labour market and future job opportunities; to say nothing of a more or less responsible climate of care and concern for the well-being and future of trainees.

The Surrogate Labour Market: In-Market Segmentation and the Adjustment of Supply to Demand

As we have already pointed out the policy of deliberately creating a surrogate youth labour market through YTS is intended to use *in-market* processes, particularly training, in a compensatory way. In practice, however, the effect of in-market factors is remarkably difficult to identify and measure because they imply that the market itself is contributing to the creation or amelioration of inequality and in this respect pre- and in-market factors usually interact on each other (Ryan, 1981 pp. 9–15). Strictly speaking it is necessary to show either that individuals who started out as different had become more alike. Or, alternatively, that 'significantly different, opportunities and rewards' have been accorded 'to otherwise comparable people' (ibid. p. 4). We do not claim to have solved that problem. What we offer in this section is a description, based upon observation and interviews backed up by quantitative data, of how the situation of trainees and schemes developed over two years of our actual fieldwork. We can thus offer some indication of how far the Scheme had gone, and how much further it had to go in accomplishing its compensatory objectives. The results we believe are at least highly suggestive that in-market processes are, on balance, confirming and extending pre-existing differentials rather than compensating for them.

(i) The Trainees

We considered that on the supply side, that is, on the trainees themselves, there were three main in-market effects associated with, though not necessarily caused by, YTS. First, of course, by joining the Scheme in the Southwich locality rather than some others, they had entered a relatively favourable segment of the wider youth labour market. Rates of placement at the end of YTS were, at just over 70 per cent, about typical for the south east as a whole but well above the official average rate for the UK as a whole (see Youthaid, 1986). As we have argued, this is one kind of effect where individuals, identically placed on pre-market criteria, have their life chances affected by the market itself.

But our case study was designed to look also at processes within the local segment. Our studies suggested that there are two further in-market processes at work. On the one hand, YTS makes possible a more refined evaluation of individual capacity than is available from traditional recruitment practices based on pre-market criteria alone. This 'fine sieve' largely extends and builds upon existing inequalities though the picture is complicated by the familial influences described above, by national policy developments, and by a large chance element. On the other hand, there are various 'moral' effects whose net impact is to isolate trainees from their peers both within and between segments. We shall consider these two effects together showing how they arise via the process of recruitment; through the varying quality of the training received; and finally at the point of transition to the 'real' labour market.

The actual *recruitment method* by which particular young people came to join occupations and schemes varied according to pre-market factors. Most of the 'top' occupations and schemes did not have to seek potential trainees at all, but rather found themselves besieged by applicants from whom they chose using often quite stringent selection methods. Interviewing trainees who had 'written round' in this way, we encountered a considerable amount of invidious self justification at the expense again of the jobless leaver. 'I wrote hundreds of letters; why can't they? You gotta make an effort or people won't come along and say "please have this job"' (female clerical trainee with five 'O' levels).

But the match of 'good trainees' to good schemes is far from perfect. Since much recruitment takes place during the final year of school, actual examination results are not known. Many organizations substituted their own tests; others relied on the mere fact of an individual being on, say, an O level course. Some, having selected a particular applicant found that the individual concerned had had multiple offers. In our own interviews we received complaints that leavers of this calibre were in short supply and this was confirmed for us by our discussions with the Careers Office. Thus, as we stated above, though the individuals with good leaving results in our samples were concentrated into the top schemes, the latter seem to have filled up with a group who had either not got the results expected or who had been 'cleared' by the Careers Service.

For the bulk of the trainees, most of whom were not particularly well qualified, the role of the Careers Service as an agent of YTS has rapidly become a central one. Many trainees, particularly at the primary end of the YTS hierarchy would speak uncomplainingly, even flatteringly of their advice. Equally, however, very poorly qualified leavers, who had found their own ideas for their future confronted by the realism of the particular Careers Officers who had interviewed them, took the opportunity to scapegoat the Careers Service for what was basically a very difficult labour market for 16 year olds in their situation. In between these two extremes the interaction between school leavers and the Careers Service is affected by the fact that the Service cannot ultimately go beyond the stipulations and perspectives of Managing Agents and work providers. The surrogate youth labour market is in this respect no different from an ordinary labour market in that it rests upon an inequality between the buyers and sellers of labour power and it is, therefore, partly the ascriptive perceptions of the former which prevail in the intersection of supply with demand.

Nevertheless, partly because of the pace at which many school leavers are assigned to schemes during a matter of weeks after school leaving, the administrative process of the Careers Service added an extra overlay to the ascriptive segmentation of the supply of trainees. This is shown best, perhaps, in the case of the few individuals who attempted to cross established divisions. We interviewed, for example, a trainee with good 'O' levels who insisted on joining a care scheme run by a voluntary agency, despite, she claimed, pressure from a Careers Officer to undertake a clerical scheme. Another interviewee had wanted to train in horticulture but because she had an 'O' level in office skills had, so she claimed been refused the Horticulture YTS Scheme. Of course, to be fair, we cannot say whether these accounts represent an accurate record of what actually transpired.

Clearly, in practice the Careers Service does not possess the same significance or fulfil the same role at all levels of the surrogate labour market. At the upper end, its function is akin to a straightforward recruiting agency matching suitable candidates to the more desirable placements though principally in situations where the organization is topping up from its list of direct applications. Below the primary sector of YTS placements, positions are often not recruited through the Careers Service at all but through family, neighbourhood and other informal networks which lead to many of the more secure and promising outlets. These informal networks often manipulate the Service — but more usually they bypass it altogether. Individual officers in fact spend much of their time dealing with those leavers who have neither formal credentials or informal contacts. Thus the salience of their placement role is constrained by the segmentation of YTS itself.

The overall effect of the YTS recruitment process was undoubtedly to increase the number of interviews and selection hurdles that have to be undergone. Plausibly, and our interviews with trainees tend to confirm this, the likelihood of crossing lines of ascriptive demarcation has in consequence become more difficult with the advent of YTS not less. Being on more or less permanent trial from the outset also reinforces the psychological individualism which the Scheme seeks to foster. At the same time there is a double stigmatization for those who, having failed to find a job on leaving school, subsequently fail to be selected for the scheme that they would prefer.

To turn now to the question of *training:* this is of course an extremely complex matter which goes to the heart of YTS and we cannot discuss it fully here. In relation to the 'in-market' effects of the Scheme upon life chances and attitudes, however, we concluded that the most salient aspects of the training centred around the relation of the formal content and 'off the job' elements to the experiences received 'on the job', that is in actual work placements. The Manpower Services Commission's blueprints conflate the training element in YTS with its unemployment function by arguing that young people who acquire 'transferable' capabilities that can be used by more than one employer will have better job prospects. In practice, the location of this transferable element varies according to the labour market segment occupied by the trainees and their schemes. Among the 'top' schemes which, as we have seen, recruit selectively and where job prospects are generally the best, the transferable element in training is located in the extensive amount of learning required for actual job performance. Both on and off the job training materials not directly related to this job element (inter personal skills, for example) tend to the discounted, even pushed aside by both trainers and trained.

Such schemes, however, account for a minority only of YTS placements, especially in a local context such as Southwich where service industry dominates the employment structure. The lower one moves down the hierarchy of occupations and schemes the greater the amount of low level service employment; and the less there is to be learned about actual job performance. Training organizations in occupations like, say, retailing, lower level catering and clerical work, or warehousing, all of which provide an impressive amount of local employment, had found difficulty in devising learning packages of sufficient length to satisfy MSC requirements, especially with the advent of two-year YTS. The transferable element thus had shifted to *off*-the-job learning. At best this meant an off the job training component only loosely connected to the actual placement of the trainee, and often associated with the award of 'credentials' which had been devised for the purpose. At worst, it was comprised wholly of elements not related to actual job performance at all, being predominantly in so-called 'social and life skills' which are not only hard to measure but are not necessarily recognized or valued by employers generally. They thus have very little effect on trainees' life chances. Worse, the attenuation of the link between placement and off the job training produces discontent, disillusionment and cynicism amongst the trainees themselves. Again the prospect arises of double stigmatization through YTS for initial failure at school.

Finally, we must consider the *entry to the real labour market* which occurs at the end of YTS. We noted earlier that many trainees once recruited to the Scheme are provided with a psychic refuge or what is in effect a moral rescue from unemployment. From this vantage they can look down upon the unemployed and YTS refusers, notwithstanding the fact that they may be themselves insecure in their tenure at work or dissatisfied with aspects of their YTS Scheme, such as the training allowance. The effect of actually obtaining a job at the end was to extend their sense of moral rescue beyond the YTS year itself. Over half of those who had got jobs saw their employment as connected with their contact with the Scheme if not always with their actual work placement. Much of their success in finding work no doubt reflected the relatively favourable employment situation in the Southwich area as a whole. The questionnaire comments showed, however, that ex-trainees who had obtained work via their placements or directly after they finish the Scheme tended to see YTS as the *cause* of their good fortune. The feeling that 'YTS worked for me' personalizes experience of the labour market and at the same time enhances the otherness of those who were not so lucky or remain unemployed.

(ii) The Schemes

We have emphasised that in the Southwich case the bulk of YTS schemes were of the privately run (formerly 'Mode A') type run on a strict commercial basis. Inevitably, therefore, the relationship *between* schemes run on business lines tended to be a potentially competitive one. Though organizations were not always aware of or willing to admit it, it seemed to us that with the establishment of YTS in the town and surrounding areas, an element of sometimes quite intense competition for likely trainees developed and where relevant for sponsors too. This competition affected not just the Agencies themselves but also, in credibility terms at least, the local FE College. Admittedly, the local MSC staff made interventions in the light of policy guidelines to control the amount of overt competition as well as overall amounts of training in the various occupational training families. With time, something akin to an equilibrium, both stimulated and controlled by the MSC was established in which agencies came to inhabit areas of market territory as recognized spheres of influence. For schemes not at the top of the hierarchy, their security of tenure in this niche largely depended upon their ability, usually through the good offices of the Careers Service, to sell work placements that could be presented as credible or meaningful to trainees; and to some extent also upon their ability to sell the trainees recruited to potential work providers.

The influence of these factors obviously affected in turn the opportunities of present and future trainees. One major reason for this was that the hierarchy of schemes so created varied in the extent to which it was likely to expose trainees to the influence of wider market forces and hence to the vagaries of sheer chance. In the current economic situation, of course, no-one was wholly immune. We have examples of trainees in 'top' YTS schemes, leading to apparently secure internal labour markets, whose work provider went out of business, or got taken over and closed down during the year. We also have examples of youngsters with very unspectacular school careers behind them who clearly flourished in the abrasive enterprise culture of an expanding small business. On the whole, however, the precariousness of work providers seemed greater at the lower levels where the less qualified school leavers were likely to be recruited. At the margins some of the actual schemes themselves, to say nothing of the work placements, proved to be insecure.

In this section, then, we have been describing some of the intricate in-market processes through which the surrogate labour market of YTS was affecting the life chance of the trainees in our case study. At best, the fact that YTS allowed scope to such factors meant that some individuals were able to compensate for pre-market disadvantages such as poor school leaving attainment. Obviously, however, it is not possible to say what would have happened to these particular individuals anyway, without the intervention of YTS. And there was little evidence that such cases were common: the main conclusion we drew was that the Scheme was merely imposing an extended and finer layer of in-market distinctions upon the pre-market segmentation of the supply of young trainees.

The situation we have described has in any case already changed. By the end of the study, local MSC officials had succeeded in removing some of the more dubious training organizations and placements at the same time as they have introduced the quality controls of two year YTS. But as we have argued elsewhere, the revised financial structure of the two-year YTS has probably had the most impact (Lee *et al.*, 1986). In the opinion of many of those we met who were closely involved with the changes the likely effect was, as one put it: 'a regression to a selective system of recruitment [to employment] via YTS which relies heavily on academic qualifications to the exclusion of other factors.' The effect of such a development would presumably be to exclude altogether the less qualified from the YTS segment within the youth labour market as a whole.

Conclusion

We began this chapter by arguing that research on current youth training policies should be trying to place them in the context of social and economic change. In particular attention needs to be given to their con-sequences for wider patterns of inequality. Hence, our own work started out from the attempts British sociologists have made to understand the factors which determine the structure of contemporary class relationships. Our criticism of much of this work was that it had concentrated far too much upon variations *between* so-called 'strata' in life chance and social perceptions, to the neglect of variations *within* them. We proposed in-stead a model of class *segmentation* developed from recent labour market theories. The most important feature of this model was the hypothesis that micro events in the labour market interpose themselves between groups of individuals and the wider structure of class inequality in such a way as to isolate their perceptions and experiences.

The relevance of this general approach to our own work, of course, is that age divisions constitute a major axis along which such labour market segmentation can, and in practice often does, arise. The youth labour market is clearly of especial interest in this regard. There is much evidence to suggest that the relation between adult and youth employment is a complex one in which young people sometimes are excluded from doing adult jobs and at others times are in direct competition with adults, according to circumstances. But more fundamentally, the ways in which the young come to participate in the labour market will affect their subjective evaluation of work and its rewards. In turn, socialisation of young workers into appropriate orientations to work is an essential element in the creation and continuance of segments in the adult economy itself. Consequently understanding the new 'staged transitions' (Roberts, *et al.*, 1986) from school to work which governments have devised in the face of high youth unemployment is highly important in grasping contemporary inequality and social divisions as a whole. This may be seen particularly in relation to the latest and, arguably most momentous of these interventions, the Youth Training Scheme, which has been the main concern here. Potentially, its effects do extend not just to the present and future life chances of young workers but also to their values and social perceptions.

It has to be said, first of all, that we saw little prospect from our case study that YTS could in itself bring about any radical improvement in the life chances of the bulk of young people recruited to it at that time. On the contrary, much of our fieldwork suggested to us that the YTS year, combined with other government measures, is not only lowering the wages of young people but also, through the in-market experiences described in the previous section, lowering their expectations as to what they can earn. Nor do we see YTS as a solution to the skill shortages which are said to hamper the growth of the economy and hence of good job prospects for young adults in future. The relatively favourable employment situation of the young people we studied in Southwich was dependent on the predominance of a number of service industries reflecting the general affluence of the south east but not necessarily contributing to the long run growth of local employment. Though the term 'subemployment' eludes easy definition it seemed to us an apt description of the job histories of the ex-trainees we followed up, to say nothing of the content of the actual jobs they were doing. Compensatory opportunities for young people to learn and then practice transferable job skills of the kind said to be short supply in the British economy were very limited. Arguably, then, YTS was, at the time of our research, fostering a significant low-wage segment in the youth labour market.

As for the effects of YTS upon the social perceptions of the trainees, we have described in this chapter three sets of potentially very divisive influences. We began by pointing out that there are significant regional disparities in the way the Scheme operates. *Ceteris paribus* one would expect these to intensify the geographical expression of differentiated life chances and orientations. But also, in any particular locality, YTS trainees themselves constitute a new and growing segment of the youth labour market as a whole which is interspersed between those with real jobs and YTS refusers and young unemployed[1]. Finally, because it acts as a surrogate labour market, YTS is itself internally segmented, especially in terms of the calibre of the training 'opportunity' on offer and the possibility of access to an internal labour market. We accept, of course, that deep divisions between segments of youth already exist as a result of such factors as education, socioeconomic background, gender and race. The YTS surrogate labour market reflects these pre-market influences just like any other labour market because from the outset they cause individuals to differ in their ascribed employability. But the main point we have tried to pursue, and which distinguishes our approach from more traditional ones, is that further inequalities develop within the between pre-market segments due to the ongoing processes of the market itself.

This divisive potential is, of course, highly relevant to some major themes in the 'stratification' tradition. Much effort has been devoted to explaining why the manual working class stratum has become more rather than less fragmented over time and why individuals have become increasingly privatized and instrumental in their attitudes. Curiously enough, the role of the labour market itself in educating people into attitudes of calculative individualism has been relatively neglected.

It is therefore tempting to speculate as to how far YTS is becoming important as an 'education' in individualism for the school leaver. We have been impressed by the changing balance of calculative and altruistic calculations which YTS implies. The strong emphasis of current training policy upon private enterprise and self help is presenting trainers and trained with a novel mix of pressures about what is owed to the young and what in turn they owe to themselves and to society through work and effort. Sustained over a period of time the effect could well be to intensify the individualism of a wide segment of British youth. Data from the Scottish leavers' survey on the attitudes of YTS trainees have revealed the highly instrumental fashion in which they come to view both the Scheme and their wider situation (Raffe and Smith, 1986). We found that many of our own respondents had been inculcated with individualistic values before they joined YTS but that they nevertheless took its moral lessons to heart in appraising their encounter with the Scheme.

The literature on the sociological sources of inflation provides one illustration of how learning the values of self-help at the personal level may have unexpected consequences for society at the system level (in this context see especially Gilbert, 1978). We observed at first hand that the acceptance of calculative individualism among YTS trainees has resulted in a critical and uneasy tolerance of the effort bargain represented by the YTS training allowance. It is conceivable then that in the long term the effects of current youth training policy may spill over into as yet unformed collective behaviour, possibly taking on some rather nasty guises. Such questions would form a useful focus for research in the future.

For the present we would simply claim, that our emphasis on sources of inequality arising from within the labour market can fruitfully be applied to the class situation of an important segment of young people. We think it also should be extended to other groups in society. It is, in fact, only at the in-market and micro level that we can discover many of the reasons why there is today considerable segmentation *within* conventional strata; and why such matters as youth unemployment remain to a surprising degree what C. Wright Mills would have called private troubles, as opposd to public issues.

Acknowledgements

The authors are grateful to David Ashton, David Raffe and Gordon Marshall for their comments and advice. They also wish to acknowledge the generous support given by the Leverhulme Trust to their work.

Note

1   Even though it may be a conscious intention of youth employment policy to make the other segments decreasingly available to school leavers it remains unclear whether such an objective will actually be achieved. Recently in the course of discussions with training organizations we have encountered suggestions that some employers are now seeking to bypass the more stringent requirements of two year YTS by recruiting school leavers at relatively low wages straight from school into jobs.

References

ASHTON, D.N., and MAGUIRE, M. (1982) *Youth in the Labour Market*, Research Paper no. 34, London, Department of Employment.

ASHTON, D.N., and MAGUIRE, M. (1986) *Young Adults in the Labour Market*, Research Paper no. 55, London, Department of Employment.

BANKS, M. and ULLAH, P. (1986) 'Unemployment and less qualified urban youth', *Department of Employment Gazette*, 94, 5, June, pp. 205–210.

BLACKBURN, R.M. and MANN, M. (1979) *The Working Class in the Labour Market*, London, Macmillan.

GILBERT, M. (1978) 'Neo-Durkheimian analyses of economic life and strife', *Sociological Review*, 26, 4, pp. 729–754.

HOCKLEY, J. (1984) 'The Implementation of the Youth Training Scheme in Three Local Labour Markets' University of Leicester, Department of Sociology.

JAHODA, M. (1982) *Employment and Unemployment — a social-psychological analysis* Cambridge, Cambridge University Press.

LEE, D.J. (1973) 'The regional factor in further education and the employment of male school leavers', Research Note', *Sociology*, 7, pp. 429–31.

LEE, D.J., MARSDEN, D., RICKMAN, P. and HARDEY, M. (1986) 'How YTS tied itself in knots', *Education Guardian*, 19 September.

MANWARING, T. (1984) 'The extended internal labour market', *Cambridge Journal of Economics*, 8 pp. 161–87.

MARSHALL, G. (1983) 'Some remarks on the study of working class consciousness', *Politics and Society*, 12, 3, pp. 263–301.

RAFFE, D. (1986) *The Context of the Youth Training Scheme — An Analysis of its Strategy and Development*, Edinburgh, Centre for Educational Sociology, University of Edinburgh.

RAFFE, D. and SMITH, P. (1986) *Young People's Attitudes to the YTS: The First Two Years*, Edinburgh, Centre for Educational Sociology University of Edinburgh.

ROBERTS, K., DENCH, J., and RICHARDSON, D. (1986): *The Changing Structure of Youth Labour Markets*, final report to the Department of Employment, University of Liverpool.

RYAN, P. (1981) 'Segmentation, duality and the internal labour market', in WILKINSON, F. (Ed.) *The Dynamics of Labour Market Segmentation*, London, Academic Press, pp. 3–20

SPILSBURY, M. (1985) 'Individual Youth Unemployment and the Local Labour Market', University of Leicester, Labour Market Studies, Working Paper, No. 10.

STAFFORD, E.M. JACKSON, P. R., and BANKS, M. (1980) 'Employment, work involvement and mental health in less qualified young people', *Journal of Occupational Psychology*, 53, pp. 291–304.

YOUTHAID (1986) 'YTS leavers survey, *Youthaid Bulletin*, 29, See also Hansard 25/7/86 col. 583–4.

8 Labour Market Segmentation and the Structure of the Youth Labour Market

David N. Ashton, Malcolm J. Maguire and Mark Spilsbury

Introduction: Approaches to the Study of the Youth Labour Market

Until recently the study of the structure of the youth labour market has attracted scant attention from sociologists and economists. However, empirical enquiries into the youth labour market, together with developments in segmentation theory, now make it possible to provide a more adequate analysis of its structure. This chapter is based on the findings of successive research projects carried out at the University of Leicester.[1] It seeks to show how the dimensions of skill, sex and age combine to create the distinctive features of the youth labour market. This market, it is argued, is comprised of eight main segments, each having its own entry criteria, which influence the allocation of young people within the labour market, and their subsequent career movement.

The hitherto limited degree of sociological study of the labour market, and especially of the youth labour market[2] is surprising, not only because there is a substantial literature concerned with the process of transition from school to work, but also in view of the centrality of the study of the labour market for our understanding of the dynamics of stratification.[3]

Research on the entry to the labour market has traditionally focussed on the effects of schooling and family background on the process of transition.[4] The placement of the young person within the labour market was usually seen as the outcome of this process, with the result that little attention was paid to the organization of the labour market. With few exceptions, this has also been true of more recent studies of the transition[5]. As a result the categories used to conceptualize the structure of the labour market have developed little from those used in popular discourse.

Elsewhere in sociology there have, of course, been conceptual developments which have a direct relevance to our understanding of the youth labour market. Work on the concept of occupational closure, careers and the position of women in the labour market all have implications for this understanding.[6] Here we advocate that this work should be integrated into a sociology of the youth labour market. This task is especially urgent as recent developments in the study of the transition, such as the numerous pieces of research concerned with analyzing the new forms of government intervention in the youth labour market have directed attention away from this issue.[7] At the experiential level a number of studies have explored the meaning of unemployment.[8] While important advances have come from these developments, in neither case has there been a focus on the need to understand the structure and functioning of the youth labour market. We believe this to be of crucial importance because the organization of the youth labour market conditions the outcomes which these two developments seek to comprehend. It does this by delineating the areas where the MSC and government can effectively intervene in the youth labour market and by determining which groups are most at risk of unemployment.

One of the few attempts to focus directly on the structure of the youth labour market has been made by Raffe, who portrays the youth and adult labour markets as being undifferentiated. While acknowledging that age is a factor in employment he argues that evidence from econometric studies, and from the MSC 1978 employers' survey, suggests that on balance 'there is substantially more competition than segregation between young people and adults' (Raffe, 1983). He goes on to agree with the conclusion of a 1978 OECD study that 'It is questionable whether, in fact, there is any such thing as a 'youth labour market' which operates separately and distinctly from other areas of the economy'. In a later paper he recognizes the possibility of the existence of a distinct youth labour market (Raffe 1985). Notwithstanding their exclusion from a wide range of jobs, he argues that, as young people are found in many sectors of the general labour market, the youth labour market is closely related to the adult market and is affected by the same factors, if not always in the same way. He concludes that 'young people are in broadly the same labour market(s) as adults: they are affected by the same factors, only more so'. (see chapter 11 in this volume).[9]

An alternative conceptualization of the youth labour market emanates from radical economists, using dual labour market theory. A leading advocate, Osterman (1980), argues, on the basis of American data, that most young people who do not go on to college, enter jobs in the secondary labour market. He gives two main reasons for this. Firstly, employers in the primary market who invest in the training of employees, prefer to hire adults, whom they regard as being more stable than young people. Secondly, young people prefer a moratorium period before they settle down. On leaving high school they have no responsibilities. 'In their lives, friends, sex, adventure seeking and travel take precedence over work. Jobs in casual and undemanding secondary firms carry few penalties for unstable behaviour' (ibid, p. 345). The result is a pattern of job hopping with intermittent spells of unemployment which is thought to be characteristic of youths.[10]

Although dual labour market theory has been utilized to analyse the British labour market (Bosanquet and Doeringer, 1973; Barron and Norris, 1976) in general, and the youth labour market in particular (Walker, 1982), its uncritical use in this context is misleading. Elsewhere we have demonstrated its inadequacies in dealing with the general labour market in the British context (Ashton and Maguire, 1984). Notwithstanding the Thatcher government's attempts at deregulation, the British labour market has a higher degree of institutional regulation. Also, a significant proportion of school leavers in Britain have traditionally entered jobs in the skilled trades, which are located in the primary market (Ashton, 1986).

In recent years Bluestone and Stevenson (1981): Edwards (1979): and Gordon *et al.*, (1982) in the United States, and Wilkinson *et al.*, in the United Kingdom, have developed ideas on dual labour markets into a theory of labour market segmentation.[11] It is this theory which we are applying to the study of the youth labour market. We believe that such developments, when used to inform empirical enquiry, can provide substantial insights into the structure and functioning of the youth labour market. Only when this has been achieved can meaningful statements be made about the relationship between the youth and adult markets.

One of the main problems with the early versions of dual labour market theory was the tendency to oversimplify our understanding of the structure of the labour market by reducing it to two non-competing groups. This stemmed from attempts to predict a firm's employment strategy from a knowledge of its industrial structure. Other work shows clearly that the same firm may utilize different strategies and that a number of factors may be important in determining the types of employment strategy adopted (Craig *et al.*, 1985). The insights in Doeringer and Piore's early work remain, in that the firm's product market, the level of competition it faces, its product or service, technology and internal organization, are all seen as important factors influencing its employment strategy, but the relationships are no longer seen as determinate. Other factors have also been identified. Gordon *et al.*, (1982) have highlighted the importance of management control systems, while Rubery and the Cambridge Labour Studies Group have pointed to the significance of forms of employment regulation, such as trade union organization, professional associations and training systems, in constraining management options, as well as identifying the importance of a differentiated or segmented labour supply (Rubery, 1978; Rubery *et al.*, 1984: Garnsey *et al.*, 1985).

The main thrust of these developments in segmentation theory has been to provide an alternative explanation of pay and job structures to that of neo-classical economics, placing the emphasis on differences in the quality of job as opposed to differences in labour quality as the main explanation of variation in rewards. Here, we are attempting to extend this approach. We use it to explain differences in employers' strategies in the recruitment and selection of young people as well as to provide a means of identifying the factors which constrain the movement of young people once they have entered the labour market.

Dimensions of Segmentation

Age Segmentation

Elsewhere we have shown how employers often make decisions which may preclude groups of workers from consideration for certain types of jobs.[12] Young people may be excluded from consideration, sheltered from competition from adults, or be in direct competition with adults. Thus, the range of job opportunities open to 16-year-old school-leavers is very different to that facing adults. Our findings have shown that most professional, administrative and managerial jobs are closed to 16-year-olds. In clerical work, some employers prefer to restrict their recruitment to young people who can be trained into the culture of the firm more easily than adults. Others will recruit from either young people or adults. In the entry to skilled manual work, age restrictions for apprenticeships result in employers only recruiting young people, usually 16-year-olds. In recruiting for semi-skilled and unskilled manual work many employers refuse to consider youths as potential recruits under any circumstances while others recruit from both youths and adults (Ashton, Maguire and Garland, 1982).

The existence of this age segmentation was confirmed by our survey of 18-24-year-olds (Ashton, Maguire *et al.*, 1986). In that survey we asked young adults if there were any reasons why young people (16-18-year-olds) would not be recruited for their job. Of the respondents who could provide a definite answer, 10 per cent of those in their first job said that young people would not be recruited. This proportion rose to 41 per cent for those in their third job. There were also differences reported in the degree of closure of jobs at different occupational levels. Three-quarters of those in their third job in professional, managerial and technician work indicated that their jobs were closed to young people, as did almost half of those in unskilled work and less than one-quarter of those in skilled work. When taken together with the findings from the employers' survey referred to earlier, this demonstrates quite clearly the effect of age discrimination in segmenting the labour market.

Sex Segregation

The impact of sex segregation in the general labour market has been well established (Hakim, 1979; Martin and Roberts, 1984; and Dex, 1985). In our own work we have been able to identify those areas of the labour market where young people of both sexes compete for jobs and those areas where segregation is greatest.[13] In general the results suggest that there is more competition between the sexes for entry into white-collar jobs than into manual jobs. However, even in white-collar work, clerical and secretarial jobs tend to be a female preserve, with males having better access to those clerical jobs offering the chance of career progression.

Sex segregation is most apparent in skilled manual work, with the craft occupations being almost exclusively male and hairdressing almost exclusively female. In semi-skilled manual, unskilled manual and sales work, there is a higher level of segregation than in the white-collar jobs, with some categories of jobs, such as machinist in knitwear, being exclusively female and other jobs, such as clicker in footwear, being exclusively male. One further aspect of the pattern of sex segregation is that at all levels of the labour market, those jobs entered by males have greater promotion or career chances than those entered by females. Thus, even in semi-skilled and unskilled jobs 62 per cent of males in our sample reported that their job offered the chance of promotion, compared with only 24 per cent of females.

Racial Discrimination

Unlike sex discrimination, racial discrimination merely makes access to existing jobs that much more difficult for certain ethnic minorities. The work of Roberts *et al.*, (1983) and Dex (1979) has shown how young blacks and Asians can obtain access to skilled manual and white-collar jobs, but in order to do so, they have to make more applications and wait longer before obtaining any success. Thus, the proportion of jobs actually open to them at all levels of the labour market is much smaller than that available for whites, with the result that blacks are disproportionately affected in their attempts to obtain access to all types of work.

Skill or Occupation Segmentation

The other main dimension of segmentation is that of skill or occupation.[14] We have identified four occupational groupings of: (a) professional, managerial, administration and technician jobs: (b) clerical, including secretarial jobs: (c) skilled manual jobs: and (d) semi-skilled manual, unskilled manual and sales jobs. The specific jobs which comprise each of these segments and the career chances they provide differs for males and females, thereby creating eight segments.

Professional, managerial, administration and technician segment
At the higher levels of the labour market, the activities of professional associations, and to a lesser extent management, have transformed the pattern of entry, denying access to 16-year-olds. Professional bodies have successfully sought to limit access to their occupations to young people with 'A' levels or preferably degrees. Accountancy, which fifteen years ago was taking substantial numbers of 'A' level recruits, is now almost exclusively a graduate profession. This is partly a response of the professions to the trend for more young people to stay on into higher education, but it also points to the desire of professional bodies to enhance their status by enforcing graduate entry. At the same time, some firms attempt to encourage 'A' level entrants, and increasingly graduates, to enter as trainee managers, because of the difficulties they have encountered in recruiting managers through the traditional channels of internal promotion. The tendency of the 'bright' young person to stay on at school has depleted the number of craft, technician and commercial trainees with managerial potential. Consequently many firms have been obliged to develop special traineeships and so encourage graduate recruitment. Also, changes in the occupational structure are increasing the proportion of technicians, managers and professionals employed by firms. In parts of the service sector, such as hotels and catering and leisure, where large firms with extensive capital resources have only recently emerged as dominant forces, there are still opportunities for access to management through the internal market for those entering at 16. However, even here, the forces of professionalism are creating pressures to enforce professional standards for new entrants.

Skilled manual and clerical segments   At the middle levels of the occupational hierarchy, firms in both the manufacturing and service sectors prefer young people with keyboard skills who can then be trained in firm specific procedures. Change in technology associated with office automation are diminishing the number of copy typing and clerical filing jobs but increasing the number of VDU operators. Here firms often prefer to recruit young people because they are more easily trained and are familiar with the technology. This is not the case among smaller firms, which tend to undertake a negligible amount of training. They prefer to recruit experienced workers who require little or no training.

The combined effect of management-union agreements on apprenticeship training and age related payment systems has been to restrict the age of entry to many apprenticeships to 16-year-olds. However, the organization of skilled manual work is currently being transformed by a number of factors. In manufacturing industry, the introduction of new technology, such as CNC machines and robotics, is starting to change the type of skills required and undermine the old concept of a time served apprenticeship imposed by the more powerful craft unions. In addition, increased competition from the United States, Europe and Japan, has led a number of firms to experiment with new forms of work organization and management techniques in an attempt to ensure greater work commitment and enhance their competitiveness. The lowering of labour costs through the reduction of manning levels, has been accompanied by the widespread introduction of a more formalized division of the labour force between 'core' and 'periphery' workers.[15] Access to 'core' jobs is gained at the expense of old forms of craft demarcation, resulting in skilled workers becoming flexible craftsmen, and increasing the degree of control exerted by the employing organization. Also, the MSC is attempting to encourage firms to move towards more flexible training in the form of a standards based modular training system. Although most firms still adhere to the old apprenticeship system, these changes will have increasing impact. Thus, the main point of entry for young people into skilled work, where they have traditionally been sheltered from direct competition with adults by age restrictions on entry, is now threatened. In other areas of the labour market, recent changes have created new 'sheltered' points of entry for 16-year-olds. In the construction industry YTS now provides the basis for the first year of the apprenticeship. This means that entry to this industry is increasingly limited to 16-year-old trainees.

Semi-skilled and unskilled manual segments In semi-skilled manual, unskilled manual, and sales work[16] a number of very different pressures operate. In firms employing capital intensive technologies, such as in the tobacco, chemicals, can manufacturing, and parts of the plastics industries, most operative jobs are effectively closed to young people because the technology requires a twenty-four hour operation. Young people are regarded as being unsuitable for shift work, either because they are seen as unreliable, especially when it comes to nightshifts, or because the jobs are highly paid and part of an internal labour market. Whatever the reason, the employer's desire to recruit only adults for such jobs is reinforced by legislation precluding young people working with dangerous machinery or substances and from working shifts.

Young people tend to be recruited in large numbers for what is conventionally termed semi-skilled work[17] in labour intensive firms, such as in the textiles, clothing, footwear and woodworking industries. The work tasks frequently require considerable skills in manual dexterity, for which a period of training is necessary. Youths are seen as being relatively easy to train in this work compared with adults and will also tolerate low levels of piece-rate earnings. However, some smaller firms will not recruit untrained 16-year-olds, as disruption to the production process occasioned by inexperienced labour is too expensive.

In retailing and distribution, unskilled and semi-skilled job opportunities for young people have been drastically affected by the shift towards a greater use of part-time workers. The increasing domination of the market by large retailers with new forms of internal organization has meant that whereas large numbers of young people were formerly employed on a full-time basis, employers now prefer to supplement a small core of full-time workers by recruiting married women to work on a part-time basis to cover the periods of peak demand. It may be, however, that in some organizations the introduction of YTS, which provides young people with a relative cost advantage, is encouraging the reintroduction of younger workers. Certainly in the hotel and catering industry, this factor, coupled with increasing demands for a trained workforce, has encouraged employers to recruit more young people. Thus, within the service sector there are contradictory pressures, some of which are reducing the opportunities for school leavers, while others are enhancing them. Evidence from France (Marsden, 1986) and the United States (Spilsbury, 1985) shows that the dominant trend is towards the elimination of full-time jobs and that young people are being displaced by adult female workers. Using UK Labour Force Survey data, Spilsbury suggests that this is also the case in the United Kingdom.[18]

One effect of these pressures on employers is to give the segments at the lower levels of the youth labour market their peculiar wedge or 'funnel' shaped character.[19] Although there are relatively few jobs available for the 16-year-old, the range of jobs open to them increases as they mature in years and obtain access to adult jobs.

Interventions in the Labour Market

The power of the various factors we have identified in segmenting the youth labour market has been sufficient to moderate the impact of recent initiatives aimed at transforming the structure of that labour market. Thus, the interventions of the MSC, through the introduction of the Youth Opportunities Programme (YOP) and, subsequently, the YTS, have so far has less widespread effect than was anticipated. Both YOP and in its early stages, YTS, were used most intensively in those industries which already employed a relatively large proportion of young people. These tended to be labour intensive industries, where young people were already seen to have a competitive advantage in terms of low labour costs. Hence the schemes proved attractive to employers in textiles, footwear, distribution, hotel and catering and miscellaneous services, in areas of high unemployment. Here the schemes have reduced the cost of training to the employer while providing twelve months vetting of potential recruits. In addition there is some evidence that the level of trainee allowances may have lowered young people's expectations about earnings (Jones, 1984). However, in the capital intensive industries, where young people have not previously had access to semi-skilled and unskilled jobs, the schemes have been less successful. Employers may have been prepared to act as managing agents out of a sense of social responsibility, but they have not necessarily been prepared to modify their recruitment procedures to accept young adults into jobs which have previously been closed to them (Turbin, 1984). Trainees have had to find work elsewhere.

In the engineering industry, which is subject to the constraints of the apprenticeship system, employers have been willing, in some instances, to treat the one-year YTS as part of the first year of apprenticeship. However, even here, given the high capital costs involved in training apprentices, the YTS allowance is not such an incentive. Also, the extent to which employers have been able to take advantage of YTS has depended in a large part on the conditions of labour supply in the local area. In areas of high unemployment where highly skilled and qualified youths are unemployed, employers have been able to use YTS as a means of recruiting apprentices. In areas of low unemployment, where competition for youth labour is more intense, employers have not used YTS to the same extent, preferring to attract the right candidates with the offer of a permanent full-time job.

This cursory treatment of the impact of YTS points to the constraints under which the scheme operates and which stem from the underlying factors which influence employers' recruitment practices and determine the shape of the youth labour market. YTS is undoubtedly having an impact on the youth labour market but this impact is essentially on the margins, and is more likely to modify its operation, than to transform it.

Labour Market Segmentation and the Young Adult's Experience of the Labour Market

The foregoing examination of the youth labour market, through an analysis of the factors which influence the decisions employers make about the type of labour they recruit, has produced a model of a segmented labour market from which a number of hypotheses can be derived about the young person's early labour market experiences. The results of our survey of the labour market experience of 1786 young adults are now used to test these ideas. The first concerns the notion that selection criteria are different for each segment. Employers recruiting for professional and managerial jobs will clearly be looking for very different qualities to those recruiting for unskilled, low paid, dead-end jobs. A second hypothesis concerns the pattern of job movement, which is different in each segment. Thirdly, if the youth and adult labour markets are different in significant respects we would expect this to be reflected in the pattern of job movement of those in the lower segments, as they mature in years and enter jobs in the adult market.

Entry Criteria

Educational qualifications are one of the few forms of apparently objective criteria available to employers in selecting school-leavers. Nevertheless, such criteria are used in very different ways when recruiting for jobs in the various segments.[20]

In recruiting for professional, technician, managerial and clerical jobs the vast majority of employers insist on candidates achieving certain minimum levels of educational qualifications, often because they are required by the relevant professional body as a prerequisite to register for qualifying examinations. Successful examination performance is thus essential before a person can be considered for most jobs in these segments. The only exception is among female clerical workers recruited for the more routine operations where lower qualifications are asked for.

For entry into skilled work, some employers ask for a minimum number of 'O' levels or CSEs, often at the request of local colleges which demand such qualifications for entry to their craft courses. Other employers, especially those not offering day release or further formal training, make no stipulations about educational qualifications, which are seen as irrelevant to job performance. However, the most common response of employers is to treat educational qualifications as a useful device for focussing their recruitment drive at pupils of a given level of ability. What they are looking for is recruits who, while not academic highflyers, nevertheless have 'some academic potential'. Whether that potential is actually realized in the examination is not seen as important.

When recruiting for jobs in the lowest segment, which we have identified as containing unskilled manual, semi-skilled manual and sales jobs, the criteria are very different. Employers view educational qualifications as irrelevant for job performance at this level. Given that the jobs are often boring and repetitive the last thing the employer wants is someone with the ambition and initiative which educational achievement is seen to signify. They are looking for people who will be content to turn up regularly, accept the discipline of the workplace and who can cope with the boredom of routine work.

The educational qualifications possessed by our sample of 18-24-year-olds who entered the different segments tended to confirm our earlier findings. As table 1 shows, it was difficult for young people without educational qualifications to enter professional, technician and managerial and clerical work. Over 70 per cent had either 'O' or 'A' levels.

Table 1:   Educational qualifications by occupations

	Educational Qualifications: Percentages					
	None	CSE	'O'	'A'	Other	
First job: males						
Prof man tech	2	20	60	15	2	n = 176
Clerical	3	12	54	32	0	n = 69
Skilled	13	41	44	0	1	n = 225
Semi-unskilled and Sales	30	37	28	4	1	n = 289
Unemployed, never had a full-time job	27	38	24	10	0	n = 104
First job: females						
Prof man tech	3	15	63	17	1	n = 86
Clerical	4	16	73	6	0	n = 266
Skilled	9	34	50	6	0	n = 56
Semi-unskilled and sales	46	31	20	1	1	n = 393
Unemployed, never had a full-time job	31	38	22	8	0	n = 107

The pattern of qualifications of those entering skilled manual work mirrored that specified by employers. A majority had 'O' level or CSE qualifications but a significant minority had none at all. Also, there was a clearly discernible difference between the distribution of qualifications of this group and those entering the segment containing the semi-skilled manual, unskilled manual and sales workers. Among the latter the majority had either no known qualifications or lower grade CSEs, reflecting the employers lack of concern about educational achievement. Indeed, the irrelevance of educational qualifications for entry to this segment is also suggested by a comparison of the distribution of educational qualifications among this group with that found among those who were unemployed and had never had a job. If employers were using educational qualifications to discriminate between applicants then we would expect the employed to be better qualified than the unemployed. In fact, the distribution of educational qualifications among those who had never been employed was almost identical to those who had been employed at some time in semi-skilled and unskilled work. This implies that educational qualifications were not being used in the selection for jobs in this segment.

These results suggest that employers are consciously using different criteria to determine entry to each of the segments. Rather than queueing applicants in terms of their potential productivity or their ability to benefit from training, no uniform criteria are used by all employers when selecting for jobs. The criteria used for determining access to the higher segments are very different in important respects to those adopted by employers when recruiting for jobs in the lowest segments.

Job Movement

Data on the 18-24-year-olds' work histories provided the opportunity to assess the impact of labour market segmentation on job movement. Our initial results indicate that the segment which a young person enters has an important influence on their subsequent pattern of job movement. Firstly, it affects their chances of changing jobs in their early years in the labour market.

Those entering the higher segments were more stable and secure in their jobs. Of the males entering professional, managerial and technician jobs approximately 70 per cent were still in their first job at the time of interview compared with fewer than 50 per cent of those who entered semi-skilled work, under 40 per cent of those in sales and fewer than 30 per cent of those in unskilled work. Those who first entered skilled manual work and clerical work were more likely to still be in their first job than those in the lower segment but did not achieve the same degree of stability as those in professional, managerial and technician jobs. The greater stability of those in the higher segments may well be a function of their more extensive training which commits them to a future in the occupation if the investment in the training is to pay off. In addition, such jobs are less likely to be affected by redundancies and other attempts to rationalize labour.

In the lower segment, learning times, especially in unskilled and sales work are very short, with the majority having learnt their jobs within a month (Ashton and Maguire *et al.*, 1986). The lack of investment in the acquisition of skills leaves individuals with little commitment to the job. If in addition, the job does not offer promotion possibilities within an internal labour market, there is little incentive for the worker to remain with the employer, should other opportunities become available.

In our sample, over half the job moves were to jobs within the same segment. Among those in the least skilled jobs, the majority who entered semi-skilled manual work moved into similar jobs, while those going into unskilled manual and sales work were less likely to enter jobs in the same category. Indeed, these jobs tended to function much like a clearing house, with those entering them coming from diverse origins, and leaving for different destinations. However, many of these destinations were other jobs in this segment. When the three categories comprising the segment are combined, almost 70 per cent of subsequent moves were to other jobs within the segment.

It may be argued that, as a significant proportion of moves are to jobs in other segments, then the barriers to movement are not particularly strong. Indeed, using similar data it has been suggested that the magnitude of such moves is evidence that segmentation theory is inappropriate (Mayhew and Rosewell, 1979). However, it can clearly be seen from table 2, which provides a comparison of actual destinations and those which could be expected, given the known distribution of all young people in the sample, that movement is not random. Further, findings in the table need to be qualified, as some of the movement from unskilled manual and sales work to professional, managerial and technician work was accounted for by young people taking fill-in jobs until they were old enough to start their training for jobs in the higher segment. A noticeable trend was for girls to leave school and work in lowly-skilled jobs, often as sales assistants, before entering nursing. Also, some of the movement from skilled manual to managerial, and from semi-skilled manual to skilled manual, was a result of progression along recognized routes within internal labour markets.

However, the existence of market segmentation is most clear in the type of downward mobility. Few of the males leaving professional, managerial, technician and clerical jobs moved into skilled manual work. Instead they had to accept semi-skilled and unskilled manual jobs. This reflects the strength of the barriers which prohibit access to skilled manual jobs to those who lack relevant experience or are over the stipulated age to start formal training.

These findings provide clear evidence of the effect of labour market segmentation on the behaviour of young people.

Conclusion

We have tried to establish some of the distinctive features of the youth labour market. Segmentation has already pointed to some of the main factors determining the general labour market. However, their significance in structuring the youth labour market has not been fully explored. What has certainly not been appreciated is the significance of age discrimination as a factor in shaping a distinctive youth labour market.

In a chapter of this length only a cursory reference has been made to the significance of the product market, internal labour market, and political factors. Other aspects of the youth labour market which have not been addressed are its local character, the differences in promotion chances in male and female segments and the impact of YTS on the pattern of entry to the various segments. Nevertheless, we believe that sufficient evidence has been presented for the idea of a distinctive youth labour market to be taken seriously.

Such an idea does not mean that the youth labour market can be regarded as being totally separate from that for adults. As a group young people do compete with adults, and despite being excluded from large parts of the general labour market as a result of that competition, most of them will in the course of time move into the adult market. For these reasons, the demand for youth labour is affected by changes in the demand for labour generally. However, because the youth labour market

Table 2: Job movement

Destination (Second or longest job)	PMT actual	Clerical	Skilled	Semi-unskilled sales	Expected distribution
		Percentage distribution of those who changed jobs			
Males first job					
Prof man tech	59	24	9	9	23
Clerical	8	52	4	4	9
Skilled	2	5	51	19	30
Semi-unskilled/Sales	30	19	36	67	38
	n = 52	n = 21	n = 94	n = 166	
Females first job					
Prof man tech	74	5	12	10	11
Clerical	17	68	16	13	33
Skilled	0	2	28	6	7
Semi-unskilled/Sales	8	25	44	72	49
	n = 23	n = 122	n = 25	n = 167	

* Represents the distribution expected if the destinations of those who moved was the same as that of the total sample.

has a distinctive structure it is inappropriate to treat it as a scaled-down version of the adult market

Once the distinctive character of the youth labour market is acknowledged, other implications become evident. It can be seen that each of the segments tends to respond in different ways to the various processes of change at work in the economy as a whole. For example, pressures producing qualification inflation may be affecting entry into segments at the middle and higher levels but having little or no impact on entry to the lower segments, where employers tend to ignore educational qualifications. Changes in the industrial and occupational structure, which stem from developments in the product market and the introduction of new technology, will also have a differential impact on the various segments. Thus, the trend towards the displacement of full-time jobs by part-time jobs can be expected to have a more significant impact on the lower segments than the higher ones, where there is still some growth in full-time jobs.

Once these labour market segments have been identified then job movement and career histories become more understandable. What was previously seen to be random movement or drifting in semi-skilled and unskilled work, can now be comprehended as being a result of the pressures of market segmentation. Having entered the higher segments workers develop commitments, which function to keep them in that occupation. They invest time and energy in acquiring job related skills which can only 'pay off' in the form of a reasonable income if they stay in that kind of work. Should they leave, alternative job opportunities are limited. For those in the middle segments, movement upwards in the form of career progression also tends to follow certain clearly defined institutional routes, as in the case of the apprentice who becomes a charge hand or foreman, and later a manager.

The final point we would wish to make, is that in attempting to understand the economic and social forces which are responsible for generating this distinctive youth labour market, we need to consider developments in the field of segmentation theory. Although it evolved initially as a means of explaining the distribution of income, the factors identified by segmentation theory are also responsible for shaping the range and direction of job movement and otherwise structuring the opportunities available to young people once they enter the labour market.

Acknowledgements

This chapter is the product of work currently being undertaken by the Labour Market Studies Group at the University of Leicester. While the authors are responsible for the drafting of this chapter, it draws on the work of Martin Hoskins, Andy Furlong and Johnny Sung.

Notes

1 These were *Youth in the Labour Market* (1977–80) a survey of 360 employers, financed by the Department of Employment; *Young Adults in the Labour Market* (1982–84), a survey of 1800 18-24-year-olds, financed jointly by the Department of Employment and the MSC; and *The Changing Structure of the Youth Labour Market* (1984–86), a study of forty major employers and secondary analysis of the Labour Force Survey, financed by the ESRC. None of these organizations is responsible for the interpretation presented here, which is that of the authors.

2 See for example, Blackburn and Mann (1979), Berg (1981), and Shervish (1983).

3 Although Weber had pointed to the centrality of the labour market, in the determination of class position, it is only recently that his insights have been developed (Giddens, 1973; Kreckel, 1980).

4 For an overview of this literature see Keil *et al.* (1966) and Ashton and Field (1976).

5 Apart from the work of Jenkins (1983), studies such as those of Youthaid (1979), West and Newton (1983) and Willis (1977), have tended to treat the structure of the labour market as unproblematic.

6 On the concept of social closure see Parkin (1974), Kreckel (1980), Lee (1981) and Friedson (1982); on the concept of career see Spilerman (1978) and Hearn (1977): and on women's experience of the labour market, see Dex (1985).

7 See Rees and Atkinson (1982) and Fiddy (1983).

8 See Roberts (1984), Coffield *et al.* (1983) Stafford *et al.* (1980) and Willis (1984).

9   Raffe's ideas on the relationship between the youth and adult labour markets are further elaborated in his critique of structural explanations of unemployment (Raffe, 1985, and chapter 11 in this volume).

10 For a further discussion of this issue see OECD (1983).

11 We are referring here to the work of the Labour Studies Group at Cambridge. Their ideas on segmentation theory can be found in Wilkinson (1981). Rubery (1984) and Garnsey *et al.* (1985).

12 This refers to the distinction between group and individual level competition, see Ashton, Maguire and Garland (1982) and Ashton and Maguire (1983). For some jobs employers refuse to recruit young people, thereby effectively closing access to large parts of the labour market; for others they will only recruit young people, thereby sheltering young people from competition with adults. This means that there is only a limited part of the labour market where young people compete with adults.

13 We did this in two ways, firstly by asking employers whether they recruited males, females or both for specific categories of work (Ashton, Maguire and Garland, 1982), and secondly by asking our sample of young adults whether they had anyone of the opposite sex working in the same job as themselves (Ashton and Maguire *et al.*, 1986).

14 Our attention was first drawn to the significance of segmentation through interviews with employers (Ashton, Maguire and Garland, 1982). Since then we have sought to use data on the job movement of young adults to refine those ideas (Ashton and Maguire *et al.*, 1986). The segments we identify here should be regarded as best current approximations. We are undertaking further analysis of the job histories of our sample which will enable us to refine them further.

15 For a discussion of the notion of 'core' and 'periphery' see Atkinson (1984).

16 Given the frequent ambiguity in sociological studies about the social location of sales workers we initially categorized them with clerical workers. However, a more detailed study of the criteria used to determine entry and their pattern of job movement suggests that they are more appropriately located with semi-skilled and unskilled workers.

17 The category semi-skilled is problematic in that many of the jobs entered by women require a fairly lengthy period of training and in that sense may be more highly skilled than comparable jobs entered by males (Garnsey *et al.*, 1985; Westwood, 1984). However, they are different in that semi-skilled jobs entered by males are characterised by greater promotion chances.

18 This refers to work currently underway on the UK Labour Force Survey data.

19 This idea is elaborated in Ashton. Maguire and Garland (1982). Some of the economic and policy implications are discussed by Hunter (1985).

20 The evidence on which this is based consists of interviews with employers, see Ashton and Maguire (1980), Maguire and Ashton (1981) and Ashton, Maguire and Garland (1982). Similar results were obtained by Hunt and Small (1981).

References

ASHTON, D.N. (1986) *Unemployment Under Capitalism: The Sociology of British and American Labour Markets.* Brighton, Wheatsheaf.

ASHTON, D.N. and FIELD, D. (1976) *Young Workers*, London, Hutchinson.

ASHTON, D.N. and MAGUIRE, M.J. (1980) 'The functions of academic and non-academic criteria in employers' selection procedures', *British Journal of Guidance and Counselling.* 8, 2, pp. 146–57.

ASHTON, D.N. and MAGUIRE, M.J. (1983) 'Competition between young people and adults', *International Review of Applied Psychology*, 32 pp. 262–9

ASHTON, D.N. and MAGUIRE, M.J. (1984) 'Dual labour market theory and the organisation of local labour markets', *International Journal of Social Economics*, 11, pp. 106–20.

ASHTON, D.N. and MAGUIRE, M.J. with BOWDEN, D. DELLOW, P. KENNEDY S. STANLEY, G. WOODHEAD, G. and JENNINGS, B. (1986) *Young Adults in the Labour Market*, London, Dept of Employment Research Paper no. 55.

ASHTON, D.N. MAGUIRE M.J. and GARLAND, V. (1982) *Youth in the Labour Market*, London, Dept of Employment Research Paper no. 34.

ATKINSON, J. (1984) 'Manpower strategies for flexible organisations', *Personnel Management*, August, pp. 24–31.

BARRON, R.D. and NORRIS, G.M. (1976) 'Sexual Divisions and the Dual Labour Market', in BARKER, D.L. and ALLEN, S. (Eds), *Dependence and Exploitation in Work and Marriage*, London, Longmans, pp. 47–69.

BERG, I. (1981) *Sociological Perspectives on Labour Markets*, London, Academic Press.

BLACKBURN, R.M. and MANN, M. (1979) *The Working Class in the Labour Market*, London, Macmillan.

BLUESTONE, B. and STEVENSON, M. (1981) 'Industrial transformation and the evolution of dual labour markets: The case of retail trade in the U.S.' in WILKINSON, F. et al. (Ed.) (1981). *The Dynamics of Labour Market Segmentation*, London, Academic Press.

BOSANQUET. N. and DOERINGER, P.B. (1973) 'Is there a dual labour market in Great Britain?', *Economic Journal*, 83, pp. 421–35.

COFFIELD, F. BORRILL, C. and MARSHALL, S. (1983) 'How young people try to survive being unemployed', *New Society*, 2, June, pp. 332–4.

CRAIG, C. GARNSEY, E. and RUBERY, J. (1985) *Payment Structures and Smaller Firms: Women's Employment in Segmented Labour Markets*, London, Dept of Employment Research Paper no. 48.

DEX, S. (1979) 'A note on discrimination in employment and its effects on black youths', *Journal of Social Policy*. 8, pp. 357–69.

DEX, S. (1985) *The Sexual Division of Work*, Brighton, Wheatsheaf.

EDWARDS, R. (1979) *Contested Terrain: The Transformation of the Workplace in the Twentieth Century*, New York, Basic Books.

FIDDY, R. (Ed.) (1983) *In Place of Work*, Lewes, Falmer Press.

FRIEDSON, E. (1982) 'Occupational autonomy and labour market shelters', in STEWART, P.L. and CANTOR, M.G. (Eds), *Varieties of Work*, London, Sage.

GARNSEY, G. RUBERY, J. and WILKINSON, F. (1985) 'Labour market structure and work-force divisions' in DEEM R. and SALAMAN, G. (Eds) *Work, Culture and Society*, Milton Keynes, Open University Press, pp. 40–76.

GIDDENS, A. (1973) *The Class Structure of the Advanced Societies*, London, Hutchinson.

GORDON, D.M. EDWARDS R. and REICH, M. (1982) *Segmented Work, Divided Workers*, London, Cambridge University Press.

HAKIM, C. (1979) *Occupational Segregation*, London, Department of Employment Research Paper No. 9.

HEARN, J. (1977) 'Towards a concept of non-career', *Sociological Review* 25, pp. 273–88.

HUNT, J. and SMALL, P. (1981) *Employing Young People*, Scottish Council for Research in Education.

HUNTER, L.C. (1985) 'The role of labour demand in youth employment and unemployment' in OECD (1985) *New Policies for the Young*, Paris, OECD, pp. 76–110.

JENKINS, R. (1983) *Lads, Citizens and Ordinary Kids*, London, Routledge and Kegan Paul.

Jones, P. (1984) 'What opportunities for youth?'. *Youthaid Occasional Paper No. 4.*

Keil, E.T. Riddell, D.S. and Green, B.S.R. (1966) 'Youth and work: problems and perspectives', *Sociological Review.* 14, pp. 117–37.

Kreckel, R. (1980) 'Unequal opportunity structure and labour market segmentation', *Sociology,* 14, pp. 525–49.

Lee, D.J. (1981) 'Skill, craft and class: A theoretical critique and a critical case', *Sociology,* 15, pp. 56–78.

Maguire, M.J. and Ashton, D.N. (1981) 'Employers perceptions and use of educational qualifications', *Educational Analysis* 3, 4, pp. 25–36.

Marsden, D. (1986) 'Youth unemployment in France', paper presented to the ESRC Workshop on Employment and Unemployment, January.

Martin J. and Roberts C. (1984) *Women and Employment; A Lifetime Perspective,* London, DE/OPCS.

Mayhew, R. and Rosewell, B. (1979) 'Labour market segmentation in Britain'. *Oxford Bulletin of Economics and Statistics.* 41.

OECD (1978) Youth Unemployment: A Report on the High Level Conference. Volume 1, Paris, OECD.

OECD (1983) *Employment Outlook,* Paris, OECD.

Osterman P. (1980) *Getting Started: The Youth Labor Market,* London, MIT Press.

Osterman, P. (1981) 'Interpreting youth unemployment, *New Society,* 57, pp. 345–6.

Parkin, F. (1974) 'Strategies of social closure in class formation' in Parkin, F. *The Social Analysis of Class Structure,* London, Tavistock, pp. 1–18.

Raffe, D. (1983) 'Can there be an effective youth unemployment policy?' in Fiddy, R. (Ed.) *In Place of Work,* Falmer Press, pp. 11–26.

Raffe, D. (1985) 'Change and continuity in the youth labour market: 'A critical review of structural explanations of youth unemployment' in Allen, S. *et al.* (Eds). *The Experience of Unemployment,* London, Macmillan.

Raffe, D. (1987) 'Youth unemployment in the UK 1979–84', in Brown, P. and Ashton, D.N. (Eds) *Education, Unemployment and Labour Markets,* Lewes, Falmer Press.

Rees, T.L. and Atkinson, P. (Eds) (1982) *Youth Unemployment and State Intervention,* London, Routledge and Kegan Paul.

Roberts, K. (1984) *School Leavers and their Prospects,* Milton Keynes, Open University Press.

Roberts, K. Duggan, J. and Noble, M. (1983) 'Youngs black and out of work' in Troyna, B. and Smith, D.I. (Eds), *Racism, School and the Labour Market,* Leicester, National Youth Bureau, pp. 17–28.

Rubery, J. (1978) 'Structured labour markets, worker organisation and low pay', *Cambridge Journal of Economics,* 2, pp. 17–36.

Rubery, J. Tarling, R. and Wilkinson, F. (1984) 'Labour market segmentation theory: An alternative framework for the analysis of the employment system', paper presented to the British Sociological Association Conference, Bradford.

Shervish, P.G. (1983) *The Structural Determinants of Unemployment,* London, Academic Press.

Spilerman, S. (1978) 'Careers, labour market structure and socio-economic achievement'. *American Journal of Sociology,* 83, pp. 551–93.

Spilsbury, M. (1985) 'Employment trends in the USA youth labour market 1979–83'. *Working Paper No 11.* Labour Market Studies Group, University of Leicester.

Stafford, E. Jackson, P. and Banks, M. (1980) 'Employment, work involvement and mental health in less qualified young people', *Journal of Occupational Psychology,* 53, pp. 291–304.

Turbin, J. (1984) *The Implementation of the Youth Training Scheme in Three Local Labour Markets,* Labour Market Studies Group, University of Leicester.

Walker, A. (1982) *Unqualified and Underemployed,* London, Macmillan.

WEST, M. and Newton, P. (1983) *The Transition from School to Work*, London, Croom Helm.

WESTWOOD, S. (1984) *All day, Every day*, London, Pluto Press.

WILKINSON, F. *et al*. (Eds) (1981) *The Dynamics of Labour Market Segmentation*, London, Academic Press.

WILLIS, P. (1977) *Learning to Labour*, Farnborough, Saxon House.

WILLIS, P. (1984) 'Youth unemployment: A new social state', *New Society*, March 29, pp. 475–7.

YOUTHAID, (1979) *Study of the Transition from School to Working Life*, London, Youthaid.

9   Rural Youth Labour Markets

Jill Turbin and Elliot Stern

Introduction

Research into youth labour markets has expanded alongside rapidly rising unemployment for young people and associated changes in the UK industrial structure. Such research has undoubtedly increased our understanding of ways young people gain access to employment opportunities and their status within the labour market. However, much of the research which has made a contribution to both theoretical and policy debates has been conducted within an urban context.[1] While this is understandable given the relative severity and visibility of youth unemployment in Britain's inner cities and major towns, measures to improve the access of young people to work and other 'remedies' for youth unemployment implicitly assume that urban and rural circumstances are the same. The research on which this paper is based[2] is one of very few attempts to examine the labour market in which young people seek employment in rural England.[3]

The research study looked at the range of work opportunities open to young people and the problem of youth unemployment in rural areas. This entailed a discussion as to whether there is a distinct rural quality about the access to work and training for those young people living outside of an urban environment. The research was also conducted with policy questions in mind. In particular it sought to clarify whether current policies to counter youth unemployment, provide training and open up access to jobs were appropriate in rural areas of England.

The research concentrated on four rural areas of England: the districts of Hambleton in North Yorkshire, Harborough in Leicestershire, the Forest of Dean in Gloucestershire and North Norfolk. The study took district boundaries as an initial point of departure, without in any way suggesting that they constitute local labour markets. Within these areas information was collected about local industrial and employment structures, training policies, and the recruitment and employment practices of firms. The research drew upon information gathered specifically for the study — interviews with employers, and young people as well as secondary sources — census material and information provided by county and district councils.

This chapter does not consider differences in employment structure and young peoples' opportunities between the four areas except where such differences are important in understanding particular issues. The main study report explores differences between areas more fully.[4] The employment structure and economic activity that have an overall effect young people across four rural areas.

The chapter is in two main parts. The first considers aspects of rural employment structure and economic activity that have an overall effect on employment opportunities for both young people and adults. For example, it discusses the nature of rural labour markets; describes rural economic activity; and highlights the characteristics of local firms. The second part of the chapter looks more specifically at the situation for young workers although it is not always possible to do this in isolation from the circumstances within the labour market for both adult and young people. Taking this problem into account we look briefly at the labour market for young people in a rural area, consider the effects of employers' recruitment and post-school training provision on job opportunities, and review the question of youth wages. The chapter concludes by drawing together some of the main themes discussed and identifies a number of policy issues particularly relevant to the enhancement of employment and training opportunities in rural areas. It should be noted that the research upon which this chapter is based was limited in scope and conceived of as a pilot study. As such it touches on many complex issues: definitions of urban and rural, the nature and even existence of rural labour markets and the position of youth labour outside of England's towns and cities. Neither this chapter nor the research on which it is based can do justice to all of these issues but it is set within this wider framework.

Employers and Employment in Rural Areas

Rural Labour Markets

There are a number of difficulties in discussing employment opportunities in rural areas. Whilst it may well make sense to consider urban employment structure within a local labour market such well defined geographic boundaries are not usually present in rural areas. Labour market studies frequently define locality in terms of Department of Employment 'travel-to-work' areas. This makes sense for urban but not rural areas, given the latter's scattered population distribution and the reliance many people living there have on urban work opportunities. Many rural areas are, for example, included within travel-to-work areas dominated by one or two urban conurbations. It would be difficult to find a rural area which could be considered purely as a local labour market. The problem of defining a rural labour market is further complicated because people living within rural areas frequently work in nearby towns and cities. Though this may reflect inadequate rural opportunities for employment, many people choose to live away from major urban centres. Dormitory villages and towns in rural areas are characterized by an absence of industrial development. These are commonly found on the fringes of urban centres of employment. Work opportunities open to young people living on the urban fringe are not limited to a rural hinterland and the study has had to take this into account. One conclusion of this research is that the employment opportunities open to the rural young have to be considered in terms of varying degrees of access to urban centres of employment.

There are employers and employees operating largely or exclusively within rural catchment areas and for these it makes sense to look at the structure and availability of work within a rural context. This is particularly the case for more isolated rural areas which accord more with notions of a self-contained labour market. In these cases young people's opportunities for work may be limited to a relatively small geographical area. However, the term labour-market has generally been used in this research to refer to a collection of firms and people operating within a given area without assuming rigid geographical boundaries.

The Four Study Areas

Rural labour markets are no more homeogeneous than their urban counterparts. The study took four districts which were different with regard to industrial base, employment structure, geographical location and levels of unemployment. Though it is not intended to fully describe these four districts a brief description is useful in order to understand the diverse nature of rural employment and set the subsequent discussion into context.

Hambleton in North Yorkshire can be described as a 'traditional' rural area, particularly where it borders Ryedale to the East and Richmondshire to the West. It is geographically isolated and economically dependent on agriculture. In the south of the district, close to the city of York and in the north where it borders Teesside, the area has an urban fringe quality. In addition the central tranche of Hambleton has excellent rail and road trunk routes: the main line to Edinburgh and the A1 both cut through the area. The central area has greater concentrations of industry and population, particularly around the two market towns of Northallerton and Thirsk. The study area was extended to include parts of Ryedale, a more isolated area although the population density of both areas is about a quarter of the national average.[5]

The Harborough district borders several urban conurbations: in the south-west its population looks to Rugby, Coventry and Birmingham, in the north it comes under the influence of the City of Leicester while the south-east looks to Kettering and Northampton. Almost half the economically active population work outside their district of residence. It is therefore difficult to see the district as an economic entity. The population of Harborough also reflects its urban fringe quality: it has a high proportion of social classes 1 and 2 amongst its residents, a substantial number of whom live in the district but commute to work in the urban areas. It has a population density less than half the national average.

The Forest of Dean has a long industrial tradition. These industries were first of all in primary or extractive activities, particularly in coal mining. The last coal mine closed in the early 1960s. Fortunately this industrial decline was accompanied by the move into the area of several large national and multi-national companies. In particular Mitcheldean became the base for Rank Xerox which at its peak employed over 4700 people. The Forest of Dean's ex-industrial status derives from the dramatic cut-back of these national and international companies located in the district, Rank Xerox now employs about 1000 people on its Mitcheldean site. The Forest's industrial tradition is reflected in a relatively high population density, a high proportion of the population engaged in manufacturing, and high rates of unemployment.

North Norfolk is a 'traditional' rural area, offering seasonal employment. A relatively high proportion of its population work in agriculture, and it is within one of the most isolated counties in England. Public transport within the district is limited and the condition of local roads makes private travel also difficult. The district's seasonal character has two bases. First, the food processing industry — with fishing along the coasts and vegetable growing inland — employs significant numbers of seasonal workers. Second, tourism is an important source of employment and revenue in both coastal resorts and inland on the Broads. Finally, North Norfolk has a below average number of young people and an above average number of elderly people. Younger people continue to leave the area to find work. In recent years many less successful hotels and guest houses have been converted to residential hotels for the elderly.

Despite their obvious differences the four areas also share common features. All four had a lower rate of unemployment than the national average.[6] Two of the areas, Harborough and Hambleton, were areas where unemployment was particularly low in comparison to Great Britain being 5.7 per cent in Harborough and 7.7 per cent in Hambleton in October 1986 as compared with a national figure of 13.4 per cent. North Norfolk and the Forest of Dean were rural areas with much higher rates of unemployment (10.2 per cent and 12.3 per cent respectively) although these were still lower than the national average. Unemployment is less visible in a rural context and this had often led to resources being concentrated in nearby urban areas where unemployment is seen as being more urgent and politically sensitive. Moveover, in many agricultural districts and tourist resorts, seasonal unemployment is regarded more as an immutable characteristic of the area rather then as an economic and social problem to be solved.

In line with national trends youth unemployment is proportionately higher than adult unemployment.[7] Even where unemployment rates are low, as in Harborough, youth unemployment rates are high and in the Forest of Dean rates of unemployment for young females were higher than the national average. In recent years, the operation of government schemes such as the YTS has reduced these rates for the school leaver group and the community programme has alleviated the problem for older young people. However, despite generally lower rates of unemployment, youth unemployment is still a particular problem within rural areas.

Other shared characteristics of rural areas are discussed in more detail in later sections. Poor public transport and road links are a characteristic of many rural areas and have an important effect on access to employment opportunities. This must be seen in conjunction with often inadequate public services and sources of information. In particular access to job seeking advice and training facilities is often difficult and this influences the range of job opportunities open to young people.

Economic Activity in Rural Areas

There are widely held stereotypes of the rural economy. These stereotypes encompass the structure of rural labour markets and the types of employers and firms to be found in a rural setting. Traditional rural activities have been seen as primarily in agricultural or in craft-based industries. Rural craft industries continue to exist in England and many have enjoyed a renaissance as part of the tourist economy. However, in absolute numbers craft-based employment is not a significant proportion of total employment in most areas. Agriculture, however, remains an important activity within much of rural England, even though numbers employed in agriculture have declined markedly over the last decade and nationally now accounts for only a small proportion of employment. Both Hambleton and North Norfolk have an economy historically based on forms of agriculture and still employ proportionately more residents in agriculture than the national average of 2.2 per cent. The comparable figures for the economically active population are 12.9 per cent in Hambleton and 11.8 per cent in North Norfolk. However, both manufacturing and service sectors employ proportionately more in both areas.

Many firms within rural areas are in some way dependent upon, or have emerged out of, an agricultural base. Whilst few people are now directly employed in agriculture, the number of firms indirectly supported can be substantial. For example, food processing industries in North Norfolk have located near their source of supply of vegetables and shellfish. In Hambleton market towns have become important centres of employment for farm services such as grain merchants, and agricultural engineers. In both areas agricultural machinery manufacture is a long standing tradition. The fortunes of many firms in the manufacturing and service sectors are bound up with current developments and changes in agriculture.

The range of employers within the manufacturing sector can be as diverse in rural as in urban areas. Some rural areas, for example the Forest of Dean, have always had a strong industrial tradition. Others, like Harborough, do not appear to have any industrial structure which sets them apart from nearby urban centres. Within less isolated parts of rural England there exist a multitude of designated areas of industrial growth, supported by the local policies and initiatives of district and county councils. An example of such industrial developments could be seen in Hambleton, where advanced factory buildings are within easy reach of the A1. This major trunk route through a rural area has attracted incoming 'footloose' firms, tempted by greenfield sites and other incentives such as low rents and rates. More isolated rural areas, such as North Norfolk, do not however have the ability to attract footloose firms. They depend on local and established industries, and as a consequence do not offer as much diversity of employment opportunity as areas such as Harborough or Hambleton.

The service sector in rural areas is generally under-developed. There are fewer supermarkets, building societies, cinemas, and other retail outlets. North Norfolk and the Forest of Dean are particular examples of areas which have relatively few employers in the service sector. This has important implications for the range of employment opportunities as well as the quality of life of local residents

Another general feature of the employment structure of rural areas is the importance of the public sector in the provision of employment. Not only is the public sector a major employer in rural areas, it is often the mainstay of local private firms. For example, District Councils may support local construction firms and County Councils support much public transport, often through school bus operations. Hence the public sector is of importance in terms of the jobs it supports both directly and indirectly. There was some variation in public sector activity within the four areas included in this study. In all areas however, cutbacks in public sector expenditure have had a depressing effect not only on jobs directly within the public sector, but on firms that relied on public agencies for their work.

Characteristics of Local Firms

The eighty firms included in this study, (twenty in each area) were chosen to reflect economic activity across the four areas. A small sample such as this could not expect to be strictly representative in any one area. Some of the main characteristics of these local firms were as follows:

The average size of employer was much smaller than might have been expected in a similar study conducted in an urban area. The smallest firm employed one person and the largest 1200. Most, however, were at the lower end of this range. Only 20 per cent employed more than 100 people whilst 36 per cent employed fewer than twenty.

Young people under 25 years of age accounted for 22 per cent of those employed in the eighty firms. Firms did not, as a general rule, employ young people in large numbers. Given the small size of firms in rural areas it is not surprising to find few employers with concentrations of young people.

The ownership patterns of firms ranged from the single owner independent business, to large subsidiary plants of multi-national companies. Within each of the four areas about half were independent local firms with a single place of trading. However, a significant number — twenty-five out of eighty — were part of a national or international group.

A third of the firms employed only full-time staff. Of those employing part-time staff the majority did not have substantial numbers of part-timers and in only sixteen firms did part-time working prove to be of any importance. The overwhelming majority of part-time work was undertaken by women, mostly in unskilled or semi-skilled positions, although clerical work also provided an important source of part-time employment.

In most firms males outnumbered female employees, and males were consistently employed in higher categories of skill than females. Even where males and females were recruited for the same level of skill, they often worked at different jobs.

Age segregation was also common, although with some jobs open to young people there is apt to be this type of initial segregation. Where young people were found working alongside adults, this was often in unskilled work, particularly alongside adult females. Young female workers are often disadvantaged in respect to the types of work for which they are considered.

Seasonal employment, although important in rural areas, is confined to certain sectors. For example, hotels will run off-season with only a skeleton staff. Hotels and other tourist related employers — such as restaurants, craft shops and other local retailers

— were important among seasonal employers. Agriculture and food processing firms also tend to increase their workforce in line with seasonal peaks of activity.

Many of the characteristics noted above are likely to be found in an urban setting. Age and gender segregation, for example, appears to be a common feature of both urban and rural employment. The significance of part-time work also mirrors urban patterns. But there are distinctive features. One is the importance of seasonal work, and a second is the small size of local firms — both in this sample and in the overall population of rural enterprises. Another distinctive feature is patterns of ownership and independence. As described earlier, the full range was encountered from the locally owned to the subsidiaries of multi-national groups. What was striking was that in some rural areas one or two subsidiary firms effectively dominated the local labour market, particularly where location was related to sources of supply, as was the case in some of the food processing industries. This often occurred alongside a significant number of small traditional, local employers.

Various consequences for rural employment can be traced back to the characteristics of firms that have just been described. Yet one of the most important conclusions of this research is that rural employment structures are not uniform. Rather the diversity of employment opportunities can be understood best by reference to the particular mix of firms and activity found in any one locality. Thus, North Norfolk firms in the sample employed higher proportions of males in semi- and unskilled work than in other areas. These firms also employed higher proportions of seasonal workers, and were often engaged in food processing activities that offered fewer skilled opportunities. By contrast, Hambleton and the Forest of Dean were favoured with firms that employed a larger proportion of highly skilled and technical staff; both areas have firms that operate in industries using, and in some cases manufacturing, advanced technology.

The particular distribution of small and large firms, the former tending to be locally owned and the latter tending not to be, also has important consequences. Small firms are less able to train, both on-the-job because of lack of supervision, and off-the-job because of a general lack of resources. Larger firms controlled by national headquarters based in a distant city, have limited autonomy to decide on recruitment, training and the disposition of labour. About a third of firms in this sample had key decisions made outside the locality in this way; and they were often the largest employers of labour.

Categories of jobs available in a rural area also relate in part to size and ownership of local firms. There is not an inevitable congruence, for example, between economic activity and available work. Large subsidiary employers often concentrate a limited range of jobs in their rural branches, and frequently, these are unskilled jobs. One feature of these firms is tht management and technical positions are filled from outside the area. They are not available to local job applicants. On the other hand an independently owned larger local firm operating in the same sector may have a broader range of jobs, from unskilled to skilled, technical and managerial, available locally.

Finally, it appears that the mix of local firms is a good indicator of the growth potential in employment terms of a local labour market. Small local indigenous firms, are constrained by the scope of their local customer markets. In areas where the public sector predominates, policies to restrain the growth of public sector employment are influential. The data from this study also suggests that locally owned rural firms with national or regional markets have been a significant source of local employment growth over recent years. The relative buoyancy of the Hambleton economy seems to be associated with a higher proportion of such independent local firms than elsewhere. In contrast North Norfolk has higher proportions of both very small local employers and larger subsidiary employers. This argument has important policy implications. It suggests why some policies to expand rural employment are more successful than others given a particular local economic structure. This has implications for all those seeking work in rural areas whether adults or young people.

Employment and Training of Young People

The Labour Market for Young People

In none of the four study areas was there any evidence of a completely separate and distinct labour market for young people. There were, of course, jobs for which young people were not considered and jobs for which employers preferred to recruit young people. There were also many instances where young people would be considered alongside adults, although in the main this was for unskilled or less commonly, semi-skilled work. However, it does make sense to consider the position of young people within the labour market separately from that of adults, because they are often disadvantaged in terms of their access to available employment opportunities. The situation facing young people has to be considered not only in terms of the occupations in which they can be found, but also in terms of the recruitment and training policies of employers. These policies and their associated practices constitute a specific rural dimension in the situation facing young rural job-seekers.

Young people's employment follows a similar pattern for that of adults in the study areas. There was a predictable difference in the numbers of young people in management and other senior positions — more evident among females than males. However, there was still a disparity between adult males and young males with respect to skilled labour and similarly, fewer young females were found in clerical work, although it still remains their most important source of employment. At all levels, however, young people in comparison to adults, are proportionately underrepresented in skilled occupations and proportionately over-represented in semi- and unskilled work.

There is nothing particularly rural about the picture painted here. However, because much of the work available in rural areas is unskilled or semi-skilled in nature, more young people enter unskilled or semi-skilled occupations. This is particularly the case in areas which have a high proportion of subsidiary industries operating in the capital intensive side of the manufacturing sector, as is the case in North Norfolk. Such firms are not only among the most important sources of employment in rural areas, but often dominate the local recruitment market conditions, set local rates of pay and powerfully influence local policy.

There are, of course, openings for skilled labour in all rural areas, many in small traditional firms and labour intensive manufacturing and engineering industries. However, the access young people have to such opportunities may be severely limited by the recruitment and training policies of employers. The decline of apprenticeships and an unwilling-ness of the smaller employer to train has led to a shortage of sheltered points of access for youg people entering work.

Rural areas such as the Forest of Dean with its strong manufacturing base, have had until recently many more skilled manual jobs than other more 'traditional' rural areas. Similarly, areas which have good road or rail links, such as parts of Hambleton, are likely to have both a greater concentration and variety of employment. This can lead to differences in occupational opportunity within a given area. For example, the opportuni-ties for young people living near these centres of employment would be very different to those facing young people in more isolated parts of the area. In some parts of rural England small high technology firms have emerged which can increase the supply of skilled or technician jobs. With the exception of parts of Ryedale, however, such new industries were not in abundance. Local policy makers and industrialists often spoke of such jobs more as a potential than an actual source of employment.

One of the more obvious features of the rural labour market was the lack of professional/career occupations open to young people. The access young people had to the available jobs in this category was likely to be diminished by the recruitment procedures of employers. Large subsidiary companies often have centralized systems of career progression and re-cruitment for managerial and professional staff. This situation was also found to some extent in the public sector, where professional and mana-gerial jobs were commonly taken by people living outside the rural area.

The prospects facing young people within a rural locality must, of course, be seen with the opportunities for working outside of the rural environment. As pointed out earlier, rural opportunities for work must include an assessment of the employment available in nearby urban areas. However, with some exceptions it appeared to be the older age groups who were most likely to commute to nearby urban areas for work. For example, many residents in Harborough did not work within the district, a significant number of these being employed in professional and/or managerial occupations. In more isolated areas, travel to such centres of employment may not be feasible or be difficult for young people without access to private transport. Even where public transport exists, young people are likely to be recruited only if there is no other option. For example, weather conditions in the Forest of Dean often make travel difficult in the winter months and local people are therefore regarded in Gloucester as less reliable than urban job seekers. Whilst young people can compete for work in major urban areas, they are likely to be disadvantaged in comparison to town dwellers. High unemployment in neighbouring urban centres may further reduce the scope for work opportunities. It is not unheard of for young people in urban areas to compete for rural jobs.

Recruitment and Access to Employment

The way in which firms recruit has been shown to affect the access young people have a jobs. The level of training provision can compound the effects of initial discrimination within the labour market by reducing the number of jobs which offer a sheltered point of access to young people. In rural areas poor opportunities for work may be the cumulative outcome of the recruitment policies of employers, poor training provision within firms and the absence of firms with internal labour markets recruiting a significant proportion of their 'career' jobs from the locality. The distribution of types of employer can also be crucial in determining the availability of sheltered points of job access for young people.

One of the most striking features of the rural workforce is how close they live to their employment. Notwithstanding the high proportion of residents working in nearby urban settlements, rural employers themselves would appear to recruit locally. The majority of employees in the study sample lived in the immediate vicinity of their place of employment usually within a five mile radius. This often required living within the same town or village. Only a small number of employees relied on public transport to get them to work, most using private transport when travel was necessary.

The recruitment of labour from a local area was usually a conscious policy on the part of the employer, many of whom stated they would only consider local people for available jobs. In a few instances there was evidence to suggest that this had occurred as a consequence of rationalization over the last few years which had effectively squeezed non-locals (that is, those from a neighbouring town or village) out of local employment.

Only 27 per cent of employers interviewed reported that transport difficulties posed recruitment problems. This was not surprising given the practice of recruiting from a small geographical area. Transport would appear to be much more of a problem for individuals than for firms in rural areas. This has particular implications for the recruitment of young people who generally do not have access to their own transport. In the four study areas, young people living in small and particularly isolated villages were restricted in the areas they could envisage seeking work. Even if they could get to a particular job, recruitment practices of employers tended to discriminate against them vis-a-vis more local job applicants.

An important exception to this generalization is illustrated by the plight of firms located within rural areas on the urban fringe. They may have poor public transport links to their rural hinterland but reasonably good links to nearby towns. Small firms in the Harborough district, where unemployment was low, complained of recruitment difficulties, because they claimed it was easier for job seekers to get to major town and urban areas than it was for people living relatively nearby to travel to their premises. Young people had a slightly different view seeing transport to major urban areas being as problematic as transport within the area.

The channels through which employers recruited demonstrated a strong tendency towards informal methods of recruitment. This could well be more important in rural areas where the 'local grapevine' is of considerable importance. This is not to say that formal methods were not-used, indeed a combination of both formal and informal recruitment channels were used for both manual and non-manual work. On the surface then formal channels such as the job centre, and advertisements in the press would be used as much as less formal means such as word of mouth. Regular use of the job centre was reported by over two-thirds of the sample, with no significant variation between areas. About a third reported regular use of the careers service. There was some indication from the survey that the organization of YTS in rural areas may have reduced the contact between the careers service and employers.

Informal processes are also important in the allocation of jobs in rural areas. Frequently employers would recruit people on the basis of their family's reputation. Young people from disadvantaged families could be eliminated from job opportunities on this basis. The importance of social networks for influencing both who got to know of vacancies and who was selected was acknowledged by young people in all four areas.

In some instances even job centres and the careers service were perceived as part of the 'local grapevine'. In order to be effective, local staff had to plug into local networks. Although this could strengthen their links with local industry, it could also shift the role of such agencies from one of enhancing job opportunities to one of job allocation.

The phenomenon of informal networks was perhaps most striking in agricultural work. Jobs on farms rarely came to the notice of job centres or the careers service. Agricultural work was often the prerogative of certain families, either the children of farmers or of farm workers. The same was true of forestry. Even when the formal system was invoked, as with YTS, 'trainees' on one farm were frequently the sons of neighbouring farmers and vice versa.

These features are likely to be more pronounced in close-knit rural communities than in urban settings. The end result is that even within a rural community entire segments of the labour market may well be closed off to some young people whilst others occupy a more favourable position. This may be a consequence of the recruitment practices of firms, or the operation of informal networks, or because of the paucity of rural transport.

Training

It has already been noted that training opportunities are restricted in rural areas. Thus the unwillingness of small firms to train and the tendency of larger firms to concentrate work needing little training in their rural subsidiaries has been commented on. Training disadvantages can often be traced back to the poor facilities and resources for education and training within the area. This is reflected in the relatively low proportion of 16-year-olds staying on at school or college, particularly in the more isolated areas. In North Norfolk for example only 38 per cent of 16-year-olds were still in full-time education. in Harborough, a less isolated rural area, this figure was 54 per cent, more in line with the national average. Neither Hambleton nor North Norfolk have a college of further education within the district and in all four study areas skill centres were distant and their courses were over-subscribed. Overall, however, the inadequacy of training facilities must be seen in conjunction with the poor range of employment opportunities in some rural areas. Low staying-on rates and the absence of colleges of further education may reflect the industrial character of an area.

The implications of these observations, all of which interact with each other, are considerable. For example, North Norfolk has a low proportion of 16-year-olds staying on at school and also lacks locally-based training and further education provision. Even YTS is affected by this with young people having to travel to Norwich, Great Yarmouth and Kings Lynn for college-based courses and off-the-job training. Employers are reportedly unwilling to release young people partly because of long journey times and partly because they are unused to training their workforce. Many local people, young and old are trapped by their lack of education and training and by their lack of physical access to resources that do exist. According to job centre managers, there are jobs available even in rural areas with few job opportunities: to those with skills, but the nearest TOPS courses are in Norwich and are heavily over-subscribed. A recent survey of Norfolk small firms[8] confirms that recruitment difficulties are greater in rural Norfolk than its urban centres and that 80 per cent of these difficulties are ascribed to skill shortages.

The Forest of Dean shares some problems in common with North Norfolk, that is, a lower percentage of 16-year-olds staying on at school compared with the country as a whole, and many small firms with no tradition of training. On the other hand it has a much stronger manufacturing sector which in the past provided apprenticeships for many male workers. Partly because of this a further education college is located in the centre of the Forest. Despite the decline of apprenticeships the College still retains a key role in training in the area and runs a major YTS scheme.

The lower skill composition of rural areas is bound to have some effect of the amount of training carried out by employers. However, this is heightened by the practice of many small firms in recruiting 'experienced' or 'skilled' labour thus fewer opportunities for skilled work, or progression within a firm, are available to young people. Many of the firms in this study trained at only a very basic level, often for a specific job within the firm. Of the eighty employers, 22 per cent only used informal methods of training (on-the-job training or 'sitting with nellie') and 21 per cent gave no training at all. Only a minority of employers used industry-based or group training programmes and less than half the employers used further education colleges as part of their training.

When training is given by firms it is almost exclusively end-on to schooling. Very little training is aimed at adults and young people over 18 years of age are frequently regarded as too old to train. Within the four study areas there was some indication that the YTS had heightened this disparity by concentrating resources still further on the school leaver group.

The YTS has become an increasingly common route into work and training opportunities in both urban and rural areas. The operation of the YTS was considered within the four study areas in order to assess its possible impact on the recruitment of young people. In rural areas YTS is less likely to be run by employers than in urban areas. Because of the number of small employers and the difficulties they have in organizing training, YTS operates largely through 'umbrella' managing agencies. For example, in North Norfolk and Harborough, the majority of YTS places are arranged through private training organizations or consortiums or, in the case of the Forest of Dean, the local college. These managing agencies provide, or arrange, the off-the-job training element of the scheme, and place trainees with employers for work experience. The consequence of this arrangement is that many small employers, for whom running their own scheme would be difficult, are able to participate. It also means that employers have less control over the selection of trainees, the training they receive and in some cases, less commitment to the scheme.

It is difficult to gauge the impact of YTS through a small survey of employers. In the four areas as a whole only 37 per cent of the employers used YTS in any way. Of those who did, there was little evidence to suggest that it had increased recruitment of young people overall. It appeared to encourage a shift from older young people to school leavers rather than opening up additional opportunities. In line with national experience there were instances where the scheme had genuinely allowed more or improved training and others where it was used instead of established, formal means of recruitment. In a rural area there may also be problems of quality control and monitoring placements due to the geographical dispersion of work placements.

Youth Wages

The level of youth wages was a contentious issue at the time this study was undertaken. The removal of young people from the statutory protection of wages councils is built on an assumption that current wage levels are to the detriment of young peoples' employment prospects. In considering this wages issue employers were asked how their employment and recruitment was affected by wage rates. Their replies were then considered in relation to the position of the firm in the local labour market.

Wage rates are generally lower than the national average in all rural areas. This was the case in the four study areas, for young people and adults alike and in fact only 15 per cent of employers reported that youth wages were too high. Even fewer employers, seven out of the eighty in the sample (9 per cent), reported that they would recruit more young people if youth wages were lower.

The issue of wages is a complex one and full discussion is beyond the scope of this chapter. However, it did not appear that wage levels adversely affected the employment of young people and in some circumstances young people were employed as cheap labour. The issue of wage levels for young people has to be seen on two interconnecting levels. First, the internal organization, market and business situation of an employer and second the position of a firm within the local labour market.

The internal organization and skill composition of a firm has implications for the employment of young people. As already noted, very few rural firms in the sample employed large concentrations of young people. In those few cases where large numbers of young people were employed it was often in labour intensive unskilled jobs, where adults and young people were in open competition for available work. In these instances, where youth and adult labour were substitutable, firms often employed young people precisely because they were cheaper than adults.

Even in the same sector firms might have quite different internal labour market and manpower strategies which influenced their wages policies. For example, one small hotel in this study traded in the relatively high value-added market for business accommodation. It was able to pay above average wages to its younger employees, but, because of the quality of the service it aimed to provide, it preferred to have a balance between younger and more experienced staff. Another small hotel in North Norfolk relied on seasonal and less profitable holiday trade. It almost entirely depended on very young workers, often school-children on holiday, who were paid very low wages.

Arguments as to the high level of youth wages frequently assume that employers always pay the lowest rate of pay. For many employers in the survey, capable of setting their own rates of pay, considerations such as quality of worker, commitment to work and motivation were as important as, if not a part of, achieving maximum profitability. In the case of the first employer, wage rates were an integral part of the internal structure of the firm and were seen as a means of securing commitment to the hotel and hence reducing labour turnover. For firms employing young people and adults in skilled occupations this was seen as being particularly important.

Wage levels in a firm could not be properly considered without reference to the local labour market. In the Harborough district with its low levels of unemployment and higher levels of average pay, a super-market manager regarded his wage rates (set for him by a London-based head office) as too low to allow him to compete locally for labour, includ-ing youth labour. In contrast a supermarket manager in the Forest of Dean faced no such problems given the less competitive nature of his local labour market.

The determinants and consequences of youth wages is part of a complex interaction between factors internal and external to the firm. In other words, as with urban so with rural firms. There were, however, at least two expressions of the youth wages issue that appear to have a particularly rural flavour. For example, local firms with particularly low levels of pay were often unable to compete in the labour market, that is, they could not attract the skilled labour that they needed, or young people for training positions. This problem was exacerbated when a significant local employer such as the subsidiary of a major national firm, dominated the wage rates the terms and conditions in a rural labour market.

A striking feature of this sample of rural firms was the number that were struggling on the margins of commercial survival. These marginal firms were concerned about all their costs, including wage costs. Their view of youth wages, namely, that they were too high, was coloured by their broader economic anxieties. Similar concerns undoubtedly exist among marginal urban firms. However the limited scope of rural markets for goods and services probably puts a higher proportion of firms on the margins of economic survival. If this hypothesis is correct then discussions about youth wages in a rural context have to be informed by these concerns. For example, there are particular implications for policy interventions to reduce unemployment which are explored more fully below.

Conclusions

This chapter has described the nature of rural labour markets and the position facing young job seekers in four rural areas. The discussion of labour markets has been shown to be problematic in rural areas, both because of the lack of geographically confined travel-to-work areas, and sometimes because of the proximity of towns and cities; nor was there any evidence of a distinct youth labour market separate from that for adults.

Many of the features of rural youth employment that have been described are recognizable also in urban contexts. For example gender segregation and the lack of commitment of small firms to training are common findings in studies of urban labour markets. Yet the study was able to identify distinctive rural aspects of the employment opportunities facing young people. For example, the predominance of very small firms and the lack of local training resources create particular problems of access for young people to more skilled jobs. There is, in any case, often a rural shortage of career type jobs because of the mix of local firms. Poor transport reduces access to training as well as to employment and encourages firms to adopt recruitment policies that are geographically restrictive. This can be further exacerbated by social networks which exclude some young people and favour others in the local allocation of jobs.

Policy questions have been raised in this chapter at several points. The limited potential in terms of employment growth of many small firms in rural areas has been noted. Yet despite the small size of most firms, employment is disproportionately vested in a few large employers. This characteristic of rural employment has been acknowledged in the long term debate about the 'branch economy' and regional development in Britain over the last thirty years.[9] Reliance on the attraction of national firms and their subsidiaries has been an important part of traditional local economic development. The fruits of this policy have accelerated the increase in the unemployment in at least two of the study areas during the recent recession. It was these larger firms which shed most labour. The need for policies to encourage and support medium-sized independent but established rural firms is one implication of the research. This would be a substantial redirection of local policy given the current emphasis on encouraging new start-ups and inward investment.

The inability of small firms to train, the lack of training facilities in rural areas and the withdrawal of larger firms from training and apprenticeships also have important policy implications. Opening up opportunities for skilled jobs with career prospects will depend in part on improved access to training resources. This may be best met at a local level, or by improving access to training resources further afield. The latter solution depends ultimately on improved public transport given the dependency of young people in particular on public transport. Improvements in public transport would also have positive consequences, indirectly, for young people by influencing the recruitment practices of employers.

There was no evidence from the study's sample of employers that lowering current levels of youth wages would improve the employment prospects of young people. Youth labour was already substituted for adult labour in many cases, precisely because of its low cost. However in skilled jobs employers were as much concerned with the quality of labour as with its costs, and in order to attract high quality applicants they expected to pay above minimum rates. It may well be possible to drive down youth wages in rural areas still further, though the implications of such a policy would have to be assessed in both ethical as well as economic terms. If the policy aim is to improve the employment prospects of young people rather than to reduce the level of youth wages a variety of measures are called for. These may include training allowances which would be particularly important for small firms unable to provide their own resources to train. Employment subsidies are also relevant especially for economically marginal firms including new firms with some prospects of future growth but currently finding it difficult to finance both employment expansion and capital investment.

Finally, any discussion of the policy implications of this research needs to recognize that measures directed exclusively at improving the employment prospects of young people are likely to have redistributional effects in other parts of the labour market, for example, by encouraging employers to substitute youth labour for female adult labour. There is already evidence from this research that the advent of YTS has such redistributional effects by improving prospects of school leavers at the expense of 'older' young people.

Notes

1   See for example, Ashton, Maguire and Garland, V. (1982).
2   This research paper is based on a one-year pilot study into the problems of youth unemployment in rural areas. It was carried out by the Tavistock Institute of Human Relations for the Development Commission between December 1985 and December 1986. For a full report see Stern and Turbin (1986).
3   It is not the purpose of this chapter to discuss previous studies based within rural areas. For an example of contemporary research into rural labour markets, see Dench (1983) and for an example of a research project which looks at the

operation of government unemployment schemes in rural areas, see McDermott and Dench (1983).

4   Stern and Turbin (1986).

5   Population densities for the four study areas and Great Britain are as follows:

	Density per hectare
Hambleton	0.57
Harborough	1.03
Forest of Dean	1.38
North Norfolk	0.85
Great Britain	2.38

6   Unemployment rates for the four areas, in April 1981 and October 1985 were as follows:

	April 1981 percentages	October 1985 percentages
Hambleton	6.8	7.7
Harborough	6.0	5.7
Forest of Dean	8.1	12.3
North Norfolk	8.1	10.2
Great Britain	9.8	13.4

(*Source*: 1981 Census of Population. Employment Gazette, November 1985, Vol. 93, No. 11)

7   Percentage rates of unemployment for young people, 16–19 years of age, in April 1981, were as follows:

	Males	Females
Hambleton	12.8	15.4
Harborough	12.8	10.9
Forest of Dean	17.4	21.4
North Norfolk	15.2	12.3
Great Britain	19.3	17.4

Source: Population Census 1981.

8   Sapsford (1985).

9   See Massey (1984) and Marquand (1979).

References

ASHTON, D.N. MAGUIRE M.J. and GARLAND, V. (1982) *Youth in the Labour Market*, London, Department of Employment Research Paper no 34.

DENCH, S.,(1983) 'A rural youth labour market — Opportunities and potentials', paper presented at the British Sociological Association Conference.

McDERMOTT, K. and DENCH, S. (1983) *Youth Opportunities in a Rural Area: A Study of YOP in Mid-Wales*, MSC, Research and Development Series no 14.

MARQUAND, J., (1979) *The Service Sector and Regional Policy*, London, Centre for Environmental Studies.

MASSEY, D. (1984) *Spatial Divisions of Labour*, London, Macmillan.

SAPSFORD, D. (1985) *A Study of Aspects of Local Economic Development Initiatives*, Economics Research Centre, University of East Anglia.

STERN, E. and TURBIN, J. (1986) *Youth Employment and Unemployment in Rural England: Report of a One Year Pilot Study in Four Rural Areas*, Development Commission.

10   Youth Rates of Pay and Employment

Ken Roberts, Sally Dench and Deborah Richardson

The Market Solution

Orthodox economic theory explains how market forces can clear unemployment if allowed to operate freely. A surplus of labour, whatever the source, is supposed to trigger a chain reaction beginning with downward pressure on wages. Labour supply should then diminish. Workers discouraged by low pay or by their difficulty in obtaining any jobs are expected to retire from the workforce permanently or temporarily for leisure, to concentrate on domestic work, or to acquire further education and training thereby upgrading their skills and market value. Simultaneously, lower wages are supposed to boost labour demand. New jobs are anticipated as entrepreneurs discover that lower wage-costs and selling-prices enable them to market more goods and services. In addition, cheaper workers are supposed to make replacing labour with capital less attractive. Neo-liberal economists argue that, given the freedom of the market, a sufficiently entrepreneurial culture will discover uses for all resources, including labour. They claim that markets are our most efficient decision-takers and resource-mobilizers and that regulating or restricting markets to reduce or mitigate so-called social costs is likely to inflict even greater longer-term social and economic damage (Littlechild, 1978; Institute of Economic Affairs, 1979; Parker, 1982).

Mass unemployment has become an international problem in the 1980s. Virtually all regions of Britain are affected to some extent, but certain sections of the workforce, particularly unskilled adults and young people, have proved particularly vulnerable, and, especially for these groups, the erosion of rigidities erected by welfare benefits, Wage Councils and collective bargaining, thereby allowing rates of pay to float downwards, has been recommended as a main plank in a strategy for returning to full employment. There is no contradiction, given neo-liberal theoretical premises, between recommending greater incentives for entrepreneurs, such as opportunities to earn and retain higher profits, and lower-wages for the already relatively low-paid. The prescriptions are complementary rather than at cross-purposes. Profitable enterprises are required to create jobs, and lower wage-costs help to make enterprises profitable.

There is evidence that the cost of employing young people contributed to the particularly sharp rise in youth unemployment after the mid-1970s. The gap between youth and adult earnings narrowed during the 1960s and early 1970s. Raising the school-leaving age, lowering the age of majority, full employment and trade union pressure all contributed to the compression of age differentials (Wells, 1983). These earlier trends appear to have made young people particularly vulnerable during subsequent recessions, shake-outs and occupational restructuring. If overpricing was a reason for the rise in youth unemployment, then it may seem reasonable to recommend lower pay to revive demand for youth labour.

Encouraging youth rates to float downwards has been among the post-1979 government's strategies for combating youth unemployment. The allowances fixed under the Youth Opportunities Programme (YOP) then the Youth Training Scheme (YTS) have been well-beneath average youth earnings, and have not kept abreast of inflation since 1978. Between 1982 and 1986 the Young Workers Scheme (YWS) subsidized youth employment provided wages were beneath a ceiling which was set between YOP/YTS allowances and average youth earnings. These measures were designed to shatter inertia and encourage youth pay to settle at 'realistic' levels where market forces would begin to clear unemployment.

Youth-adult pay differentials have widened since 1979. This part of the chain-reaction has worked, but there has been no revival of youth employment. Is this only because more time and patience are required? Should more of the same medicine be prescribed? (Minford, 1983). Young people are being relieved of Wage Council 'protection'. Further reductions in their social security entitlements, even denying supplementary benefit to under-18-year-olds thereby withdrawing the 'option' of unemployment, are also being considered.

No-one argues that exorbitant pay has been the sole reason for the steady rise in youth unemployment since the 1960s, or the particularly sharp rise since the late-1970s. Some writers emphasize straightforward demand deficiency and argue that new entrants have always borne an exceptionally heavy share of rising unemployment (Makeham, 1980; Raffe, 1984). Others stress how structural economic and technological changes have eradicated many jobs, especially the less skilled occupations that 16-year-olds once entered (Ashton and Maguire, 1983). Structural explanations encourage a search for structural remedies, such as the reform of education and training to align beginners' capabilities with changing job requirements. Alongside its search for a market solution the government has also backed these theories by authorizing the Technical and Vocational Education Initiative (TVEI) and the YTS which will train young people for up to two years from 1986. No-one denies that, all other things being equal, the cheaper young people become absolutely and relative to adults, the greater will be the demand for their services. However, there is a debate over how much credibility to attach to structural explanations, and how much reliance to place on structural remedies as opposed to simply allowing market forces to operate.

Up to now the debate on youth pay and employment has been conducted purely in theoretical terms, or aided by aggregate national data on trends in employment and rates of pay. However, the manipulators of this data acknowledge that correlations are not the same as causation. There is still a dearth of information on how youth rates of pay are actually fixed, how these rates influence employers' and young people's actual behaviour and, therefore, the likely effects of lower rates on the quantity and types of jobs available to school- and scheme-leavers.

Our study helps to fill this particular gap. The evidence is from parallel surveys during 1984–85 among managements in 308 establishments, and 854 17-18-year-olds from three local youth labour markets — Chelmsford, Liverpool and Walsall. The firms were quota samples from thirteen business sectors, and ranged in size from a minimum of five employees to as large as were operating in the areas. The young people were random samples of the age-group from local schools who had completed full-time education and entered the local labour markets. The firms supplied information on trends in employment — in the size, structure and composition of their workforces, about the jobs for which young people were preferred, eligible and excluded, about their uses of government schemes to promote youth training and employment, and on rates of pay at 16, 18 and for adults in different occupations. The young people gave details of their careers since leaving school in jobs, on the Youth Training Scheme and periods of unemployment, and about their incomes, earned and unearned. Those who were unemployed when interviewed were also questioned on their wage aspirations and the minimum pay they would accept.

This evidence sheds new light on how employers' and young people's labour market behaviour responds to variations in rates of pay and, we will argue, undermines confidence in the ability of the pay mechanism and market forces to clear youth unemployment in Britain in the 1980s. Our evidence shows that pay is only one of several influences on employers' and young workers' labour market behaviour, and is decisive in too few cases to sustain realistic hopes of cheaper youth labour draining the current pools of unemployment, especially in Britain's more depressed areas. Indeed, we will explain why the low pay 'solution' to youth unemployment is likely to aggravate an already serious problem of unemployment among young adults. Instead of lower youth pay encouraging employers to create stepping stones or bridges to adult rates and occupations, our evidence suggests that low-paid youth employment is currently

leading young adults into dead-ends and exposing them to an unemploy-
ment/poverty trap from which claimant roles may offer the most realistic
prospect of adult life-styles.

Rates of Pay

Firms were questioned about pay in the occupations to which 16-18-year-
old males, then females, were most likely to be recruited, and the findings
are in table 1. The 17-18-year-olds who were in employment were asked

Table 1: Employers survey: Earnings by sex and occupation (in percentages).

	Prof/tech		Clerical/sales		Skilled		Other	
	M	F	M	F	M	F	M	F
Age 16:								
Under £30	–		4	3	12	61	2	–
£30–39	9		7	18	20	26	15	21
£40–59	65		78	65	61	13	67	70
£60–79	17		13	13	6	–	13	9
£80–99	4		–	1	1	–	3	–
£100–149	4		–	–	–	–	–	–
£150–199	–		–	–	–	–	–	–
£200+	–		–	–	–	–	–	–
Age 18:								
Under £30	–		–	–	–	8	–	–
£30–39	–		7	5	4	21	–	–
£40–59	18		27	34	25	50	26	39
£60–79	46		57	52	46	21	52	53
£80–99	27		10	9	22	–	12	5
£100–149	10		–	1	3	–	10	2
£150–199	–		–	–	–	–	–	2
£200+	–		–	–	–	–	–	–
Adult rate:								
£30–39	–		–	–	–	–	–	2
£40–59	–		3	3	–	22	9	19
£60–79	12		22	42	11	52	30	44
£80–99	12		50	39	18	19	35	24
£100–149	60		13	16	55	4	22	10
£150–199	16		9	1	16	4	4	–
£200+	–		3	–	–	–	–	2
Age when adult								
rate paid								
16	–		–	1	–	–	–	3
17 or 18	23		27	31	18	24	56	60
19, 20, 21	64		57	59	77	72	39	35
22–25	14		10	6	3	4	5	2
Older	–		7	3	3	–	–	–
TOTAL	28		33	139	76	27	77	62

Table 2: Young people's survey: Occupations, gender and pay

Gross weekly pay	Managerial/ professional/ Technical	Clerical		Sales		Apprentice/skilled		Other	
	Male	Male	Female	Male	Female	Male	Female	Male	Female
-£30	4	–	1	4	4	2	9	1	4
-£40	4	–	7	19	21	11	52	19	19
-£60	29	17	47	35	51	45	35	33	50
-£80	39	50	36	31	17	28	4	25	17
-£100	18	21	6	11	6	11	–	10	8
Over £100	7	12	3	–	–	3	–	12	2
n	28	24	101	26	47	112	23	96	52

about their gross earnings and this evidence, organized by occupation and sex, is in table 2. These twin sources of information are wholly consistant and complementary, but the employers' evidence is the more comprehensive in covering pay at 16 and 18, the full adult rate, and the age from which this applied. The findings are complicated in detail, but the main messages are straightforward.

Boys earned slightly more than girls in similar occupations, not so much at 16 as at 18 and later. Among boys the earnings of craft apprentices, technician and professional trainees began to push well clear of office, sales and unskilled pay after age 18. Among girls there was a different occupational pay hierarchy. Female apprentices, mainly in hairdressing, clothing and leather goods, were behind at 16 and never caught up. Girls' sales, clerical and unskilled jobs offered similar pay until age 18, after which office salaries continued to rise whereas the others had already reached, or were close to full adult earnings.

There were slight mean differences between, but enormous variations in youth and adult rates for males and females in similar occupations. In the firms we surveyed, starting pay for 16-year-old male apprentices and unskilled workers, and for female sales ad clerical staff, ranged from under £30 to over £80 per week, and this was reflected in the 17-18-year-olds' reported earnings.

Geography and local labour market conditions do not explain these variations. Table 3 compares rates of pay in those occupations for which sufficient numbers of firms supplied information in Liverpool, Walsall and Chelmsford. Female clerical staff commanded higher pay in Chelmsford where there was a much stronger demand for this type of labour than in the other areas. However, in all other occupations the ranges of youth and adult rates, for males and females, were similar within each of the three areas. The local labour markets were not fixing going rates for different types of labour with which local employers then conformed.

The absence of clearer inter-area differences is surprising, given the different balances between supply and demand in the local labour markets. Only 8 per cent of the Chelmsford 17-18-year-olds were unemployed when interviewed, compared with 28 per cent in Walsall and 41 per cent in Liverpool. Sixty-one per cent of unemployed respondents said that they were prepared to work for less than £40 per week. The Walsall and Liverpool employers would have experienced little difficulty in attracting youth labour, certainly to sales and unskilled jobs, at such rates of pay, but only a minority were taking advantage.

How Youth Rates Are Fixed

Explaining intra-occupational and intra-area inequalities in youth pay requires attention to how employers fix beginners' rates. The figures

Table 3: Employers Survey: Pay by area (in percentages)

	Female sales and clerical			Males skilled			Males unskilled			Females unskilled		
	Liverpool	Walsall	Chelms-ford	Liverpool	Walsall	Chelms-ford	Liverpool	Walsall	Chelms-ford	Liverpool	Walsall	Chelms-ford
Age 16:												
Under £30	5	3	2	11	15	8	5	–	–	–	–	–
£30–39	18	34	6	16	15	29	19	14	11	28	19	15
£40–59	52	53	86	58	69	54	62	68	72	61	77	69
£60–79	25	9	4	16	–	4	14	9	17	11	4	15
£80–99	–	–	2	–	–	4	–	9	–	–	–	–
£100–149	–	–	–	–	–	–	–	–	–	–	–	–
£150–199	–	–	–	–	–	–	–	–	–	–	–	–
£200+	–	–	–	–	–	–	–	–	–	–	–	–
Age 18:												
Under £30	–	–	–	–	–	–	–	–	–	–	–	–
£30–39	4	9	2	5	8	33	35	20	24	56	24	50
£40–59	33	44	28	25	15	29	39	64	52	33	69	42
£60–79	49	41	62	45	62	25	13	4	19	–	7	8
£80–99	14	3	8	25	15	13	13	12	5	–	–	–
£100–149	–	3	–	–	–	–	–	–	–	6	–	–
£150–199	–	–	–	–	–	–	–	–	–	6	–	–
£200+	–	–	–	–	–	–	–	–	–	–	–	–
Adult rate:												
£30–39	6	–	2	15	3	16	15	–	14	22	10	7
£40–59	42	53	32	10	27	12	30	28	33	44	50	36
£60–79	40	34	42	60	57	52	30	45	29	17	33	29
£80–99	10	13	24	15	13	20	19	24	24	11	7	14
£100–149	2	–	–	–	–	–	7	3	–	–	–	14
£150–199	–	–	–	–	–	–	–	–	–	6	–	–
£200+	–	–	–	–	–	–	–	–	–	–	–	–

Age when adult rate paid												
16	2	–	–	–	–	–	–	–	–	5	–	7
17 or 18	40	26	27	15	24	12	63	44	62	79	48	57
19, 20, 21	51	62	65	85	66	84	30	48	38	16	52	29
22–25	2	12	4	–	3	4	7	7	–	–	–	7
Older	4	–	4	–	7	–	–	–	–	–	–	–
TOTAL	52	42	52	20	30	25	27	29	21	19	30	14

Table 4: Employers survey: earnings by size of firm and occupation

	Female sales and Clerical				Males skilled		Male unskilled		Female unskilled		
	−25	−100	−500	Over 500	−25	−100	26–100	101–500	−25	−100	−500
Age 16:											
Under £30	9	2	—	4	18	13	—	—	—	—	—
£30–39	9	25	27	—	23	21	21	5	13	28	19
£40–59	70	66	59	70	59	58	74	77	75	72	69
£60–79	9	7	15	26	—	4	5	14	13	—	13
£80–99	4	—	—	—	—	4	—	5	—	—	—
£100–149	—	—	—	—	—	—	—	—	—	—	—
£150–199	—	—	—	—	—	—	—	—	—	—	—
£200+	—	—	—	—	—	—	—	—	—	—	—
Age 18:											
Under £30	4	—	3	—	5	4	—	—	—	—	—
£30–39	44	8	40	4	46	13	35	8	69	42	18
£40–59	44	40	51	75	36	54	48	67	25	58	71
£60–79	4	44	6	21	9	25	17	8	6	—	6
£80–99	4	8	—	—	5	4	—	17	—	—	—
£100–149	—	—	—	—	—	—	—	—	—	—	6
£150–199	—	—	—	—	—	—	—	—	—	—	—
£200+	—	—	—	—	—	—	—	—	—	—	—
Adult rate:											
£30–39	—	—	—	—	—	—	15	—	5	—	—
£40–59	8	4	49	28	26	4	33	36	32	32	—
£60–79	44	43	40	48	22	7	41	24	37	47	47
£80–99	24	41	9	24	35	68	11	32	16	21	29
£100–149	24	13	3	—	17	22	—	8	11	—	18
£150–199	—	—	—	—	—	—	—	—	—	—	—
£200+	—	—	—	—	—	—	—	—	—	—	6

Age when adult rate paid											
16	–	–	–	4	–	–	–	–	5	5	–
17 or 18	21	33	33	35	17	13	75	54	38	68	53
19, 20, 21	67	60	61	50	74	81	21	38	52	26	47
22–25	13	8	–	4	4	4	4	8	5	–	–
Older	–	–	6	8	4	4	–	–	–	–	–
TOTAL	25	54	36	26	23	27	27	25	19	19	17

themselves are sufficient to undermine the view that local markets set going rates with which firms then comply. We interviewed many employers who were aware that they were paying well in excess of the rates necessary to attract the quantity of labour required, but had no intention of changing their apparently irrational ways.

Larger firms tended to offer the higher wages (table 4), and one reason was that their rates were usually agreed through collective bargaining. Another reason was the operation of company-wide pay structures with which rates in particular branches and departments had to conform. Only 36 per cent of establishments in the employers' surveys were sole places of trading, and only a minority, 39 per cent of multi-site companies, gave local managements complete discretion in setting or negotiating pay. Recruitment, training and promotion decisions were more likely to be delegated to local levels. Managements in multi-site companies explained the advantages in company-wide pay agreements and structures. They feared leap-frogging, and wanted to avoid sections of their workforces feeling unfairly treated. In firms where these considerations applied, managements argued that trying to force youth rates down to local market levels would distort the companies' pay structures, and might provoke such industrial relations trouble as to outweigh any savings.

Other firms, small as well as large, believed that it served their own long-term interests to treat recruits more generously than competitor companies. Managements emphasized that youth pay was only a minute fraction of their total wage-bills and an even smaller proportion of total costs, and that they preferred to offer over-the-odds to attract good quality applicants, select the best, then boost their morale and motivation. They wanted young recruits to feel fairly treated, not exploited. In contrast, other firms saw no reason to offer more than the local market rates. Some managements had to be cost-conscious because their businesses were marginal; a common situation in clothing and catering establishments. Others were taking conscious decisions to save on wage-costs then cope with any motivation, morale and turnover problems in other ways.

Employers do not respond uniformly to common external labour market conditions which would allow youth rates to float downwards. Neither the employers' situations nor values are uniform. Hence the wide inequalities in earnings among young people from the same areas, with similar qualifications, in jobs of similar status that make apparently similar demands. These inequalities provoke complaints from all quarters. Young people on low pay complain of exploitation and, as explained below, are particularly likely to quit. Employers who offer 'good money' complain about low-wage cowboy competitors giving the younger generation huge chips on the shoulder. Low-wage employers also complain about young people with exaggerated ideas of their worth, trade unions that demand high starting rates, and managements who succumb to these pressures. Employers who offer £30 to beginners can protest that they are paying the fair, market rate.

A point to emphasize about inter-firm differences in youth rates is that the inequalities rarely arise because managements lack knowledge of labour market conditions, or are prevented by outside obstacles from lowering their rates to market levels. Managements' reasons for paying more than markets require usually arise from conceptions of their companies' own interests in avoiding internal anomalies, maintaining harmonious industrial relations, and preserving the quality and motivation of their workforces.

Pay and Recruitment

The market solution to youth unemployment begins to stall at the first hurdle with a selective rather than an across-the-board response when an abundance of youth labour presents opportunities to hold or force rates down and widen age differentials. The solution also stalls at a second crucial stage because, according to our evidence from employers, lower wages, even if introduced, do not lead to increased youth recruitment in the majority of companies.

Table 5 divides firms into extreme groups of 'youth' and 'adult' companies according to whether 16-18-year-olds were above- or below-average proportions of their current workforces *and* recruits during the previous year, then compares their rates of pay. This evidence confirms that relatively low youth wages are associated with relatively high youth recruitment and employment, but this was never in doubt. The debate concerns the strength of the relationship, and the same evidence shows that some firms were recruiting few young people despite low starting rates, while others with much higher rates of pay were well-into youth recruitment.

All firms were asked if they were likely to take-on more young people in the event of their wage-levels being reduced. Only 11 per cent said that they would 'definitely' or even 'possibly' do so. Some were amazed by the suggestion that youth pay might fall even lower, but the majority explained how, 'That isn't the way things work here' youth recruitment was determined by other, overriding considerations. Firms that were cutting-back and reducing their establishments, the situation in most large companies, explained that they would be unable to absorb new blood at any price. Natural wastage had nearly always been the firms' first-resort job-cutting strategy. It can reduce recruitment to a trickle for years and create situations where wage costs can make little difference to hiring levels or choices because of the overriding need to slim.

Firms that recruited young people to apprenticeships and other jobs with extended training were more likely to be gearing intakes to

Table 5: Rates of pay in youth and adult firms

	Female sales/clerical		Male skilled		Male unskilled		Female Unskilled	
	Youth	Adult	Youth	Adult	Youth	Adult	Youth	Adult
Pay at 16								
Up to £29	3	3	25	5	5	–	–	–
– £39	24	23	18	10	21	6	23	18
– £59	68	53	57	70	74	56	77	59
– £79	6	20	–	15	–	33	–	24
– £99	–	3	–	–	–	6	–	–
– £149								
Pay at 18								
£30 – £39	3	7	7	–	–	–	–	–
– £59	38	30	32	16	45	–	39	28
– £79	56	37	36	58	50	64	57	56
– £99	3	24	21	26	5	14	4	6
–£149	–	2	4	–	–	23	–	6
–£199	–	–	–	–	–	–	–	6
Adult pay								
£30 – £39	–	–	–	–	–	–	–	5
– £59	8	2	–	–	19	–	17	10
– £79	53	26	11	4	52	19	65	40
– £99	28	49	21	8	24	39	9	25
–£149	11	21	57	58	5	35	9	15
–£199	–	2	11	29	–	8	–	–
£200 and over	–	–	–	–	–	–	--	5
Adult pay at age								
16	3	–	–	1	–	–	–	–
17, 18	39	29	7	17	72	46	73	53
19–21	56	60	85	74	28	50	27	42
22–25	–	9	4	4	–	4	–	5
Older	3	2	4	4	–	–	–	–
Number of firms	36	45	28	24	21	26	23	20

anticipated skill requirements than current starting rates. Managements explained that there would be no point in excess training however cheap the trainees, while it remained necessary to replenish vital skills and maintain balanced age-structures even when wage and other training costs became onerous. Cutting-back on training, even under severe financial pressure, was usually deplored and regretted as a false economy.

Other employers explained that they would be unable to replace adults with cheap teenagers because the latter would be unable to do the jobs, or would be so less productive or expensive to supervise that they could not be good bargains at any price. Many firms were 'rationalizing' their workforces, which meant different things in different places, but invariably meant that accommodating inexperienced young people was becoming more difficult. Rationalization sometimes meant organizing the workflow and workforce so that everyone did more, and to ensure that no spare-hands such as novices were carried. Some firms were introducing core-periphery employment structures. Core members with relatively well-paid and secure employment were expected to be flexible, multi-skilled and experienced. There was a trend towards using part-time and temporary labour in peripheral jobs. Married women were normally pre-ferred in part-time employment. The employers believed that unem-ployed teenagers wanted and needed full-time work. Adults were usually preferred for temporary posts since there seemed no point or need to train novices.

The Young Workers Scheme

Only a minority of firms were interested in taking advantage of prevailing market conditions, forcing or holding youth rates down, and increasing youth recruitment. Twenty-three per cent of establishments had used the YWS for which wages had to be beneath £42.50 in 1984, the time of our survey, to qualify for the full £15 subsidy. Some firms had not used the scheme because the YTS was considered more suitable. Others explained that they were unable to lower their rates to qualify or to derive any benefit from cheap school-leavers for various combinations of the reasons listed above. It had never occurred to most of these managements that they could or should reduce their wage-levels to qualify for the YWS.

All employers were asked their views on the main government mea-sures for promoting youth training and employment then in operation-the YWS and the YTS. On the YTS most employers who understood the scheme, participating or not, mentioned advantages and drawbacks. Opin-ions on the YWS were more sharply polarized. Users were mostly pas-sionately in favour. They appreciated the subsidy as cash in the bank, a real incentive to take-on young people and offer real jobs, not mere work experience or training. They also approved the scheme's simplicity; it was easy to qualify and involved relatively little red tape. Non-users were sometimes unaware of the YWS or indifferent, but others were completely opposed. They objected to government handouts to low-wage competi-tors, and argued that the scheme was pushing the economy backwards instead of promoting successful companies that could afford better wages.

Firms using the YWS were located in all areas and sectors, except public services which were ineligible. Clothing and leather goods, and engineering firms were the most likely to be participating. The scheme was being used most frequently to employ females in unskilled jobs, but it was certainly not confined to these occupations. Apprentices, trainee techni-cians, sales and clerical recruits were also being subsidised. The main features that distinguished YWS-users were their size — small to medium, being non-unionized, and expanding. They tended to be small but growing companies whose managements were anxious to contain all costs including wages. Hence their active interest in cheap teenagers. Only 6 per cent of YWS users had qualified by lowering their beginners' rates. The remainder were previously low-wage companies and were benefiting from the windfall supplied by the YWS. Age differentials in these firms were not particularly wide. Both youth and adult rates tended to be below-average.

As already mentioned, only 11 per cent of firms said that they were likely to recruit more young people if their wages could be reduced, but in replying to this question a number of managements argued that it was not 16 and 17-year-olds' high rates that inhibited their employment so much as the application of adult rates at age 19 or 18, before recruits were fully-experienced, mature, settled and productive. Once-upon-a-time 21 was the generally recognized age of majority, and until 1972–73 the statutory school-leaving age was 15. The transitional period has since been shortened at both ends and, according to some managements, returning to a longer transition would make young people more attractive. Over a half of the firms surveyed had unskilled males and females on full adult rates by age 18 (see table 1). However, some managements who advocated a longer transition pointed out that the YWS was no help on this score. Indeed, in some firms YTS allowances and youth pay beneath the YWS ceiling were aggravating situations where young adults' pay rose steeply at age 18.

Only 13 per cent of firms that were using the YWS claimed to have substituted youth for adult labour since the scheme became available. The greater part of this employment subsidy seems to have been 'deadweight' (Rajan, 1985). Most users were already low-wage companies, recruiting cheap young people, and were treating the YWS as a bonus. Some explained that the scheme had tipped the balance against decisions to replace young people with adults. Low pay and employment subsidies were thereby helping to retain some jobs on youth labour markets, and, according to our evidence, such jobs are currently amounting to a growing proportion of employment accessible to less-qualified young people.

Higher-wage firms tended to have ceased recruiting school-leavers to sales, clerical and unskilled jobs. The better-paid jobs still nominally open to young people were mostly in larger, unionized firms that were reducing their workforces and, in practice, not recruiting. Moreover, whenever sales, clerical and unskilled jobs became vacant in these firms there were usually plenty of experienced adult applicants. Managements who had once found it necessary to recruit streams of young people and adults to keep their offices, sales forces and production lines fully-staffed had discovered, amidst rising unemployment, that there was no longer any need to bother with inexperienced school-leavers.

A New Underclass

The wider debate on youth pay has tended to ignore the views of young people themselves, together with the effects of pay on their labour market behaviour and life-styles. It seems to have been tacitly assumed that 16—18 year olds who live with their parents have minimal income needs and domestic responsibilities, and therefore will suffer no harm if their wages are forced down. After all, it can be argued, teenagers who remain in full-time education until 18 rarely qualify for any grants or allowances.

Eighty per cent of our 17-18-year-old Chelmsford respondents were living in 'normal' family situations with two parents including an employed father, but only 61 per cent in Walsall and 51 per cent in Liverpool. The spread of adult unemployment and the rise in divorce and separation are now denying many teenagers hitherto normal family environments. The years between school-leaving and marriage used to be described as a 'brief flowering period' in working class communities, whereas unemployment, low wages and training allowances often intensify family poverty during this life-stage.

We collected information on our 17-18-year-olds' involvement in various types of out-of-home recreation during the four weeks preceding the interviews. There were no consistent 'occupational class' differences, but participation rates were clearly related to income. The highest paid participated most frequently in the widest range of activities, the lower-paid did less, and the unemployed had the most impoverished leisure. Low pay and unemployment mean that teenagers lack the spending power to acquire motor transport, and to go out on most evenings to clubs, discos and other youth scenes. Young unemployed respondents and those on low wages resented these restrictions. Many lower-paid working teenagers saw no good reason why they should be deprived compared with peers in better-paid but otherwise similar jobs.

High pay does not guarantee job satisfaction but low pay, beneath the levels achieved by other members of individuals' reference groups, can be a source of acute dissatisfaction. Whether respondents felt satisfied and settled in their jobs, or whether they were discontent and keen to move, depended mainly on two sets of job characteristics — the pay and prospects (see table 6). Individuals were prepared to tolerate low pay when the training and prospects promised longer-term rewards. They were also willing to stick-it-out in careerless jobs if the pay was all right. In contrast, many young people in low paid, careerless occupations felt abused as slave labour, and were mostly seeking better deals.

The highest rates of labour turnover were from low-paid unskilled and sales jobs which led nowhere in particular. Only 32 per cent of 17-18-year-old respondents whose first jobs were unskilled were still in these occupations when interviewed. Approximately a half of their departures had been voluntary. Young people in low-paid jobs without

Table 6: Young people's survey: pay, occupation and job stability (in percentages)

	Managerial/ professional/ technical		Clerical		Sales		Apprentice/ skilled		Other	
Gross Pay	High	Low	High	Low	High	Low	High	Low	High	Low
In a job hope to keep	71	54	55	57	68	50	63	60	54	43
Settled for time being but not permanently	14	23	27	29	18	32	33	23	28	30
Intend to move, but not taking action yet	10	8	11	3	–	4	2	12	11	13
Looking for another job	5	15	6	10	14	14	2	5	7	15
n	21	13	64	58	22	50	48	85	57	88

Notes: Definition of pay levels: high = over £60 a week
low = £60 a week or under

prospects tend to be constantly searching for something better, often to the chagrin of employers who complain about the young employees' attitudes. Young people who feel exploited are often willing to quit 'trash jobs' even at the risk of unemployment if and when they become too fed-up with the work, bosses or wages. However, our respondents' job departures were as likely to have been involuntary as voluntary. Many had been forced out by closures and redundancies which can be constant threats in marginal businesses that hire cheap teenagers. Some young people had been dismissed for simply growing too old for the subsidies or youth rates on which they were recruited.

Our evidence suggests that labour market conditions in the 1980s are re-creating the dead-end youth jobs that became infamous before the Second World War. Full employment subsequently drove these jobs from the market. Employers found it necessary to offer genuine training or opportunities to progress towards normal adult earnings in order to attract any youth labour. Blind-alley jobs are now being reinvented and some of the clearest examples are the youth niches supported by government measures — YWS jobs, and youth training that leads back to external labour markets after employers provide and sometimes benefit from a period of work experience.

It might be argued that there have always been some low-paid youth jobs in which neither the employers nor employees expected or wanted life-long relationships. However, the situation in the 1980s presents problems that did not arise during the post-war decades of full employment. Firstly, there are now insufficient youth jobs, even the dead-end variety, to keep all young people fully occupied. Market forces may depress youth pay in some firms, particularly for less-qualified school-leavers who enter sales and unskilled occupations. These forces may help to preserve some low-wage youth jobs, but they are unable to override other trends and tendencies — the decline in demand for unskilled labour, and the ease with which experienced adults can be hired — so as to balance supply and demand in most areas' youth labour markets. The net result is that sub-employment — intermittent employment and unemployment — has become one of the more attractive early career patterns facing less-qualified school-leavers. Secondly, it has become more difficult for young people to step from youth to adult occupations and pay. So many experienced adults with good work records have joined the queue of job-seekers that young people may never advance from the back.

We asked employers about the qualities sought when recruiting 19-25-year-olds. When seeking skilled labour managements expected individuals in this age-group to be ready trained or exceptionally qualified. When filling non-skilled posts the firms were not necessarily interested in specific training or skills though 'relevant experience' was invariably an asset. More than anything else, the employers were impressed by stable and preferably progressive career histories. Few employers were unwilling to hire any unemployed person, but many explained their suspicions of the longer-term unemployed. Did they lack initiative? Would they find it difficult, maybe impossible to adopt regular work habits? Firms were equally suspicious of applicants who had left former jobs without 'good reason'. Redundancy was considered an acceptable excuse. Simply quitting or having been dismissed were regarded differently.

A problem confronting less qualified school-leavers in the 1980s is that the state of their local labour markets prevents many from building the steady work records that, in time, would assist their transitions to adult occupations and pay. Moreover, the wider youth-adult pay differentials become, the less the likelihood of employers offering good money being prepared to take chances with inexperienced, formerly unemployed or sub-employed young people. The wider the age differential, the greater the incentive for employers seeking cheap labour to replace one generation of beginners with another instead of offering career and pay structures that would tempt their employees to settle.

Most 17-18-year-old respondents had been unemployed at some time since leaving school. The majority had detested the experience. Low-paid and insecure jobs were considered preferable, though not as life-sentences. For 16-18-year-olds even low-paid jobs are more remunerative than unemployment. This is why 61 per cent of the unemployed were willing to work for less than £40 per week. They were prepared to take low-paid jobs, but then often felt exploited rather than grateful.

Responses to low-paid employment must change as age and domestic responsibilities increase young adults' benefit entitlements. If and when young people move from parental homes into independent accommodation, especially if they are then supporting dependent children, the minimum wages that they can afford to take rise considerably. Those who are unable to obtain jobs with adult pay may thereby discover that it does not pay to work at all. Claimant roles, supplemented if possible by casual, no-cards, cash-in-hand work, begin to look positively attractive.

It would be misleading to say that such individuals opt for unemployment. They gravitate into, then become trapped in the predicament because they have no alternatives. Further education and training offer no escapes. Young people who fail to cross the good 'O' level threshold are likely to discover that further qualifications have virtually no vocational value. The young adults currently at risk of becoming a long-term unemployed underclass are mostly products of the YTS. Only 6 per cent of our respondents had remained continuously unemployed since leaving school despite the scheme's availability. The young people's problem, especially in Walsall and Liverpool, was the likelihood of youth training leading back to external labour markets and unemployment. The low-paid youth jobs that some obtained were turning into blind-alleys rather than stepping-stones.

There are long-term costs to over-reliance on the low pay solution to unemployment among school-leavers. Forcing youth rates of pay well beneath the welfare minimum that societies such as Britain can afford and be persuaded to concede erects an unemployment/poverty trap which is currently threatening to create an underclass of long-term, potentially lifelong claimants. The size of the group at risk varies from place-to-place. Such a stratum is now present even within generally prosperous areas such as Chelmsford. In places such as Liverpool it could contain up to a quarter of the adult population in the 1990s. By then the cohort that we studied will be rearing a new generation, including many acutely deprived children.

During 1986 government measures to promote youth training and employment received yet another overhaul. The YTS is being enlarged from one to two years, whereupon the YWS is being phased-out and replaced by another low wage/job subsidy scheme for the 18 age group. A parallel wage enhancement scheme to encourage long-term unemployed adults to take low-paid jobs is also being introduced. Attempts to price the unemployed into jobs are being intensified, not abandoned with the demise of the YWS. The two-year YTS followed by a spell on subsidized youth rates could help to recreate the extended transition to adult wages that many employers would prefer, except that the subsidies will expire when young workers are still receiving less than half average adult pay. The chances are that blind-alleys will simply close at 18+ instead of earlier. Ignoring the immediate costs of employing school- and scheme-leavers will not avert the longer-term dangers sketched above. We are not advocating higher pay for beginners. The implication of our evidence is rather that market mechanisms and solutions to contemporary youth unemployment must be complemented by other measures to balance labour demand and supply, and to ensure that youth jobs are transitional, not dead-ends.

Acknowledgements

The research on which this chapter is based was funded by the Department of Employment, but the views expressed are solely the authors'.

References

ASHTON D. and MAGUIRE, M. (1983) *The Vanishing Youth Labour Market*, London, Youthaid Occasional Paper 3.

INSTITUTE OF ECONOMIC AFFAIRS (1979) *Job 'Creation' — or Destruction?*, London, Institute of Economic Affairs.

LITTLECHILD, S.C. (1978) *The Fallacy of the Mixed Economy*, London, Hobart Paper 80, Institute of Economic Affairs.

MAKEHAM, P. (1980) *Youth Unemployment*, London, Research Paper 11, Department of Employment.

MINFORD, P. (1983) *Unemployment: Cause and Cure*, Oxford, Martin Robertson.

PARKER, H. (1982) *The Moral Hazards of Social Benefits*, London, Institute of Economic Affairs.

RAFFE, D. (1984) 'Change and continuity in the youth labour market: A critical review of structural explanations of youth unemployment' paper presented to the *British Sociological Association Conference*.

RAJAN, A. (1985) *Job Subsidies: Do they work?*, Sussex, Institute of Manpower Studies, University of Sussex.

WELLS, W. (1983) *The Relative Pay and Employment of Young People*, London, Research Paper 42, Department of Employment.

11 Youth Unemployment in the United Kingdom 1979–84

David Raffe

Introduction

Much of the current concern about unemployment in the UK is focussed on young people. Youth unemployment has risen faster than adult unemployment in recent years and is now at a substantially higher percentage rate; it also gives rise to concern about its long-term effects on the social, psychological and vocational development of individuals, as well as its more short-term effects on crime, delinquency and social disorder. Most government spending on employment and training measures for unemployed people is directed towards young people.

This chapter examines the problem of youth unemployment in the UK in the first half of the 1980s. 1979 is included as a 'baseline' year of relative stability against which subsequent changes can be assessed. 'Youth' unemployment is defined as that of young people under 20, although any such age demarcation is somewhat arbitrary; the legal age of majority in the UK is 18, but the transition from youth to adult labour markets is a less abrupt one as the range of available opportunities progressively changes. The first part of the chapter is descriptive, and examines the level, rate, duration and distribution of youth unemployment during the 1980s; the second part assesses various explanations for the level of youth unemployment and for its recent large increase.

The Level and Pattern of Youth Unemployment: A Statistical Overview

The level of youth unemployment since 1970

Figure 1 shows the total number of teenagers officially recorded as unemployed in Great Britain every January since 1970 (UK figures are not available before 1979). The three unbroken lines show unemployment totals for, respectively, 18-19-year-olds, all under 20-year-olds excluding school leavers, and all under-20-year-olds.

In British unemployment statistics 'school leavers' are defined as unemployed people under 18 years of age who have not entered any employment since leaving full-time education. School-leaver unemployment has a marked seasonal cycle, with annual peaks following the main school-leaving date in the summer. Partly for this reason school leavers are often excluded from the reported totals, but this can be misleading. As the average duration of unemployment increases and school leavers take longer to find jobs, a larger proportion of unemployed under-18s have had no job since school and therefore count as school leavers in the statistics. This trend is clearly seen in figure 1, where school-leaver unemployment is represented by the distance between the top two unbroken lines. This has risen faster than other under-18 unemployment and figures which omit school leavers therefore understate the upward trend.

Before 1979 unemployment figures are only available by age for two months, January and July. The January series is incomplete due to industrial action in 1974 and 1975. As a result the July series is often used to represent trends in youth unemployment, but this is inappropriate, partly because the July figures are heavily weighted towards relatively short-term unemployment, and partly because they are particularly affected by institutional and statistical changes. In the 1970s these changes caused the July figures to exaggerate the underlying increase. A change in school-leaving regulations in 1976 allowed young people to leave school at the end of May rather than at the end of the school term; this brought the annual peak of school-leaver unemployment forward from August to July and accounted for a substantial increase in the recorded youth unemployment count between July 1975 and July 1976. In the 1980s institutional and statistical changes, discussed in the following section, caused the July youth unemployment totals to understate the underlying increase. As a result July data tend to exaggerate the extent to which the current (mid-1980s) level of youth unemployment was generated during the 1970s, and underestimate the extent to which it is a product of the 1980s.

Figure 1 therefore uses the January figures which are less biased in this respect. These show that teenage unemployment in Great Britain rose steadily over much of the 1970s, with a temporary downturn after January 1972[1] and another downturn in 1978. Both downturns coincided with a fall in all-age unemployment; the earlier one also coincided with the raising of the school-leaving age (from 15 to 16 years) in 1972/73, the later one with the introduction of the Youth Opportunities Programme (YOP) for unemployed school leavers in 1978/79.

Although youth unemployment grew during the 1970s it grew much more, in absolute terms, during the first half of the 1980s. The net increase in youth unemployment during a single year, 1980, was greater than the net increase during the whole of the 1970s. The recorded increase between January 1980 and January 1984 was nearly twice as large

Figure 1: Youth and all-age unemployment: Great Britain, January, 1970-1984

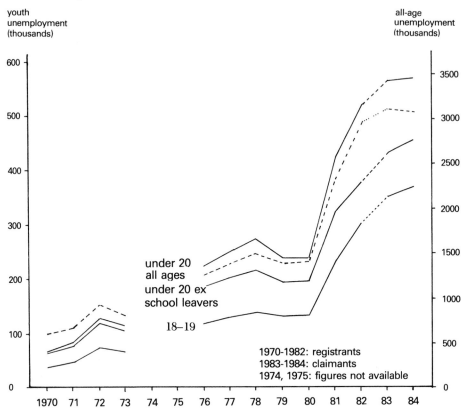

Source: *Employment Gazette, various issues*

as that during the 1970s, despite the institutional and statistical changes (discussed below) which affected the 1980s figures.

The rest of this chapter focusses on the changing problem of youth unemployment in the 1980s, the period in which the largest post-war increase occurred. The year 1979 is used as a baseline for comparisons: since the underlying trend was stable during 1979 the effect of subsequent changes should be relatively unaffected by the choice of month used for the comparison.

The Level of Youth Unemployment 1979–1984

Figure 2 shows the quarterly totals of teenagers officially recorded as unemployed in the UK from 1979–84. The data are broken down in the

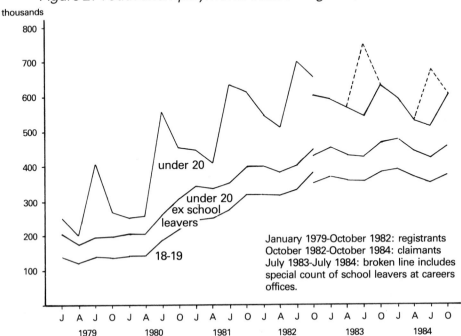

Figure 2: Youth unemployment: United Kingdom, 1979-1984

thousands

under 20

under 20
ex school
leavers

18-19

January 1979-October 1982: registrants
October 1982-October 1984: claimants
July 1983-July 1984: broken line includes
special count of school leavers at careers
offices.

same way as in figure 1, and reveal the seasonal pattern of school-leaver unemployment, with a peak in July usually falling to a trough the following April. Among non-school-leavers the opposite seasonal pattern tends to prevail — with a trough in the summer months — but this is relatively weak and in figure 2 is swamped by the longer-term trend.

The trend in figure 2 is clearly upward, although the figures tend to understate the underlying increase due to the effects of three institutional and statistical changes.

The first change concerns young people's propensity to register as unemployed. The level of unregistered youth unemployment in the UK, although difficult to measure precisely, appears to have been generally low. In the late 1970s a study found that even in inner-city areas, where the problem of non-registration was believed to be greatest, only 10–14 per cent of all youth unemployment was unregistered in three of the four cities studied (Roberts *et al.*, 1981: the fourth city, London, was exceptional with over 40 per cent unregistered). There is no reliable evidence of recent changes in young people's propensity to register as unemployed. It is possible that the longer duration of unemployment has increased the proportion that is registered, but any such effect is likely to have been outweighed by the effects of changes in benefit entitlements in 1981. From that date summer-term school leavers did not become eligible for supplementary benefit until the September after leaving school; some leavers may have deferred registration, and this may account for the somewhat smaller quarterly increases in registered school-leaver unemployment in July 1981 and 1982 compared with 1980.

The second change was the switch, in October 1982, from registrants to claimants (unemployed people receiving benefit) as the basis for the unemployment count. The effect was to reduce the recorded unemployment total, partly because registrants not receiving benefit were thereafter excluded from the count, and partly because the new computerized procedure was quicker to take account of people leaving unemployment. In October 1982 the effect of the change on the youth unemployment count was to reduce by 51,700 the (old-basis) estimate of 655,300. However, the effect varies over the year, and is most pronounced in the July figures, when the 'bulge' of summer-term school leavers, not entitled to benefit, completely disappears from the new-basis total. In the summer months separate counts have been kept of unemployed school leavers registered at careers offices; these are indicated in figure 2 by the broken lines for July 1983 and July 1984, but the peaks still underestimate youth unemployment for those months as they exclude unregistered unemployment, school leavers registered only at job centres and all young people other than school leavers who were registered but not receiving benefit.

The third change to have affected the recorded trend in youth unemployment is the growth and development of government schemes for the young unemployed. The numbers participating on the two largest schemes, the Youth Opportunities Programme (YOP) 1978–1983 and the Youth Training Scheme (YTS) from 1983 are shown in table 1.[2] Only unemployed young people were recruited on to YOP, and once on the scheme they were expected to continue their job search and leave the scheme if they found work; on the criteria of availability and seeking employment they should therefore be regarded as unemployed. In principle this is not true of YTS, which is not restricted to the unemployed, but seeks to attract entrants in preference to ordinary jobs, and which expects its trainees to remain on the scheme for its duration. However, in practice many young people have entered YTS because they were unemployed, and many YTS trainees have continued their job search and have been prepared to leave the scheme if they found employment. Whether or not YOP or YTS trainees should properly be regarded as 'unemployed' it is clear that both programmes kept the recorded total of youth unemploy-

Table 1: Young people on youth opportunities programme or youth training scheme (thousands): Great Britain, January, 1979–84

	Current Trainees			Total entrants in year
	16	17–18	16–18	
1979	46	25	71	162
1980	52	28	80	216
1981	96	52	148	360
1982	129	69	198	553
1983	170	91	261	543
1984	222	55	277	354

Note: Figures subject to rounding. Estimates of current trainees are approximate. Totals for entrants in year double-count young people who enter more than one scheme.

Source: Manpower Services Commission.

ment below the level it would otherwise have reached.[3] Moreover, since YOP in particular grew at a faster proportionate rate than youth unemployment (a result of increasingly ambitious undertakings to unemployed school leavers) its effect was to reduce the extent to which the underlying increase in youth unemployment, as well as its current level, was reflected in the published statistics. Younger members of the age group have been most affected: YOP was open to 16-18-year-olds, although most of its entrants were under 18, and it was targetted primarily at school leavers, whereas YTS has been targetted particularly at 16-year-olds with most unemployed 18-year-olds ineligible to enter.

A concurrent change, which has also affected mainly the younger members of the age group, has been an increase in participation in full-time education after 16; full-time students rose from 28 per cent of the 16-18 age group in 1979 to 33 per cent in 1983, largely in response to the scarcity of employment (DES, 1985).[4]

As a result of all these changes the official figures for youth unemployment not only understate the current level of youth unemployment on most definitions, but also understate the underlying increase in youth unemployment since 1979. The extent of this understatement is greatest for school leavers and other under-18s, and the July figures are the most affected. As measured at any of the other three months for which data are available (January, April or October), youth unemployment increased between 1979–1984 by a factor of 2.3 to 2.6, depending on the month chosen for the comparison; this is still a low estimate of the increase that would be observed on any consistent definition. Although the observed increase among under-18s (1.8 to 2.1) is substantially smaller than that among 18–19 year-olds (2.8 to 3.0) this probably reflects the fact that the three factors discussed above had a greater impact on recorded

Table 2: Estimated youth unemployment rates, 1979–84

Source	Date	Scope	Age group	1979	1980	1981	1982	1983	1984
Unemployed as % of age group									
DE1	(January)	GB	under 18	6.1	5.8	10.2	11.9	×11.9	11.2
			18–19	7.8	7.7	12.9	16.5	×19.2	20.3
			under 20	6.9	6.8	11.6	14.2	×15.6	15.9
DES1	January	E & W	16	7.4	7.1	13.8	14.2		
			16–18	8.1	7.7	13.8	16.7		
DES2	January	GB	16	6.2	5.8	12.0	12.3	×14.1	12.7
			16–18	7.4	7.1	12.6	15.2	×16.8	16.9
LFS	April–June	GB	16–18	5.5		×15.0		×18	
SSLS	March–April	Sc	SLs	6.8		11.9		13.8	12.0
Unemployed and schemes as % of age group									
DE2	(January)	GB	under 20	9.0	9.0	15.6	19.6	×22.7	23.5
DES1	January	E & W	16	11.0	10.9	21.1	23.9		
			16–18	10.9	10.7	22.4	23.9		
DES2	January	GB	16	11.4	11.5	22.4	26.1	×32.8	37.4
			16–18	10.1	10.1	18.0	22.4	×26.2	27.0
SSLS	March–April	Sc	SLs	12.5		24.7		31.3	33.8
Unemployed as % of employed and unemployed									
DE3	January	UK	under 18	13.5	13.1	21.7	25.2	×25.8	24.5
			18–19	10.8	10.9	18.1	22.8	×26.1	27.0
DES1	January	E & W	16	13.4	13.1	28.3	33.4		
			16–18	11.8	11.2	21.0	27.2		
DES2	January	GB	16	11.7	11.2	23.6	31.8	×43.0	41.9
			16–18	10.7	10.3	19.3	24.8	×29.0	28.6
LFS	April–June	GB	16–19	8.9		×22.9		×27	
GHS	Annual Average	GB	16–17	14.8	19.4	27.8			
			18–19	9.6	13.8	19.5			
			16–19	11.9	16.2	22.6			
SSLS	March–April	Sc	SLs	10.0		19.7		27.9	26.8

Unemployed and schemes as % of employed and unemployed and schemes

DES1	E & W	16	January	18.8	18.7	37.6	45.9	×63.7	68.0
		16–18		15.2	14.8	27.1	34.9		
DES2	GB	16	January	19.5	19.8	39.8	49.8	×39.0	39.1
		16–18		14.1	14.0	25.5	32.7		
SSLS	Sc	SLs	March–April	17.0		33.8		46.7	50.8

Note: Definitions of unemployment, employment, etc, vary between sources: see accompanying notes on sources. All estimates are subject to rounding error. Major discontinuities in series are indicated by 'x'.

Sources

DE1: based on published unemployment figures (1979–82: registrants; 1983–84: claimants) and provisional population estimates. The unemployment figures refer to January, the population figures to June: no adjustment has been made to allow for this seasonal difference.

DE2: calculated as for DE1 with the addition of estimates for the numbers on YOP or YTS schemes in January (see table 1).

DE3: estimated unemployment rates prepared by the Department of Employment. The numerator is the January unemployment count by age (see figure 2); it is expressed as a percentage of unemployment plus employment, the latter being obtained by applying age breakdowns from the Labour Force Survey to figures for the total number of employees in employment, with adjustments to allow for seasonal patterns and the years between Labour Force Surveys (see 'Unemployment rates by age', *Employment Gazette*, September 1983, p. 411). The employment estimates are unreliable, partly because of the assumptions involved in interpolation and adjustment, and partly because of the weaknesses of the Labour Force Survey data (see below).

DES1: based on estimates of the educational and economic activity of the age group, published in DES (1983). These use data from several official sources, including: DES statistics of students in full-time education; DE figures for registered unemployment, combined with DHSS age details and LFS estimates of unregistered unemployment; and MSC figures on YOP trainees. Estimates of employment are residuals and probably subject to the widest margin of error. Age groups are defined as at 31 August of the previous year.

DES2: based on estimates published in DES (1985). These differ from DES1 in several respects, including: the wider coverage (Great Britain); unemployment figures include only registered (to 1982) or claimant (from 1983); the employment figures, being residuals, therefore include all other unemployed.

GHS: the General Household Survey. Based on households, this does not provide satisfactory population estimates, but since little proxy interviewing is used, the quality of data is likely to be high (compare LFS below). Unregistered unemployment is included. Sample numbers are relatively small for finer age divisions (lowest base n in table 2 is 443). The data are supplied by Joan Payne: see also Payne (1985).

LFS: based on published tables from the EEC Labour Force Survey. The discontinuity between 1979 and 1981 is caused by major changes in the sampling and fieldwork procedures. The discontinuity between 1981 and 1983 is caused by a change in the treatment

Table 2: continued

of full-time students in the published tables. For 1979 and 1981 full-time students are excluded from the economically active; in 1983 they may be recorded as employed, unemployed (seeking work) or neither. The data are further affected by their restriction to residents in private households (making estimates based on the population unreliable) and by the substantial use of proxy interviewing, which may have particularly affected young people, and which probably resulted in some confusion of special employment measures with employment. Unregistered unemployment is included.

SSLS: based on self-reports of a sample of the previous summer's school leavers (of all ages) in a postal survey (the Scottish School Leavers Survey). The occupational and industrial composition of employment in Scotland is broadly comparable to that in the rest of the UK. The 1984 estimates are based on relatively small sample numbers (lowest base n in table 2 is 642); sample numbers for earlier years are several times larger. From table 1 of Raffe (1987).

unemployment among younger members of the age group. This is particularly noticeable in the years after 1982, when the changed basis for the unemployment count and the replacement of YOP by the year-long YTS both contributed to a fall in the recorded unemployment total among under-18s.

The Rate of Youth Unemployment

The figures discussed so far describe levels, not rates, of youth unemployment. The 16–19 age group grew at an annual rate of rather more than two per cent (an annual increment of some 50,000) until 1981; a smaller increase in 1982 was followed by a gradual decline. Subject to changing rates of participation in the labour market, therefore, one might expect the increase in the rate of youth unemployment to have been somewhat smaller than the increase in its level.

There are two problems in estimating youth unemployment rates. The first is conceptual, and concerns the definitions of unemployment and of the base by which it is divided to yield a rate. The definition of unemployment, and related problems of measurement, have been discussed above; the definition of the base is equally difficult since, with the development of special measures such as YOP and YTS, and with growing numbers remaining in or entering full-time education because of the scarcity of employment, the definition and identification of young people who are economically active have become increasingly problematic. Table 2 presents estimates based on four different definitions of unemployment rates — respectively excluding and including schemes such as YOP from the definition of unemployment, and using the population or the 'economically active' as the base. The definitions vary further across the sources used, for example with respect to the treatment of the unregistered unemployed.

The second problem is empirical, and concerns the inconsistency, scarcity or unreliability of the data needed to estimate youth unemployment rates. This particularly affects estimates of young people in employment, needed as part of the base for estimates based on the economically active. The unemployment rates in table 2 are derived from a variety of (mainly published) sources. Not all the sources are independent: data from the Labour Force Survey, for example, are also used in the calculation of the DES1 and the DE3 rates (although different LFS estimates are used in each case). The sources differ in several other respects including the age group or area covered, the date of measurement, definitions, sampling arrangements and methods of data collection. The principal differences are described in the notes on the sources for table 2. Many of the estimates in the table are also subject to wide margins of error.

Despite these differences, and despite the wide variation in estimated rates in table 2, most of this variation can be attributed to differences in the population, the broad definition of the unemployment rate and the year of measurement. When unemployment rates are based on the whole age group, the younger cohorts generally have lower rates than the older ones. However, basing unemployment rates on the economically active reverses this pattern, and when schemes are taken into account the observed relative disadvantage of the younger cohorts increases further. Indeed the table shows how much the estimated unemployment rate for 16 year-olds or school leavers depends on the inclusion or exclusion of schemes. More generally, the table suggests that any attempt to provide an unproblematic estimate of the rate of youth unemployment at a given time should be viewed with scepticism.

Different ways of estimating youth unemployment rates may yield different conclusions about the trend in these rates as well as about their level. The first set of estimates — expressing the unemployed as a percentage of the age group — tends to show a smaller proportionate increase in unemployment than the other sets. This reflects, first, that the 'economically active' have declined as a proportion of the age group, and second, that definitions which exclude schemes tend to indicate a slower rate of growth of unemployment than definitions which include schemes.

The Duration of Youth Unemployment

Among under-18s the average duration of unemployment, as recorded in official statistics, tended to rise over the period, but the rise was neither continuous nor consistently reflected in a relative growth of the two longest duration categories, of twenty-six and up to fifty-two weeks and over fifty-two weeks (table 3). Among 18-19-year-olds there was a larger and more consistent increase in duration: in 1980 one quarter (24.9 per cent) of the unemployed had been out of work for over 26 weeks, whereas by 1984 this figure was approaching one half (46.4 per cent). (Among all age groups the January 1984 proportion was 55.3 per cent).

The data refer to uncompleted (current) spells of unemployment. Data on completed spells of unemployment have only been available since the new basis for collecting unemployment statistics was introduced in October 1982. The median duration of spells of unemployment completed between January and April 1984 was 9.5 weeks for under-18s and 15.9 weeks for 18-19-year-olds, compared with 14.2 weeks among all age groups (DE, 1984).[5] Outflow data complement these figures: between January and April 1984 the number of under-18s leaving unemployment was 52.1 per cent of the average number of unemployed; the corresponding proportion was 35.1 per cent among 18-19-year-olds and 32.7 per cent among all age groups.

The official data therefore suggest that the average duration of unem-

Table 3: Duration of unemployment (uncompleted spells) in weeks, by current age (percentages): Great Britain, January, 1979–84

		1979	1980	1981	1982	1983	1984
Under 18							
Up to 6		37.6	41.3	29.6	27.1	29.0	25.3
Over 6 and up to 13		21.3	23.7	21.6	19.8	18.1	17.8
13	26	19.0	19.1	24.0	28.9	32.9	35.2
26	52	18.0	13.7	22.8	19.2	14.6	12.6
52		4.1	2.2	2.1	5.0	5.4	9.1
Total		100.0	100.0	100.1	100.0	100.0	100.0
18–19							
Up to 6		27.5	27.6	19.8	14.7	14.9	14.6
Over 6 and up to 13		22.8	24.2	22.4	17.5	14.5	13.2
13	26	22.0	23.3	27.2	25.1	25.9	25.7
26	52	17.6	16.2	22.4	24.0	22.4	19.8
52		10.1	8.7	8.1	18.7	22.3	26.6
TOTAL		100.0	100.0	99.9	100.0	100.0	99.9

Note: 1979–82: based on registrants; 1983–84: based on claimants.
Source: Employment Gazette

ployment among 18-19-year-olds rose rapidly between 1979–84 and by 1984 their position was near the average for all age groups, whereas among under-18s duration rose more slowly and remained well below the average. However, these data are also affected by the institutional and statistical changes described earlier. The change in benefit regulations in 1981, and more particularly the switch to a claimant-based count in 1982, reduced the recorded average duration of unemployment. In 1983 and 1984 school leavers who had become unemployed in June or July were only recorded as having entered unemployment in September, reducing the recorded duration of their unemployment by two or three months. Moreover, many young people left unemployment to enter YOP or YTS; these schemes have not only thus reduced the observed duration of youth unemployment spells, but also accompanied a change in the nature of young people's labour-market movements. In the 1970s and earlier decades youth unemployment was largely frictional, comprised of relatively short intervals between jobs; it was part of a pattern of 'frequent job changing' which reflected the restricted (secondary) labour-market opportunities available to many young people but which appeared to have few adverse personal or occupational effects in the long term (Roberts, 1968; Phillips, 1973; Baxter, 1975; Cherry, 1976). Between the late 1970s and the early 1980s the pattern changed, at least among younger members of the age group, to one of frequent movements in and out of schemes. The amount of movement in and out of jobs declined sharply (Jones, 1984; Raffe, 1984a).

As a result the relatively low duration of unemployment among under-18s, and its relatively small increase since 1979, obscure a sharp increase in the proportion who had never experienced employment. This is partly reflected in the increased proportion of 'school leavers' to other unemployed under-18s in figures 1 and 2 (although the targetting of special measures on school leavers reduces the observed effect). More direct evidence is available for Scottish school leavers: the proportion of labour-market entrants who were non-employed (unemployed or on YOP) about a year after leaving school rose from 19.3 per cent to 49.9 per cent between 1977–83; but the proportion of the non-employed who had experienced some employment since leaving shcool fell from more than two-thirds in 1977 to less than one-sixth in 1983 (Raffe, 1984a).[6]

There has, therefore, been a powerful underlying tendency for the duration of youth unemployment to increase during the 1980s, although especially among under-18 year-olds this tendency has been partly obscured by the effects of special measures and (in the official statistics) by the effects of statistical changes. This conclusion has two important implications. First, arguments that youth unemployment is not a serious social or psychological problem, based largely on the earlier patterns of short-term youth unemployment, are inapplicable to the 1980s. Second, in the 1980s the problem of youth unemployment has increasingly become a problem of the failure of young people to secure employment rather than their failure to remain in it.

The Distribution of Youth Unemployment

The youth labour market is substantially segregated on lines of gender, with very large differences in the occupational distributions of males and females (DE, 1982; Ashton *et al.*, 1982). Some difference between the impact of rising unemployment on males and females might therefore be expected. Unemployment grew faster among young males than young females over the period, reflected in a rising male proportion of the unemployed (table 4). The unemployment rates calculated by the Department of Employment also show a steeper rise among males than among females, although among under-18s this started from a position where the female rate was somewhat higher than the male rate, with a switchover between 1980 and 1981.

Young people with few or no qualifications have been at considerably greater risk of unemployment, and at least in part this appears to reflect the direct influence of qualifications (MSC, 1978; Roberts *et al.*, 1981; Lynch, 1987; Main, 1985). The incidence of unemployment has also been significantly higher among young people from large families, working class homes or homes where other members of the household were unemployed (Raffe, 1984b; Main, 1985; Lynch, 1987). Youth unemploy-

Table 4: Youth unemployment by sex: United Kingdom, January, 1979–84

		1979	1980	1981	1982	1983	1984
Males as % of unemployed							
Under 18		51.6	51.0	54.6	55.8	55.8	56.7
18–19		54.4	54.0	57.4	58.5	58.9	58.0
*Estimated unemployment rates**							
Under 18	males	13.0	12.5	22.3	26.7	27.7	26.9
18–19	females	14.2	13.7	21.0	23.5	23.7	21.9
	males	11.2	11.3	19.8	25.5	29.4	30.2
	females	10.3	10.4	16.1	19.8	22.4	23.6

*Unemployed as percentage of employed plus unemployed. See notes on series DE3 in Table 2.
Sources: *Employment Gazette*; Department of Employment

ment thus coincides with, and aggravates, existing patterns of social and economic disadvantage. Young blacks have experienced higher unemployment than young whites, with a much greater gap between them than would have been expected on the basis of other disadvantages listed above (Roberts *et al.*, 1981; Lee and Wrench, 1983, MSC, 1984; Lynch, 1987). In Northern Ireland the same has applied to Roman Catholics (Cormack *et al.*, 1980), but in Scotland, which also has a significant Catholic minority, the higher unemployment rates of young Catholics can be attributed to their relative social, educational and regional disadvantage (Main and Raffe, 1983a).

Finally, there have been wide variations in the opportunities for young people in different local labour markets (Sawdon *et al.*, 1981; Ashton *et al.*, 1982). Youth unemployment has also been unevenly distributed within local labour markets, for example with heavy concentrations in inner-city areas, but much of this appears to reflect the uneven distribution of young people with different levels of individual disadvantage (Lynch, 1987).

Most of the evidence on the distribution of youth unemployment comes from one-off studies, many of them conducted during the late 1970s rather than the 1980s. There is little systematic evidence on changes during the period of rapid increase in the early 1980s, although crude comparisons of studies conducted at different times do not suggest that any of the dimensions of inequality have become less salient. With respect to educational qualifications, however, there is rather firmer evidence of increased polarization: studies of school leavers in Birmingham (Jones, 1984) and Scotland (Raffe, 1984a) and of young people in Britain covered by the General Household Survey (Payne and Payne, 1985) all report widening differences between qualified and less qualified over periods of rising unemployment; Payne and Payne suggest that the observed effect might have been even greater had their data included young people on schemes for the unemployed. One should be wary of generalizing to other dimensions of inequality, but it is possible that the general effect of rising unemployment in the 1980s has been to exacerbate social differences and divisions among young people. Moreover, the increased duration of youth unemployment has added a further dimension of inequality: the longer the period for which a young person has been unemployed, the poorer his or her chances of subsequent employment (Lynch, 1984).

The Relation of Youth to Adult Unemployment

The relation of youth to adult unemployment can be understood in two ways. At a micro and longitudinal level, today's unemployed young people may become tomorrow's unemployed adults. Not only is the early experience of unemployment correlated with a greater probability of unemployment in later years among members of the same age cohort, but there is some evidence that young people entering the labour market in depressed periods may suffer continuing occupational disadvantage relative to other cohorts (Payne, 1985).

At a macro level, one reason for the particular policy interest in youth unemployment is that it has grown much faster than adult unemployment. In January 1970 teenagers accounted for 11 per cent of British unemployment; by 1984 this proportion had risen above 18 per cent. The growth was not steady: teenagers' recorded share of total unemployment remained relatively stable during the principal period of study, 1979–84. However this obscures two countervailing trends: 18-19-year-olds' share of total unemployment increased, whereas that of under-18-year-olds declined after 1978. The decline among under-18s may be largely due to the institutional and statistical changes discussed earlier, especially the growth in special measures, which particularly affected this age group. Without these factors the upward trend would probably have continued. Nevertheless, the youth unemployment rate in January 1984 was considerably higher than that of older age groups. The Department of Employment's estimated rate (series DE3 in table 2) was 24.5 per cent among under-18s and 27 per cent among 18-19-year-olds; among other age groups it ranged from 8.5 per cent (35-44-year-olds) to 19.3 per cent (20-24-year-olds).[7]

Although youth unemployment has risen more than adult unemployment the year-by-year sequence of changes has followed the adult pattern very closely (figure 1). This is consistent with the view that youth unemployment rises and falls alongside adult unemployment but with disproportionately large fluctuations: since adult unemployment generally increased over the period, so did youth unemployment but to a greater degree. Analyses across local labour markets also reveal a close relationship between levels of adult and youth unemployment (Makeham, 1980; Main and Raffe, 1983a).

Summary: The Level and Pattern of Youth Unemployment

Although the definition of precise rates is somewhat arbitrary, youth unemployment in the UK had reached an historically high level by 1984. This level is substantially a product of the 1980s. Although institutional, statistical and policy changes have tended to mask the fact, particularly with respect to under-18s, the greater part of the present (mid-1980s) problem reflects changes that have occurred since 1979. Over this period youth unemployment has also changed from a relatively short-term, frictional problem to one of much longer duration, where such labour-market movements as still occur tend to be in and out of schemes rather than in and out of jobs. The unequal distribution of youth unemployment persists and may have been intensified.

Several of these conclusions reflect current processes in the youth labour market. The evidence on dynamics suggests that the problem is increasingly one of young people's failure to secure jobs rather than their failure to keep them. The concentration of youth unemployment among the disadvantaged is consistent with a job-queue model of occupational selection. Above all, the evidence points to close links between the adult and youth labour markets; the same factors may affect both markets even if their impact on young people is proportionately greater. These considerations are relevant to the explanation of youth unemployment, discussed in the next section.

Alternative Explanations for the Increase in Youth Unemployment

Suggested Explanations

Five factors have been widely canvassed as full or partial explanations for the recent increase in youth unemployment. The first four refer respectively to quantitative and qualitative changes on the demand and supply sides of the labour market.

The first, 'cyclical', explanation attributes youth unemployment to the recession, that is to deficient aggregate demand. As has been seen, youth unemployment levels have changed closely in line with adult unemployment in recent years, even if youth unemployment tends to have risen faster.

The second explanation alleges that structural shifts in the composition of labour demand have disadvantaged young people relative to adults. These shifts are seen as linked with industrial change, occupational change (either of an upskilling or deskilling nature) or a switch from full-time to part-time employment.

233

The third explanation points to demographic trends and the effects of the baby boom of the early 1960s. The size of the 16–19 age group rose through much of the 1970s, and continued to rise to a peak around 1982. This rise may have been partly offset, in the most recent years, by a decline in economic activity rates, although precise estimates of the latter are unreliable.

Fourth, ministers of different governments have attributed youth unemployment in part to the poor standards or attitudes of school leavers.[8]

Finally, youth unemployment has been attributed to a rise in the earnings of young workers relative to adults. However relative earnings have not in fact risen since 1975, and have tended to fall during the 1950s (table 5).[9] Comprehensive data on earnings on a consistent age basis are only available since 1974; the more restricted data for earlier years show a substantial increase in relative earnings in the early 1970s, although with significant differences between males and females.[10] Part of this increase reflects the changed age composition of young workers following the raising of the school-leaving age in 1972—73.

Time-Series Studies

The British debate about the macroeconomic determinants of youth unemployment has been dominated by analyses of time-series data. One of the

Table 5: *Relative earnings of young workers (percentages): Great Britain, April, 1974–84*

	Males		*Females*	
	Under 18	*18–20*	*Under 18*	*18–20*
1974	38.2	60.2	56.3	74.6
1975	40.6	62.0	57.6	73.9
1976	39.2	60.6	54.3	72.7
1977	40.3	60.8	55.1	73.9
1978	40.0	61.4	54.5	73.8
1979	39.7	61.0	56.0	74.6
1980	38.8	60.8	54.9	73.2
1981	38.8	58.7	53.1	71.1
1982	38.7	57.6	52.3	70.4
1983	36.4	56.7	49.2	69.0
1984	34.9	55.6	48.3	67.9

Note: The table refers to gross weekly earnings of full-time employees whose pay was not affected by absence, and reports the average earnings of young employees as a percentage of the average earnings of employees aged 21 and over. Age is measured as at 1 January.

Source: New Earnings Survey.

simplest and commonest approaches uses youth unemployment itself as the dependent variable and estimates the size and significance of several hypothesized explanatory variables. Analyses of this type have been reported by Makeham (1980), the OECD (1980), Lynch and Richardson (1982) and Layard (1982). They all report a cyclical variable (usually all-age or adult unemployment or notified vacancies) to be highly significant, but reach different conclusions about the other suggested explanations. A time-trend variable — possibly reflecting the effect of structural changes in labour demand — is significant in the OECD study but not in Makeham's.[11] A demographic variable is found to be significant by the OECD and Layard, not significant by Makeham and significant for females but not males by Lynch and Richardson. The relative earnings or labour costs of young people are found to be insignificant in models which use adult unemployment as the cyclical or demand variable (Makeham; Lynch and Richardson; Layard) but significant (sometimes marginally) when the registered vacancies series is used instead (Lynch and Richardson; Layard).

These studies confirm the importance of aggregate labour demand but reach no other consistent conclusion, although they suggest that any other influence may be relatively weak. Their conclusions are sensitive both to the specification of the model and to the time period covered (Junankar and Neale, 1987); they extend at most to 1979 and their ability to explain the developments of the 1980s is doubtful (Lynch and Richardson, 1982).

More recent approaches assume a disequilibrium model of the youth labour market, which is estimated (either exogenously or endogenously) to have moved from excess demand to excess supply around 1971. The implication of this is that analyses which straddle the switch in the market may not yield sensible results. Moreover some variables, including relative earnings, might have had more influence during the later period when the market was demand-constrained than during the earlier period when it was supply-constrained, but this influence would be obscured or confounded in analyses which did not take account of the switch in the market. The disequilibrium model similarly casts doubt on analyses which estimate demand functions for youth labour from data covering periods of excess demand. In practice such analyses reach widely diverging conclusions (Abowd *et al.*, 1980; Hutchinson *et al.*, 1984).

The disequilibrum approaches therefore estimate separate demand functions (or demand and supply funcions simultaneously) for the periods of excess supply (Merrilees and Wilson, 1979; Wells, 1983; Rice, 1984). All these studies report a significant effect of relative earnings or labour costs, although not consistently. For example, Wells finds no significant effect of relative labour costs on the employment of 18-19-year-olds of either sex, and no consistent effect for females under 18. All studies report a cyclical variable to be highly (and with the exception of Wells) consistently significant.

Although the disequilibrium analyses have attracted considerable attention, their alleged superiority should be viewed with scepticism. Their value is undermined by major problems of model specification,[12] which in turn are aggravated by two further difficulties which are particularly salient for the disequilibrium approach.

First, the analyses rely upon data sources of limited scope and doubtful validity. The main dependent variable, youth employment, is estimated in part from the EEC Labour Force Survey: this is only available for alternate years, and the survey, which is household-based, allows proxy reporting and this is likely to affect the quality of data for young workers particularly. (Among other problems the survey is believed to distinguish poorly between employment and special measures). The data on relative earnings also pose problems; two different sources, not wholly compatible, are needed to cover the period, and one of these (the October earnings enquiry) is highly restrictd with respect to the age categories and the occupations covered.

Second, a consequence of the disequilibrium approach is that estimates for the period of excess supply are based on a very small number of observations (years); and since some data series are incomplete and require interpolation or extrapolation the true degrees of freedom are of the order of half a dozen or fewer.

Both the quality and the quantity of available data are therefore inadequate to sustain the interpretations placed on the disequilibrium analyses, whose conclusions appear in any case to be highly sensitive to model specification.[13] More generally, all the time-series analyses need to be seen in historical context. They are largely based on the 1970s or earlier periods; they appear not to be generalizable to the 1980s (Lynch and Richardson, 1982; Wells, 1983) and they do not satisfactorily take account of the increasing influence of special measures on the youth labour market after 1978. They therefore fail to cover the period of greatest increase in youth unemployment. Their most controversial conclusion, about the effect of relative youth earnings, largely reflects the coincidence of an increase in relative earnings and a rise in youth unemployment before 1975: relative earnings did not vary much in the late 1970s (table 5). Moreover the quantitative implications of this conclusion should be borne in mind. Rice (1984) presents the only disequilibrium analysis which permits the (lagged) effect of relative earnings on youth unemployment to be quantified: she calculates that relative earnings explain 32.6 per cent of the rise in youth unemployment between 1974–78 among males, and 22.4 per cent among females. However, most of the rise in youth unemployment has occurred since 1978, so the contribution of relative earnings to rising youth unemployment over the whole decade 1974–1984 is very much smaller than this — and the *net* contribution may be around zero if the effects of declining relative earnings in the 1980s are taken into account.

The main conclusion of the time-series studies is that declining aggregate demand is a significant cause of rising youth unemployment: on all other factors, including the relative pay explanation, the evidence is equivocal. However, the quality of evidence from these studies is poor. The dominant influence of time-series analysis in the economic debate about British youth unemployment is difficult to justify.

The Youth Labour Market

To explain the rise in youth unemployment it is necessary to complement time-series analysis, not only with a more historically grounded approach to the study of trends, but also with evidence from other types of study on the institutions, structures and processes within the youth labour market, paticularly as these affect the relationship with the adult market. All these things vary across local labour markets but a number of generalizations are possible.

On the supply side of the youth labour market, there is no evidence of a decline in educational standards (Choppin, 1981); in formal terms, as measured by qualifications, these have risen. However as more of the abler and more qualified young people have continued in full-time education, the average level of attainment of young people entering the labour market at 16 has declined in relative if not in absolute terms. This may explain why some employers have perceived a decline in the calibre of young workers, although a larger number of employers have perceived either no change or an improvement (MSC, 1978). Criticisms of the quality of young workers have been widespread, especially in the late 1970s, but there is little evidence that this has in fact declined; similar criticisms have been voiced throughout the twentieth century (Reeder, 1979). In any case, if the rise in youth unemployment were in part attributable to the declining calibre of young people it is hard to see why this should have occurred during the 1980s when any beneficial impact of the Great Debate of 1976/77 might have started to take effect. Arguments that young people have lost the 'work ethic' or developed unfavourable attitudes to work are even less well founded. Unemployed young people may develop various behavioural or cultural responses to help them cope with unemployment, their expectations of finding work may be lowered and their attitudes towards looking for a job may become less positive; but these are all consequences not causes of unemployment (Roberts *et al.* 1981 and 1982; Ullah and Banks, 1985; Jones, 1985). Indeed the underlying commitment to employment appears to be remarkably enduring (Warr *et al.*, 1985). In the past, young people in Britain held highly 'realistic' expectations for their future employment. Recent studies reveal a continuing realism, governing young people's expectations for wages among other occupational criteria (Sawdon *et al.*, 1982; Lynch, 1983).

With respect to the demand side of the labour market, young people have access to a more restricted range of jobs than any other age group (Jolly *et al.*, 1980). They are excluded from wide areas of employment, including jobs demanding higher education and those affected by legal restrictions. Examples of the latter include jobs involving shiftwork, driving, the sale or handling of alcohol, and some kinds of machinery.

On the other hand most jobs to which young people do have access are also open to adults: one study of employers concludes that only apprenticeships are the 'preserve of young people alone' (MSC, 1978); another identifies clerical and sales work as a further 'sheltered' area, although in this latter study only a minority of employers of any type of labour had jobs for which they only recruited young people (Ashton *et al.*, 1982).

The identification of young people as 'secondary' workers (Bosanquet and Doeringer, 1973) may be misleading. There is much less occupational segregation in terms of age than in terms of sex. Although young workers enter jobs that are, on average, lower paid, less skilled and less secure than adults', a significant minority enter 'primary' employment, to which young people have greater access in Britain than in the other EEC countries or the USA (Ryan, 1983). In other words, young people are found within many (but not all) sectors of the general labour market; the youth labour market is closely related to the adult market, affected by the same factors if not always in identical ways.

Some commentators have suggested that the relationship between youth and adult labour markets has changed, to the disadvantage of young people, but the evidence for this is inconclusive. Total employment in the more youth-intensive industries has not declined substantially more than in other industries. Thus, school leaver employment in Scotland declined by 45 per cent between 1979–83, but only 1.3 per cent of jobs were lost due to the disproportionate representation of school leavers in industries whose total employment levels were declining more rapidly (Raffe, 1984c; Main and Raffe, 1983b).[14] With respect to occupational shifts, it has variously been argued that young people have been progressively disadvantaged by a long-term process of upskilling, by deskilling, or by a shift from full-time to part-time employment (Williamson, 1983; Finn and Frith, 1981; Ashton and Maguire, 1983). However, these arguments tend to rest upon inadequate trend data, to make conflicting assumptions about changes in general labour-market processes, and to mistake the (reversible) effects of recession for long-term structural changes. There are further problems of generalization from the evidence, most of which is based on studies of particular labour markets or industries: some changes in the structure of occupational demand may cancel each other out as far as their effects on young people are concerned. The effects on young people of changes in the occupational structure are difficult to determine, but their net impact has probably been small.[15] These arguments, it should be stressed, concern the effects of the changing *composition* of employment on young people; to the extent that the effects of structural changes are mediated by changes in the *level* of employment, they may affect young people through the processes described below.

Given that young people are represented within many sectors of the general labour market, and that they have not been substantially affected by the changing composition of employment consequent on sectoral shifts, the analysis then turns on the degree of substitutability between adult and young workers, and on employers' criteria for choosing between them where at least the possibility of choice exists. Three factors appear to be relevant.[16]

First, the different training needs of young people may lead employers to discriminate with respect to age when recruiting workers. This frequently works to young people's disadvantage: the value of their output to an employer may be low during training (making the recruitment of young people more of an investment decision), the training itself may be costly and many employers are ill-equipped to provide it. On the other hand young people's relative flexibility and lack of ingrained work habits make them relatively attractive to some employers as a raw material to be trained up and moulded to employer-specific requirements.

Second, young people's perceived personal and behavioural characteristics are a major consideration in employers' recruitment decisions with respect to age. Such traits as motivation, reliability, maturity and discipline are consistently mentioned by employers as important criteria both for choosing among young people and for choosing between young people and adults; young people are typically perceived as less satisfactory workers than adults on most of these criteria. These considerations may be made more important by the need to work with expensive or dangerous machinery and by employment protection legislation, both of which are seen by employers as increasing the risks of employing young people.

Third, the relative wages of young people — particularly apprentices — may influence recruitment and employment decisions. However, most employers appear to regard relative wage costs as a comparatively minor consideration: the costs of supervision and control, training and the associated disruption of production, and in particular the 'risk' involved in hiring inexperienced and untried young workers, are widely seen as more important.

Much of the evidence on employers' preferences between young people and adults refers, if implicitly, to 'group-level' competition, where decisions to recruit particular (age) groups are taken in advance, as distinct from individual-level competition where individual adults and young people compete for the same jobs. Employers tend to be less critical of young people as individuals than as a group. Moreover, most employers who discriminate in terms of age do so flexibly, and often without any clearly articulated policy (Livock, 1983). A majority of young people are recruited through channels (such as informal networks, or by direct application) which are not age-specific (Clarke, 1980). The boundaries between youth and adult labour markets are therefore flexible, and the proportions of young people and adults recruited to vacancies are likely to be influenced by their relative proportions among job-seekers. One implication of this is that the effects either of structural changes in the demand for labour or of changes in the size of the age group may be dissipated across other age groups, cushioning their impact on young people. This is confirmed by analyses across local labour markets, which show the local youth unemployment rate to be unaffected either by the industrial structure or by the relative size of the age group, but to be closely related to the adult unemployment rate (Makeham, 1980).

Nevertheless, there is a wide range of jobs which young people are capable of filling but for which employers tend to prefer adults, subject to the flexibility described above. Young workers tend to occupy the rear of the 'job queue' of potential recruits to these occupations (Thurow, 1976), and are only likely to be hired when the aggregate demand for labour is sufficient. This sensitivity to cyclical fluctuations is aggravated by the relative concentration of young people in occupations which are themselves more vulnerable to recession.

It is further aggravated by the dynamics of the youth labour market. Some employers seek to maintain an age balance among their current stock of employees (including those who agree apprentice-journeyman ratios with unions), but in other cases young people may be more affected by flows of vacancies than by levels (stocks) of employment. All the young people in employment at any given time have been recruited within the previous four years – most of them much more recently than that. The youth labour market includes a disproportionate number of job-seekers, particularly new entrants but also (at least until the recent decline in turnover) a large number of job-changers. As a result the employment of young people more than of any other age group is determined by recent levels (and patterns) of recruitment, as distinct from levels of employment. Among other things this makes the youth labour market very sensitive to the structure of internal labour markets which could be designed either to focus all recruitment on young people or to exclude them completely (Ashton *et al.*, 1982).[17] Above all, however, this factor increases young people's sensitivity to recession, since this is typically accompanied by a much steeper fall in recruitment than in total employment, as employers stop new recruitment rather than sack existing staff. This effect is aggravated by the tendency of employers also to reduce investment in training in a recession.

Labour-market processes therefore serve to cushion the impact of structural and demographic changes affecting young people, but they make youth employment disproportionately sensitive to changes in the general level of demand. This explains why youth unemployment has risen more than adult unemployment over a period when the latter was generally rising; it also explains how the current problem is increasingly manifested in a failure of young people to find jobs rather than a failure to keep them. Young people are in broadly the same labour market(s) as adults; they are affected by the same factors, only more so.

Summary: The Causes of Youth Unemployment

In assessing explanations of youth unemployment it is important to identify the period of time over which explanations are believed to hold, and to distinguish between continuing determinants of the *level* of youth unemployment and factors which account for its *increase* over a given period. The former include all those factors in which a (potential) change would contribute to a change in youth unemployment; the latter include only those factors in which an actual change contributed to the actual change in youth unemployment during the period.

Of the determinants of the *level* of youth unemployment, aggregate demand is of paramount importance. Its effect is disproportionate, with young workers more affected than adults by changes in the general level of demand. Conversely, the effect of the size of the age group is to some extent cushioned by the flexibility of the boundary between youth and adult labour markets. The same applies to the effect of the composition of aggregate labour demand. The 'quality' of youth labour may influence the level of youth unemployment, although this influence is difficult to measure through empirical analysis, which cannot easily assess the importance of variables which have not varied.[18] However, this effect is likely to be small within the 'realistic' range of variation which policy measures can influence, especially since the aspects of 'quality' most valued by employers appear to be experience, personal qualities and other traits which cannot easily be developed through such measures. Finally, young people's relative wage costs may also influence youth unemployment levels but their influence is relatively small compared either with that of the aggregate level of demand or with that of the other (non-wage) considerations which influence employers' recruitment decisions.

Much of the evidence reviewed above relates to the 1970s or to earlier decades. Although claims of a dramatic break in the labour market should be treated with caution, relationships may have changed in the 1980s. The dynamics of youth unemployment have changed as, with lengthening duration, it has become less of a frictional problem and more of a problem of initial absorption into employment; the macroeconomic relationships may have changed at the same time. Moreover, policy measures such as YOP, YTS and the Young Workers Scheme may, in addition to their direct effect on youth unemployment, have encouraged employers to structure recruitment and employment more on age lines; they may also have encouraged more firms to articulate policies for youth employment, whether motivated by self-interest, paternalism or obligation to the community (Chapman and Tooze, 1984). In the long run such changes might strengthen the boundaries between youth and adult labour markets and further weaken the influence of relative wage costs: taken to extremes they might replace the youth labour market with a youth training market, subject to very different influences, but that day is still some way off.

The discussion now turns to the factors which caused the *increase* in youth unemployment between 1979–84. The statistics presented earlier in this chapter revealed the current problem to be largely a problem of the 1980s and the result of changes since 1979. By far the most important explanation of the rise in youth unemployment over this period is the recession. If relative earnings had any influence this was to restrain the growth in youth unemployment, since relative earnings fell between 1979–84. There is no evidence that the 'quality' of youth labour deteriorated over the period: if anything the reverse. Changes in the industrial structure made a negligible contribution to the increase in youth unemployment after 1979; changes in the occupational structure, perhaps precipitated by the recession, may have had some influence but their net effect is likely to have been small. Similarly, demographic changes may have contributed to the rise in youth unemployment, although these changes were reversed during the period and their effects were offset by declining rates of economic activity.

Much of the research on the causes of rising youth unemployment in the UK refers, explicitly or implicitly, to changes that took place in the 1970s. Although this typically identifies 'cyclical' changes as the main explanation it allows for some influence of demographic factors, of higher relative earnings and perhaps of structural changes in labour demand. The story is somewhat different for the much larger increase in youth unemployment during the 1980s. Apart from the 'cyclical' effect all of the suggested factors either failed to move in the appropriate direction during this period or moved in a way that fails to match the uneven growth of youth unemployment and in particular its sudden upsurge in 1980. The massive rise in youth unemployment during the 1980s is almost wholly the result of the recession.

Conclusion

Youth unemployment in the UK has been recognized as a problem at least since the early 1970s. However, the current problem, at its current level, is very largely a product of the 1980s. Not only has the level of youth unemployment undergone a massive increase since 1979, albeit partly masked by the effects of statistical and institutional changes and by special measures, but the qualitative experience of youth unemployment has changed, particularly with respect to its lengthening duration.

Much of our knowledge of the social and psychological consequences of youth unemployment dates from the 1970s or earlier periods (Cherry, 1976; Stafford *et al.*, 1980; Roberts *et al.*, 1982). The effects of the experience of youth unemployment in the 1980s, and in particular its long-term effects, are largely unknown. But while employment remains a central normative feature in the social and cultural life of young people as well as of adults, as well as an accepted step towards adulthood, the implications of the current problem are disturbing and they may be aggravated by its unequal distribution.

Yet, whatever its specific consequences, the causes of the recent rise in youth unemployment are substantially the same as the causes of the rise in adult unemployment. The preceding analysis failed to identify factors specific to the youth labour market that have caused youth unemployment to rise substantially since 1979; instead it explained why the factors which caused adult unemployment to rise should have affected youth unemployment disproportionately. By the same token, specific remedies for youth unemployment — whether focussed on training, wages, or any other target — can have only a modest effect on the problem, except insofar as they simply remove young people from the workforce, if adult unemployment is not also reduced.

Acknowledgements

This chapter was commissioned by the International Labour Office, by whose permission it is included here. The author is grateful to Brian Main and Michael Shelly for helpful comments and discussions, to David Ashton, Malcolm Maguire, Catherine Marsh, Joan Payne and Mark Spilsbury for comments on an earlier draft, and to officials of the Department of Employment, the Department of Education and Science and the Manpower Services Commission for advice on statistical sources. The author is responsible for any errors and for the opinions expressed in the chapter. Crown copyright material is used by permission of HMSO.

Notes

1 The July figures show a continued decline between July 1972 and July 1973, a slight increase to July 1974, a sharp increase to July 1975 and a much smaller increase to July 1976, except among school leavers affected by the change in regulations.

2 Although the number of trainees on YTS in January 1984 was greater than the number on YOP in the previous year, the total number of entrants (including re-entrants) fell. This apparent discrepancy reflects the longer duration (one year) of YTS: the median length of YOP schemes was six months. Both schemes, run by

the Manpower Services Commission, cover Great Britain only. See Rees (1983) for an account of the corresponding schemes in Northern Ireland.

3   The precise scale of this effect is difficult to determine: since a number of YOP and YTS places have substituted for or incorporated ordinary jobs their effect on recorded unemployment at any one time may have been somewhat smaller than the current number of trainees.

4   In 1984 the proportion dropped back to 31 per cent, probably as a result of the introduction of the Youth Training Scheme.

5   The median duration of completed spells appears shorter than the median duration of current uncompleted spells because of the different sampling basis; each spell of unemployment can only be recorded as a completed spell once, but it may be recorded as an uncompleted spell several times, in proportion to its duration. Longer spells therefore form a larger proportion of current (uncompleted) spells than of spells completed in a given period.

6   These data refer to the Scottish regions of Fife, Lothian, Strathclyde and Tayside, and therefore do not correspond precisely to the data in table 2.

7   This range excludes the over-60-year-olds, among whom changed benefit regulations produced a spuriously low unemployment rate.

8   For example, the Labour Prime Minister (James Callaghan) in October 1976, and the Conservative Lord Young in January 1985.

9   The fall between 1975–81 is partly the result of the increasing concentration of young people in low-paying jobs (Wells, 1983). This may also be true of the change between 1981-84, although there may be an offsetting influence if special measures such as YOP tended to substitute for lower-paid jobs.

10   The October enquiry shows a relatively steady rise in the earnings of young males relative to adult males between 1968–76; for females the rise is concentrated in one year, 1972–73, and this is offset by a decline in the other years so that relative earnings of young females *fell* between 1968–76, partly because of the effects of equal pay legislation on adult women's earnings. See Wells (1983, table 1) and Marsden (1987).

11   Makeham's conclusions are equivocal with respect to females.

12   Some of the problems of model specification are as follows. The notion of an unproblematic switch from supply- to demand-constrained regimes assumes a unique and homogeneous market, but wide geographical differences, in particular, make this too simple an assumption (Ashton *et al.*, 1982): some local youth labour markets may be in a state of excess supply while others are still in a state of excess demand. The demand functions are largely specified in terms of 'stock' variables, whereas a consideration of labour-market dynamics suggests that flow variables (entrants to the labour force, vacancies, etc) might be equally important. The demand for youth labour is assumed to be independent of the age composition of job-seekers, contrary to the evidence of most accounts of the search and recruitment process. The influence of special measures is not satisfactorily allowed for. These problems are aggravated by the inadequacies of the data, discussed in the text: for example some of Rice's (1984) 'supply-side' influences might equally be interpreted as demand-side influences.

13   See note 12. This discussion follows several points raised in Junankar and Neale's (1987) critical review. However, most of these points apply to time-series analyses of the youth labour market in general, particularly those based on the disequilibrium approach (on account of its more demanding data requirements and limited degrees of freedom), not (as Junankar and Neale imply) to specific models or techniques.

14   Equivalent analyses for the UK are not currently available; the industrial structure of Scotland is broadly similar to that of other parts of the UK so there is some expectation that similar results would obtain.

15 A more detailed critique of the structural arguments is provided by Raffe (1986).
16 The account in the following three paragraphs is based on studies of employers reported by MSC (1978), Hunt and Small (1981), Markall and Finn (1981), Ashton *et al.* (1982) and Livock (1983).
17 With the exception of Ashton *et al.*'s (1982) study this potentially important area has received very little research attention with respect to young people.
18 Whereas the 'quality' of youth labour may vary at a micro level, the labour-market analysis presented here suggests that extrapolation from micro to macro relationships is invalid.

References

ABOWD, J., LAYARD, R. and NICKELL, S. (1980) *The Demand for Labour by Age and Sex*. Working Paper no. 110, London School of Economics, Centre for Labour Economics.

ASHTON, D. and MAGUIRE, M. (1983) *The Vanishing Youth Labour Market*, London, Youthaid.

ASHTON, D., MAGUIRE, M. and GARLAND, V. (1982) *Youth in the Labour Market*, Research Paper no. 34, London, Department of Employment.

BAXTER, J. (1975) 'The chronic job changer: A study of youth unemployment', *Social and Economic Administration*, 9, pp. 184–206.

BOSANQUET, N. and DOERINGER, P. (1973) 'Is there a dual labour market in Great Britain? *Economic Journal*, 83, pp. 421–35.

CHAPMAN, P. and TOOZE, M. (1984) *Youth Training in Scotland: A Review of Progress*, Dundee, University of Dundee, Department of Economics.

CHERRY, N. (1976) 'Persistent job-changing: Is it a problem? *Journal of Occupational Psychology*, 49, pp. 203–21.

CHOPPIN, B. (1981) 'Is education getting better?', *British Educational Research Journal*, 7, pp. 3–16.

CLARKE, L. (1980) *The Transition from School to Work: A Critical Review of Research in the United Kingdom*, London, HMSO.

CORMACK, R., OSBORNE, R. and THOMPSON, W. (1980) *Into Work? Young School Leavers and the structure of Opportunity in Belfast*, Belfast, Fair Employment Agency.

DEPARTMENT OF EDUCATION AND SCIENCE (1983) *Educational and Economic Activity of Young People aged 16–19 in England and Wales from 1973–74 to 1981–82*, Statistical Bulletin no. 2/83. London, DES.

DEPARTMENT OF EDUCATION AND SCIENCE, (1985) *Educational and Economic Activity of Young People aged 16 to 18 years in Great Britain from 1974 to 1984*, Statistical Bulletin no. 5/85, London, DES.

DEPARTMENT OF EMPLOYMENT (1982) 'First employment of young people', *Employment Gazette*, 90, March pp. 117–20.

DEPARTMENT OF EMPLOYMENT (1984) 'Unemployment flows: Detailed analysis', *Employment Gazette*, 92, pp. 347–53.

FINN, D. and FRITH, S. (1981) *Education and the Labour Market*, E353, Block 1, Unit 4. Milton Keynes, Open University Press.

HUNT, J. and SMALL, P. (1981) *Employing Young People: a Study of Employers' Attitudes, Policies and Practices*, Edinburgh, Scottish Council for Research in Education.

HUTCHINSON, G., BARR, N. and DROBNY, A. (1984) 'The employment of young males in a segmented labour market', *Applied Economics*, 16, pp. 187–204.

JOLLY, J., CREIGH, S. and MINGAY, A. (1980) *Age as a Factor in Employment*,

Research Paper no. 11, London, Department of Employment.

JONES, P. (1984) *What Opportunities for Youth?* Occasional Paper no. 4, London, Youthaid.

JONES, P. (1985) 'Youth and unemployment: An alternative approach', mimeo, University of Oxford, Department of Social and Administrative Studies.

JUNANKAR, P. and NEALE, A. (1987) 'Relative wages and the youth labour market', in JUNANKAR, P. (Ed.) *From School to Unemployment: The Labour Market for Young People*, London, Macmillan.

LAYARD, M. (1982) 'Youth unemployment in Britain and the US compared', in FREEMAN, R. and WISE, D. (Eds) *The Youth Labor Market Problem*, Chicago, University of Chicago Press.

LEE, G. and WRENCH, J. (1983) *Skill Seekers*, Leicester, National Youth Bureau.

LIVOCK, R. (1983) *Screening in the Recruitment of Young Workers*, Research Paper no. 41, London, Department of Employment.

LYNCH, L. (1983) 'Job search and youth unemployment', *Oxford Economic Papers*, 35, pp. 595–603.

LYNCH, L. (1984) 'State dependency in youth unemployment: A lost generation?'. Working Paper no. 184, London School of Economics, Centre for Labour Economics.

LYNCH, L. (1987) 'Individual differences in the youth labour market: A cross section analysis of London youth', in JUNANKAR, P. (Ed.) *From School to Unemployment? The Labour Market for Young People*, London, Macmillan.

LYNCH, L. and RICHARDSON, R. (1982) 'Unemployment of young workers in Britain', *British Journal of Industrial Relations*, 20, pp. 362–72.

MAIN, B. (1985) 'School-leaver unemployment and the youth opportunities programme in Scotland', *Oxford Economic Papers*, 37, pp. 426–47.

MAIN, B. and RAFFE, D. (1983a) 'Determinants of employment and unemployment among school leavers: Evidence from the 1979 survey of Scottish school leavers', *Scottish Journal of Political Economy*, 30, pp. 1–17.

MAIN, B. and RAFFE, D. (1983b) 'The industrial destinations of Scottish school leavers 1977–1981', *Fraser of Allander Institute Quarterly Economic Commentary*, 8, February, pp. 37–49.

MAKEHAM, P. (1980) *Youth Unemployment*, Research Paper no. 10, London, Department of Employment.

MANPOWER SERVICES COMMISSION (1978) *Young People and Work*, Manpower Studies no. 19781, London, HMSO.

MANPOWER SERVICES COMMISSION (1984) *Labour Market Quarterly Report*, September.

MARKALL, G. and FINN, D. (1981) *Young People and the Labour Market: A Case Study*, Inner Cities Research Programme no. 5, London, Department of the Environment.

MARSDEN, D. (1987) 'Youth wages and employment in the EEC', in JUNANKAR, P. (Ed.) *From School to Unemployment? The Labour Market for Young People*, London, Macmillan.

MERRILEES, W. and WILSON, R. (1979) *Disequilibrium in the Labour Market for Young People in Great Britain*, Discussion Paper no. 10, University of Warwick, Manpower Research Group.

ORGANISATION FOR ECONOMIC COOPERATION AND DEVELOPMENT (1980) *Youth Unemployment: the Causes and Consequences*, Paris, OECD.

PAYNE, J. (1985) 'Changes in the youth labour market, 1974–1981', *Oxford Review of Education*, 11, pp. 167–80.

PAYNE, C. and PAYNE, J. (1985) 'Youth Unemployment 1974–1981: The changing importance of age and qualifications', *Quarterly Journal of Social Affairs*, 1, pp. 177–92.

PHILLIPS, D. (1973) 'Young and unemployed in a northern city', in WEIR, D. (Ed.) *Men and Work in Modern Britain*, Glasgow, Fontana.

RAFFE, D. (1984a) 'The transition from school to work and the recession: Evidence from the Scottish school leavers surveys, 1977–1983', *British Journal of Sociology of Education*, 5, pp. 247–65.

RAFFE, D. (1984b) 'School attainment and the labour market', in RAFFE, D. (Ed.) *Fourteen to Eighteen*, Aberdeen, Aberdeen University Press.

RAFFE, D. (1984c) 'The effects of industrial change on school-leaver employment in Scotland: A quasi-shift-share analysis', mimeo, University of Edinburgh, Centre for Educational Sociology.

RAFFE, D. (1986) 'Change and continuity in the youth labour market: A critical review of structural explanations of youth unemployment', in ALLEN, S. *et al.* (Eds) *The Experience of Unemployment*, London, Macmillan.

RAFFE, D. (1987) 'Small expectations: the first of the Youth Training Scheme', in JUNANKAR, P. (Ed.) *From School to Unemployment: The Labour Market for Young People*, London, Macmillan.

REEDER, D. (1979) 'A recurring debate; education and industry', in BERNBAUM, G. (Ed.) *Schooling in Decline*, London, Macmillan.

REES, T. (1983) 'Boys off the street and girls in the home: Youth unemployment and state intervention in Northern Ireland', in FIDDY, R. (Ed.) *In Place of Work*, Lewes, Falmer Press.

RICE, P. (1984) 'Juvenile unemployment, relative wages, and social security in Great Birtain', mimeo, University of Sussex, Department of Economics.

ROBERTS, K. (1968) 'The entry into employment: An approach towards a general theory', *Sociological Review*, 16, pp. 165–84.

ROBERTS, K., DUGGAN, J. and NOBLE, M. (1981) *Unregistered Youth Unemployment and Outreach Careers Work: Final Report Part One: Non-Registration*, Research Paper no. 31, London, Department of Employment.

ROBERTS, K., DUGGAN, J. and NOBLE, M. (1982) 'Out-of-school youth in high-unemployment areas: An empirical investigation', *British Journal of Guidance and Counselling*, 10. pp. 1–11.

RYAN, P. (1983) 'Youth labour, trade unionism and state policy in contemporary Britain', paper presented to the International Working Group on Labour Market Segmentation, Aix-en-Provence.

SAWDON, A., MATTHEWS, P. and WARNOCK, D. (1982) *Unemployment and YOP in the Inner City*, London, Youthaid.

SAWDON, A., PELICAN, J. and TUCKER, S. (1981) *Study of the Transition from School to Working Life*, Volume 3, London, Youthaid.

STAFFORD, E., JACKSON, P. and BANKS, M. (1980) 'Employment, work involvement and mental health in less qualified young people', *Journal of Occupational Psychology*, 53, pp. 291–304

THUROW, L. (1976) *Generating Inequality*, New York, Basic Books.

ULLAH, P. and BANKS, M. (1985) 'Youth unemployment and labour market withdrawal'. *Journal of Economic Psychology.*

WARR, P. BANKS, M. and ULLAH, P. (1985) 'The experience of unemployment among black and white urban teenagers', *British Journal of Psychology*, 76, pp. 75–87.

WELLS, W. (1983) *The Relative Pay and Employment of Young People*, Research Paper no. 42, London, Department of Employment.

WILLIAMSON, B. (1983) 'The peripheralisation of youth in the labour market', in AHIER, J. and FLUDE, M. (Eds) *Contemporary Education Policy*, London, Croom Helm.

Notes on Contributors

DAVID ASHTON is senior lecturer in sociology at Leicester University and a member of the Labour Market Studies Group which, for the last nine years, has undertaken a number of research projects into youth employment and unemployment. His publications include *Young Workers* (with David Field, Hutchinson 1976), and *Unemployment Under Capitalism* (Wheatsheaf, 1986).

PAT AINLEY is a researcher who studied Social Anthropology at Cambridge (1971) and has taught in East London schools for several years. On the basis of his teaching experiences he completed a PhD at Goldsmiths' (1986). He has written widely on education and training issues, including *From School to YTS* (forthcoming Open University Press)

SHANE BLACKMAN is currently working as a part-time lecturer at Thames Polytechnic. As a member of the Girls And Occupation Choice Project 1983/1987 (Institute of Education, Sociological Research Unit) he published a number of papers on developing anti sexist material, curriculum development and the new vocationalism (TVEI and YTS).

PHILLIP BROWN is currently a researcher at the Institute of Criminology, University of Cambridge. He has written a number of articles and is the author of the book *Schooling Ordinary Kids: Inequality, Unemployment and the New Vocationalism* (Tavistock, 1987).

ANDREW CHURCH was a postgraduate student in the Department of Geography, Queen Mary College, (University of London), researching a PhD thesis on the redevelopment of London Docklands. He is now a lecturer in geography at Birkbeck College, London University and author of several papers on regeneration in London Docklands.

SALLY DENCH studied Geography and Economics at Exeter University. She became involved in youth labour market research as a post-graduate, and has since worked on several research projects and is co-author of *The*

Changing Structure of Youth Labour Markets. She is currently a Research Associate in the Department of Sociology at Liverpool University.

ANDY FURLONG is a Research Fellow at the Centre for Educational Sociology at Edinburgh University where he works on the Scottish Young People's Surveys. Prior to this, he was attached to the Labour Market Studies Group at Leicester University where he wrote a PhD thesis on the effects of Youth Unemployment on the transition from school.

MIKE HARDEY graduated in Sociology from the University of Essex in 1982. He was a Research Officer on the Leverhulme YTS Project until 1987 and is now a Research Fellow at the University of Surrey.

SUSAN HUTSON is a Senior Research Assistant in the Department of Sociology and Anthropology at University College, Swansea. Trained as an anthropologist, she has worked in part-time teaching and research in Swansea since 1978.

RICHARD JENKINS is a Lecturer is Sociology, University College, Swansea. He has undertaken research in Belfast, Birmingham and Swansea. Among his publications are *Hightown Rules* (1982), *Lads, Citizens and Ordinary Kids* (1983) and *Racism and Recruitment* (1986).

DAVID LEE graduated from the London School of Economics in 1959 and has since held research and teaching posts at the universities of Birmingham and Sheffield. He moved to the University of Essex in 1969 and is now Senior Lecturer. His publications include work on vocational education and social mobility; on apprenticeship and craft unionism; and the deskilling controversy. He is author with Howard Newby of the text *The Problem of Sociology.*

MALCOLM MAGUIRE is a Research Fellow in the Labour Market Studies Group at the University of Leicester. After graduating from Hull University he worked on a number of research projects in the field of youth, training and labour markets. He has published widely on the topic of youth employment and is co-author of a number of research papers, the latest being *Young Adults in the Labour Market* (1986).

DENNIS MARSDEN trained as a scientist. He has held social research posts at the Institute of Community Studies, Salford University (formerly C.A.T.) and the University of Essex where he is now Reader in Sociology. His publications include *Education and the Working Class,* and *Working Class Community* (both with Brian Jackson). *Mothers Alone: Poverty and the Fatherless Family, Workless: an Exploration of the Social Contract between Society and the Workers,* and a Fabian Pamphlet, *Politicians, Equality and the Comprehensives.*

DAVID RAFFE is Reader in Education and Deputy Director of the Centre for Educational Sociology at the University of Edinburgh. He has worked at the CES since 1975, and has been involved in the design conduct and analysis of the Scottish Young People's Surveys (formerly Scottish School Leavers Surveys). His current research interests include secondary and further education, the youth labour market and education and training initiatives for 14–18 year-olds.

DEBORAH RICHARDSON read economics at Lancaster University, then business studies at Durham. She was a research worker on, and is co-author of the Department of Employment funded study, *The Changing Structure of Youth Labour Markets*. She is currently employed at the National Girobank in Bootle.

PENNY RICKMAN graduated in Sociology from the University of Essex in 1982. She is now Senior Research Officer with the Leverhulme YTS Project.

KEN ROBERTS is Reader in Sociology at Liverpool University, and is a co-author of *The Changing Structure of Youth Labour Markets*. His previous books include *Youth and Leisure* (Allen and Unwin, 1983), and *School-Leavers and their Prospects* (Open University Press, 1984).

MARK SPILSBURY graduated in economics from the University of Bradford. After doctoral research into the effects of unions on wages he joined the Labour Market Studies Group at Leicester University. He has published papers on unions and youth employment and is co-author (with D.N. Ashton and M.J. Maguire) of the forthcoming book Re-Structuring the Labour Market: the Implications for Youth (Macmillan, 1988).

ELLIOT STERN studied economics and political science at London University before joining the Tavistock Institute in 1968. In addition to the study of rural youth employment, he has recently undertaken research into the effects of information technology on the spatial location of work and evaluations of adult training schemes. He currently coordinates a programme of research in the employment policy and vocational training field at the Tavistock Institute.

JILL TURBIN studied sociology at Essex University. She undertook doctoral research into the youth labour market and government training measures at Leicester University. In 1984 she joined the Tavistock Institiute of Human Relations to work on a project on rural youth unemployment. She is currently researching in the field of education and training at the Tavistock Institute.

CLAIRE WALLACE is a Senior Lecturer in Sociology at Plymouth Polytechnic. She worked before that as a Research Fellow at the University of Kent. She has just completed a book called *For Richer, For Poorer. Growing Up In and Out of Work*, (Tavistock, 1987).

Index

Index